United States Army
Aviators' Clothing,
1917–1945

ALSO BY C.G. SWEETING

United States Army Aviators' Equipment, 1917–1945 (McFarland, 2015)

United States Army Aviators' Clothing, 1917–1945

C. G. Sweeting

McFarland & Company, Inc., Publishers
Jefferson, North Carolina

This book is a republication of *Combat Flying Clothing: Army Air Forces Clothing During World War II* (Washington, D.C.: Smithsonian Institution, 1984).

LIBRARY OF CONGRESS CATALOGUING-IN-PUBLICATION DATA

Sweeting, C. G.
United States Army aviators' clothing, 1917–1945 / C.G. Sweeting.
pages cm
Includes bibliographical references and index.

ISBN 978-0-7864-9396-8 (softcover : acid free paper) ∞
ISBN 978-1-4766-1809-8 (ebook)

1. United States. Army Air Forces—Uniforms—History. 2. United States. Army Air Forces—Equipment—History. 3. World War, 1914–1918—Equipment and supplies. 4. World War, 1939–1945—Equipment and supplies. I. Title.

UG1163.S928 2015   358.4'114097309041—dc23   2014047493

BRITISH LIBRARY CATALOGUING DATA ARE AVAILABLE

© 2015 C.G. Sweeting. All rights reserved

No part of this book may be reproduced or transmitted in any form or by any means, electronic or mechanical, including photocopying or recording, or by any information storage and retrieval system, without permission in writing from the publisher.

On the cover: Type A-2 summer flying jacket originally worn during the war by Lt. Col. (later Brig. Gen.) Robert W Waltz, 390th Bomb Group, Eighth Air Force (Smithsonian National Air and Space Museum); World War II airplane (Melissa Madia/Thinkstock)

Printed in the United States of America

McFarland & Company, Inc., Publishers
Box 611, Jefferson, North Carolina 28640
www.mcfarlandpub.com

Contents

Preface   1

Introduction   3

1. Problems in the Development of Flying Clothing   5
2. The Manufacture and Supply of Flying Clothing   11
3. Research and Testing of Flying Clothing   24
4. Heavy Winter Shearling Flying Suits   32
5. Electrically Heated Flying Suits   43
6. Other Types of Flying Suits   51
7. Other Items of Body Clothing   68
8. Headgear   87
9. Handwear   108
10. Footwear   119

Appendices

   A. "Program of the Personal Equipment Laboratory," *The Personal Equipment Officer* 2, no. 2 (c. 1946), p. 1.   134

   B. "Kit, Clothing and Equipment, Flyer," Technical Order no. 00-30-41, Headquarters, Army Air Forces, Washington, D.C., April 16, 1942.   135

   C. "Kit, Flyer's Clothing and Equipment," Technical Order no. 00-30-41, Headquarters, Army Air Forces, Washington, D.C., October 20, 1945.   137

   D. "Clothing—Refinishing Sheep Shearling Type Flying Clothing," Technical Order no. 13-1-10, Headquarters, Army Air Forces, Washington, D.C., October 16, 1943.   147

E. "Preliminary Tests on Durability of Flying Clothing" Memorandum Report no. ENG-49-695-2S, Aero Medical Laboratory, Materiel Command, Wright Field, Ohio, April 12, 1944.   149

F. Type Designation Sheets, Wright Field, Ohio, 1920s through World War II.   154

G. The Preservation of Vintage Flying Clothing and Accessories.   160

Abbreviations   168

Notes   170

Bibliography   175

Index   177

Preface

Since 1945 almost every aspect of air operations in World War II has been examined in detail. The aircraft, aces, and air combat in particular have been discussed in numerous books and articles. A notable exception to this growing store of knowledge is the subject of flying clothing and accessories, particularly the items worn by American airmen during their many hard-fought campaigns around the world between 1941 and 1945. This gap in information, however, is not due to disinterest in flying clothing and its important role in winning the war. Rather, it indicates the absence of reference sources on the development and manufacture of flight materiel.

This book is my attempt to document the development, procurement, and utilization of the flying clothing worn by the airmen of the U.S. Army Air Forces (AAF) during World War II. I hope it will stimulate further research that will bring to light additional information of value.

Space limitations prevent the inclusion of the countless variations, modifications, and unauthorized items of flying clothing and equipment that were used by the AAF. Many garments that did not conform exactly to the original specifications were made—and will frequently be found today. This is mainly because numerous minor changes and improvements were introduced during the manufacturing process, or in the field, without changing the type numbers. In general, service uniforms and mechanics' clothing also fall outside the scope of this study. Additional articles of clothing and equipment will be covered in a subsequent work to be published at a later date. That work would include such items as ballistic protective gear, oxygen masks and devices, parachute systems, anti-g garments, and survival equipment.

For the collector, a word of caution is in order. As the economics of supply and demand dictate, when the market values of historic items increase beyond their current manufacturing costs, reproductions appear. Some reproductions serve a useful purpose: for example, they allow the owners of vintage aircraft to wear appropriate apparel without wearing out scarce original garments. Copies of AAF shearling jackets and Type A-2 leather jackets, with authentic looking labels, are currently being produced. Other replicas—including helmets, goggles, badges, and insignia—are also in wide circulation. Copies of the CBI patch originally made some forty years ago are being manufactured today in the Far East. Unfortunately, these reproductions are frequently offered as originals and must be examined very carefully, so that the buyer realizes that a modern reproduction is being purchased.

Information and photographs for this study were obtained from a number of sources, as well as through the examination of original specimens in the collection of the National Air and Space Museum (NASM). I wish to thank the individuals who assisted me and to express my appreciation for the special contributions made by Donald Huxley of Johnstown, New York, former chief of the U.S. Air Force Clothing Branch, and Robert Lehmacher of Burbank, Illinois, a well-known authority on flying clothing and accessories. Both generously offered their expertise and kindly consented to review my final manuscript. Walter J. Boyne, the director of NASM, provided suggestions and encouragement. George A. Petersen of Springfield, Virginia, furnished useful reference material, while Dr. Von D. Hardesty, associate curator of the NASM Aeronautics Department, offered valuable advice. Last, but not least, Donald S. Lopez, deputy director of NASM, was particularly helpful since, as a flyer with the AAF during World War II, he used or wore many of the types of items discussed in this book.

Introduction

In the early days of aviation flying airplanes was fraught with many hazards and difficulties. The open aircraft of that era usually caused pilots and passengers great discomfort with their deafening roar, splattering oil, and icy wind, not to mention the lashing rain or snow.

The first civil and military aviators braved the elements in whatever clothing they considered appropriate. Leather coats and goggles, such as those worn by motorcyclists, and football helmets were a few of the items of apparel that proved useful in the early years of flight.

By 1911 helmets and other special items of clothing for aviators were being offered for sale by various firms, and by 1913 entire catalogs devoted to flying clothing and equipment were available from companies in the United States and Europe.[1]

The beginning of World War I in 1914 created a great demand for military uniforms in Europe, and this included flying clothing for the services. The thousands of army and navy aviators entering service needed suitable garments, so new designs were produced to meet the requirements of wartime flying. A similar situation confronted the U.S. Army when the United States entered the war in April 1917. The small Army air arm, then part of the Signal Corps, expanded immensely and required quantities of flying clothing suitable for winter and summer use. These needs were supplied at first by allied nations and by civilian clothing purchased off-the-shelf. The origins of many items of flying clothing used in World War II can be traced back to military developments initiated in World War 1.[2]

During the period between the wars the development of aviation clothing was determined almost entirely by the progressive changes and advances made in military aircraft. As new aircraft could fly increasingly higher and faster, their crewmen required improved types of flying garments and accessories. During World War II advanced aircraft designs, changing tactics, and the pressing demands of worldwide combat operations not dreamed of even a few years earlier also accelerated the development of suitable clothing for the Army Air Forces. But research and development were only part of the story. Manufacturing and supplying so great a variety of flight gear in such huge quantities during the war provided American industry with one of its greatest challenges.

As a spin-off of technology, flying clothing has an evolution that is an important part of the broader history of aviation. Flight materiel must be available in adequate quantity when and where it is needed, but most important, it must be rigorously practical: it must work and be effective, even in the crucible of combat.

The fact that almost all important difficulties were overcome so that adequate quantities of serviceable flying clothing and accessories could be supplied to the Army Air Forces during the war is a tribute to the dedicated civilian and military personnel concerned with development and procurement, as well as to the members of the American clothing industry.

1

Problems in the Development of Flying Clothing

From the freezing temperatures of the Arctic to the sweltering jungles of the South Pacific, Army Air Forces (AAF) personnel flew countless combat missions throughout World War II. Providing the clothing worn by the various crewmen aboard the many different types of aircraft was a monumental task, to say the least.

The development and production of flying clothing and accessories over the years have involved many difficult and unusual problems. Flying clothing proved to have design needs far different from those of ordinary garments. The varying factors of human nature and the body also caused complications. During World War II the great variety of item requirements, the highly specialized clothing needs, and the rapid increase in procurement needs together imposed a tremendous burden on both development and production facilities. Some of the problems were resolved rather slowly during the war: they were complicated by a shortage of experienced personnel in all phases of design and production and by rapidly changing requirements in flying clothing caused by the unexpected shifts in military tactics, airplane design, and operation. By 1945, however, solutions had been found to almost every problem.

Criticism of flying clothing supplied by the Army was nothing new. As far back as World War I, complaints had been made about the suitability and availability of flying clothing, especially for the Air Service of the American Expeditionary Forces (AEF) in Europe. An Aviation Clothing Board was established by the Army on September 17, 1917, to supervise the development and production of flying clothing. By the time the Armistice was declared, large quantities of flying gear were being delivered to the Air Service, and for reasons of economy this stock continued in use for many years after the war. As the nation slipped deeper into economic depression during the early 1930s, funds for the development and procurement of flying clothing became even more limited than they had been during the previous decade. New types of flying gear were eventually introduced, but not all of the items proved satisfactory in actual use. In 1932 an official of the Office of the Assistant Secretary of War wrote to the commanding general at Wright Field, Dayton, Ohio, where most flying-clothing development was centered, that there was "very extended and bitter criticism of the winter flying suits in the service and those which were now being produced."[1] Brigadier General H.C. Pratt, commanding general of the Materiel Division, responded, "I don't believe that there has been any project in the Division [Materiel] in which it has been so difficult to obtain a satisfactory solution or a uniform consensus of opinion. Almost all the ideas everyone has suggested have been

Exhibition of various types of flying clothing prepared by the Clothing Branch, Personal Equipment Laboratory, at an AAF Fair in 1945. (SI Photo 80-20352)

tried out and so far no one solution has been satisfactory."[2] Ten years later, in 1942, just as great a diversity of opinion and amount of criticism in the Materiel Division itself seemed to remain. A survey of officers at Wright Field, expressed in a memorandum report, indicated that among the reporting officers there was "a great diversity of opinion of requirements for flying clothing and an equal diverse criticism of present equipment."[3]

The report further outlined the severe criticism of the shearling flying suits that were then in use and pointed out that the design and standardization of flying clothing could best be made by personnel who had actual combat experience in the various theaters of operation. To better accomplish this, a Liaison Branch of the Personal Equipment Laboratory was organized at Wright Field in 1944. This branch gathered information from the combat and other areas and transmitted it to the various interested branches of the laboratory.

The Clothing Branch and individuals at McCook and Wright fields responsible for flying clothing and accessories learned that they needed to cooperate with the engineers and technicians in charge of oxygen, radio, and other equipment and with the aeromedical specialists and similar experts, but this teamwork did not always occur. Cooperation with the Army Quartermaster Corps (QMC) also left something to be desired.

The situation was further complicated by the overlapping activities and conflicting in-

1. Problems in the Development of Flying Clothing

Typical outfit worn by Army Air Service aviators during and after World War I. The brown leather flying coat, gauntlets, helmet, and goggles were often worn over the khaki or olive drab service uniform, which included breeches, and leather leggings or boots. The plane is a modified DH-4. (SI Photo A4868E)

terests of the QMC and the Army Air Corps (beginning in 1941, the Army Air Forces), which caused some delays in acquiring clothing at critical periods. During the early part of World War II, before the Air Corps's clothing program was fully developed, information developed by the QMC concerning cold weather clothing and equipment was slow in being used. Air Corps personnel in Alaska at the time preferred to use QMC ski and mountain-troop clothing, and civilian items, instead of their own heavy winter shearling flying clothing, which they deemed unsatisfactory.

The mission traditionally assigned to the QMC included developing and procuring clothing for all branches of the Army, of which

The ball turret on a Boeing B-17 showing the limited space available for the gunner. 303rd Bomb Group, Eighth Air Force, England, June 6, 1943. (SI Photo 80-20353)

the Air Corps was one. However, in its quest for self-determination during the war and in an effort to better satisfy its special requirements, the AAF rebuffed attempts by the QMC to become involved with flight gear. Bradford Washburn, a noted authority on the Arctic and a civilian special consultant, first to the Office of the Quartermaster General (OQMG) and then to the AAF, carefully studied the clothing situation in the AAF, and especially the results of the Army Alaskan Test Expedition, in June and July 1942. He concluded:

1. The QMC has maintained that it should have full control over the development and distribution of personal equipment for all branches of the Armed Forces of the United States.
2. The AAF, on the other hand, contend that their relatively small and unique requirements demand special attention all along the line: in research, development, production and distribution. The flying personnel of the AAF represent less than 3% of the entire U.S. Army. These men need highly-specialized personal equipment to meet the greatest climatic extremes and physiological strain encountered by any personnel in the Army.
3. Because of these special requirements, and the need of special design and high-quality materials to meet them, the entire personal equipment program of the AAF should be in the hands of the Air Technical Service Command (ATSC).
4. In order, however, for personnel of the ATSC to operate a satisfactory program of research, development and production of this equipment, it will always be of vital importance that they be in constant contact with the [Army] Quartermaster, the Navy and the technical missions of foreign nations.[4]

Washburn considered the clothing situation to be extremely critical at that time, and in his formal report he stated that the AAF clothing unit's staff was too small and inexperienced to develop and test flying clothing adequately. There was also insufficient cooperation between the AAF Materiel Center and the Special Forces Section, OQMG.[5] The acting director of the Equipment Laboratory, however, rejected Washburn's report. After discussing the matter with the chief of the Engineering Division and the commanding general at Wright Field, Washburn resigned his position with the Materiel Division and made a report in person to General H.H. Arnold, commander in chief of the AAF. That report resulted in an investigation of the clothing unit, and a number of changes in both personnel and administration eventually took place.

Another reorganization subsequently occurred in the fall of 1943. The Clothing Branch was separated from the Equipment Laboratory, Washburn returned to Wright Field, and AAF clothing was temporarily established as a special project under the personal supervision of the commanding general,

Materiel Command. In April 1944 the Personal Equipment Laboratory was organized in the Engineering Division of Materiel Command, and the Clothing Branch was absorbed into it.[6] One man who worked in that laboratory during the war—Donald Huxley, the civilian chief of the Clothing Branch from World War II until 1975—later said that the work performed there was very important, not only to the AAF during the war, but to the postwar U.S. Air Force (USAF) as well.[7] (The program of the Personal Equipment Laboratory around the end of World War II was outlined in an article in a periodical for personal equipment officers.[8])

Adequate production was another problem complicated by the special characteristics required in flying clothing. The supply of skilled labor was often inadequate, special materials were frequently limited, and specialized equipment was sometimes necessary. Special sewing machines, for example, were needed to attach the wiring in electrically heated flying clothing. Over the years it was learned that manufacturers who were familiar only with the fabrication of commercial clothing found the special drawings and specifications for flying clothing particularly difficult to comprehend and follow. (Such production problems and shortages are further discussed in Chapter 2 of this book.)

From its beginning the development of flying clothing presented many problems with pattern, style, fit, and comfort. Patterns had to be standardized so that the number of types could be kept to the minimum. Other suit design concerns included the choice of color; the use of one- or two-piece styles; the ease of donning and removal; the size, position, and number of openings; the use of buttons or zippers; and the position, number, size, and shape of pockets.

Extensive research was performed by the Aero Medical Laboratory (AML) at Wright Field to determine the quantities and sizes of the various types of garments needed by flying personnel and the proper integration of all items such as helmets, goggles, and oxygen masks. Another important medical and operational consideration was the accessibility that clothing allowed to an injured part of a flyer's body when first aid was required. Apparently, this was

One of the improved types of winter flying outfits introduced during 1943 consisted of the Types B-11 jacket and A-10 trousers. Featuring a cotton-fiber wind- and moisture-resistant outer shell with a deep alpaca-wool pile lining, this suit was a big improvement over previous types, including the shearling suits. This P-51C fighter pilot is also wearing an AN-H-16 winter helmet and A-14 mukluks. (SI Photo 81-330)

given insufficient emphasis until well into the war, since combat reports in 1943 indicated that the thickness and inaccessibility of flying clothing in use at that time prevented the quick application of first aid, especially at high altitudes. As a result of combat experience, more openings were incorporated into new types of suits, which also made them more comfortable and easier to put on and take off.

One of the most common complaints concerning flying clothing was that it was uncomfortable, and this remains a concern even in the Air Force of today. Psychological and physiological factors included health conditions, amounts of activity, and the greatly varying needs of different parts of the body; materials, weight, heat, cut, and sizing also had to be considered. Further complicating the designing of suitable clothing were the length of the missions and the degree of inactivity faced by pilots and gunners in cramped fighter plane cockpits and aircraft turrets, respectively.

Clothing requirements changed along with the designs, variety, and functions of aircraft; the increasing number of types and length of missions; the duties of crew members; the use of closed cabins; and aircraft heating and pressurization. The global scope of World War II with its emphasis on long, high-altitude missions posed further difficulties, while the number and variety of flying outfits needed for all-weather use around the world added to the production problems. (Flying clothing, worn by various crewmen at the beginning and end of the war, was listed in Technical Orders no. 00-30-41, "Kit, Clothing and Equipment, Flyer," April 16, 1942; and "Kit, Flyer's Clothing and Equipment," October 20, 1945—included in this book as Appendixes B and C.)

The flying clothing of World War II was constructed of many types and combinations of materials, including cotton, rayon, nylon, wool, sheep shearling, camel hair, leather, fur, rubber, spun glass, wire, metals, and other substances. Some of these had to be fireproofed, waterproofed, or mothproofed; often they needed to be resistant to mildew and to damage by such elements as oil, gasoline, and salt water. Unfortunately, processing a fabric to increase one desired characteristic sometimes decreased another one. For instance, waterproofing some fabrics reduced their porosity and ventilation, which were especially important when moving from warm, humid regions or altitudes to freezing conditions in a short period of time.

Flying clothing required reliable materials and high-quality construction to function satisfactorily. Lt. Col. A.P. Gagge, of the AML, investigated the unsatisfactory flying clothing used by AAF units operating from England during the winter of 1943–44. In his report he stated: "Approximately 50% of all combat casualties returning from missions are a result of frostbite. Failure of electrically heated equipment has accounted for from 15% to 30% of all frostbites." Colonel Gagge reported that at first frostbite constituted 70 percent of all combat casualties but that by the end of 1943 the proportion had been reduced to between 15 and 20 percent. He also indicated that a lack of training in the proper use of flying clothing, as well as the deficiencies in the available clothing, contributed to the many cases of frostbite.[9] The decrease in the number of cases of frostbite at that time probably resulted mainly from an improved training program for AAF flying personnel in how to use their flying clothing properly. In 1943 nonflying personal equipment officers were assigned to units where they were responsible for maintaining and repairing "personal, protective, and emergency equipment" and for training personnel in its use. This equipment included flying clothing, oxygen equipment, flyer's armor, parachutes, and related items.

These were but a few of the problems facing the designers and manufacturers as they began to produce the greatest quantity of flying clothing in history.

2

The Manufacture and Supply of Flying Clothing

The investigation by Lt. Col. A.P. Gagge in 1943–44 dramatically underlined the importance of flying clothing. He reported that the number of AAF bombers going out on a combat mission was determined more by the amount of adequate clothing available than by any other factor.[1]

The shortages of certain items of flying clothing were even more pronounced in operational areas outside the European theater. Allied strategy after the United States entered the war made defeating Germany its major priority. The Army in the Asiatic-Pacific Theater did not begin to receive any priority in war materiel until the fall of 1944. This plan proved to be the correct course to follow, but it made prosecuting the war against Japan more difficult.

Priorities and Shortages

Several factors led to the shortage of flying clothing during much of World War II. Flying clothing, of course, was just one of the many essential categories of war materiel urgently needed for the great expansion of the U.S. and Allied armed forces, and for the conduct of the war on a global scale. In marshaling the United States' resources for the all-out war effort in 1942, it soon became apparent not only that research and development needed expansion but also that the U.S. manufacturing base required major alteration and enlargement so all of the necessary materiel required for victory could be produced.

An intricate set of priorities governed the production of weapons, equipment, and supplies. Limited raw materials required continuous allocation amid rapid industrial expansion. Synthetic materials, including rubber, had to be developed. Skilled and unskilled labor had to be mobilized and assigned to vital war production programs. Various manufacturing facilities needed to be adapted to war production quickly and efficiently, especially during the first two years of the conflict. This prodigious undertaking was not accomplished without difficulty.

The Army and Navy reached an agreement early in the war to standardize common articles of flying clothing and equipment, as well as ordnance and other items, for use by both services (and the Marine Corps), as well as the British forces. The pattern for this collaboration had been established for ordnance long before Pearl Harbor through the work of the Army-Navy Munitions Board and other activities. During the war this program was intended to cut development time and costs, increase production, and facilitate distribution of similar items. The standardized items were identified by an *AN* specification number, e.g., "AN-J-3." The *AN* indicated that the article was a standardized Army-Navy item, the *J* showed that it was a jacket, and the 3 stood for "type 3." The *AN* clothing concept, however, was not totally successful; each service preferred to procure most items of flying clothing to its own specifications. Still, hundreds of other items in the supply system, especially aviation ordnance, were standardized, and some of them are still used today. By the end of the war the only *AN* item of flying clothing still listed as a *standard* article for issue to AAF personnel was the AN-H-16 winter flying helmet, though some other items of *AN* clothing continued to be issued as limited standard.

A principal obstacle to the mass production of flying clothing was the inability of many commercial clothing firms to meet the precise specifications of the military procurement program. Often these companies lacked the requisite equipment and trained personnel. For example, after the AAF decided in 1943 to shift production from sheep shearling flying suits to wool- and alpaca-pile garments, it learned that proper manufacturing facilities would be difficult to obtain, even though sufficient raw materials were available. A decision to change thread type in the AN-H-15 flying helmet provided another case in which unforeseen technical or mechanical difficulties developed in production. The chief of the Supply Division at Wright Field reported:

> Recent instructions were issued to change the thread in the AN-H-15 helmet from cotton to nylon. Although this is a simple change and apparently should cause no difficulty, it developed that the machines on which the helmets were made would not operate with nylon thread without modification which required a part not immediately available. Production stopped even though the supply of helmets sewed with cotton thread was not sufficient to meet issue requirements.[2]

Wartime shortages of certain essential materials sometimes caused delays in production, as well as changes in the methods of construction. For instance, in the spring of 1943 a scarcity of brass caused a serious shortage of slide fasteners (commonly known today as "zippers," a patented trade name). The zippers made of substitute materials, such as steel and zinc-plated alloys, had proved unsatisfactory: corrosion of these substitute metals had rendered hundreds of flying suits useless, since a small amount of corrosion might prevent the necessary quick removal of a heavy flying suit or other items of clothing during an emergency landing in water. Similarly, a shortage of natural materials also stimulated the development and use of synthetic materials. Sometimes this was an improvement, as in the case of nylon.

The manufacture of electrically heated flying clothing provided peculiar problems. Special sewing equipment was developed to stitch the heating elements onto the inside of the inner layer of the F-3 suit. The wires used in the suits, gloves, and other articles of electric clothing were intended to withstand 250,000 flexings or bendings without breaking. Until May 1944, however, no existing commercial wire could meet that specification. After extensive testing, a series of wires was developed from three alloys composed of silver, beraloy, and BB bronze. Produced in both flat and round forms for use as heating elements, the new wires were an important milestone in the development of electrically heated garments.[3]

The complicated organizational relationships of the agencies responsible for the development, testing, standardization, procurement, and distribution of flying clothing sometimes interfered with the effective functioning of the flight clothing program. The jurisdictional relationship between the AAF and the QMC concerning flying clothing was particularly important. Procurement had to be initiated so far ahead of the time when equipment was needed that items were frequently outmoded before they arrived, and the time necessary to initiate changes also could be quite long. For example, when consideration was given to the procurement of new types of fabric clothing that had been designed to meet the requirements of the long-range, high-altitude bomber missions over Europe, it was learned that procurement had already been initiated for the old-type shearling clothing through July 1, 1943. The new types of flying clothing were not obtained by the autumn of 1943—a supply failure that had serious consequences, as Colonel Gagge's report revealed.[4]

Memories of pilots and gunners who served in combat overseas between 1943 and 1945 provide further evidence of the AAF's failure to clothe its personnel adequately. One pilot, Lt. Royal D. Frey, who began flying long-range sorties from England on December 28, 1943, recalled in 1980 the futility with which he and his colleagues tried to keep warm during high-altitude missions:

> The Allison manifold heater on the P-38J was worthless and the cockpit temperature could reach -55° F. at 30,000 feet. The standard shearling flying clothing was available but was too bulky to wear in the P-38 cockpit. Since no suitable AAF flying clothing was available for a fighter pilot, we were issued U.S. Army tank crew jackets and bib trousers which we wore over our regular uniforms and long underwear. The P-38J was not wired for the electrically heated "blue-bunny" flying suit at that time. We also wore GI high-top shoes and winter flying boots (Type A-6). On our hands we wore silk gloves, chamois gloves over the silk, and gauntlets over the chamois, all British equipment. A few of us lucky ones in the 55th Fighter Squadron had well-used RAF (Royal Air Force) helmets given to us by our British friends but the rest of the pilots wore AAF winter helmets which were quite similar. We all had AAF goggles and low-pressure oxygen masks (the A-14, I seem to recall). I bought a brown scarf in Stamford because we had no issue scarfs available. Despite the above, we froze! After a couple of hours at altitude, the only thing that still functioned was the brain because the brilliant sun kept the head warm. Electrical switches were extremely difficult to operate because of no finger movement—usually you accomplished this by a "whole-arm" movement, hoping you had a fingertip alongside the switch you wished to actuate. All-in-all, I would estimate that combat effectiveness was reduced by 40 to 50% because of the extremely low temperatures in which we had to sit for up to five plus hours. Needless to say, the extreme cold tended to have an invigorating effect upon one's bladder. Any attempt to get through all that tank suit, uniform, and long underwear to use the relief tube was futile.[5]

The deficiencies in the Materiel Command's procurement procedures in 1943 centered mainly around three factors: the marked differences between the final manufactured products and the samples approved by the Equipment Board at Orlando, Florida; the "unconventional methods" for placing contracts; and the lack of "advanced materials planning." During the early part of 1944 these conditions were almost entirely corrected by the Clothing Branch at Wright Field, which adopted a policy of preparing detailed specifications and patterns for guidance and control in the production of each article of flying clothing. Manufacturers with contracts received copies of the master patterns from the Clothing Branch, along with detailed descriptions of each operation. Any deviation from the standard patterns or materials was carefully checked by inspection. This arrangement secured "quality control" in the production of flying clothing.

During 1944 other actions were taken by the Clothing Branch to improve the manufacture and supply of flying clothing. These included: (1) preparing specifications for component parts; (2) conducting simulated tests on all materials and clothing; (3) training inspectors and preparing detailed manuals for their use; (4) eliminating deviations by manufacturers; (5) securing a better understanding of the special AAF clothing needs and problems by the manufacturers through joint conferences; and (6) engaging the services of skilled, experienced designers of commercial clothing.

According to Major F.E. Miller, chief of the Clothing Branch from May 3, 1944, to October 31, 1944, most of the problems encountered had originated primarily in the rapid and unexpected changes in aerial warfare.[6]

By late 1944 the improved types of flying clothing were generally in good supply and clothing became a negligible factor in causing frostbite.[7] Gradually, the AAF stopped pooling clothing at unit level and issuing it out daily for maximum utilization.

Many of the items of clothing and equipment produced during the war were used by the AAF after the end of hostilities and by the

An exhibit prepared by the Personal Equipment Laboratory at Wright Field on August 24, 1945, featured a display of items worn by the fully equipped AAF crewman. The back chute with Type C-2A para-raft kit, the one-man life raft Type C-2, and the Type B-4 life vest at left should be noted. (SI Photo 80–20354)

USAF after it was established in September 1947. A few articles could even be found in service after the Korean War.

Temperature Zones

Before World War II clothing provided for Army aviators was divided into "summer" and "winter" groups. The worldwide activity of the AAF after 1941, however, made it obvious that "summer" and "winter" did not exist for a force that operated at many altitudes and latitudes. That situation posed both engineering and supply problems: First, the AAF had to secure a system of clothing that would meet flyers' needs wherever they went, in temperatures ranging from -50° to 122° F (-50° to 50° C). After that was accomplished, the new clothing had to be distributed efficiently with consideration given to the annual temperature variations common to each base being equipped and to the types of missions to be flown from those bases. Flawless accomplishment of such efficiency was extremely difficult, especially in view of the AAF's great expansion and global deployment. Unfortunately, the emphasis and pressure early in the war for equipment required to sustain Alaskan-Arctic operations and to solve the very large problems encountered by the Eighth and Fifteenth Air Forces in high-altitude flying eclipsed the interest in developing an overall system of clothing until late 1944.

To facilitate the planning, distribution, and use of flying clothing, specialists attempted to establish five "temperature zones" covering the range of temperatures in which flyers operated. Items of clothing were classified by the zones for which they were best suited. Each of the

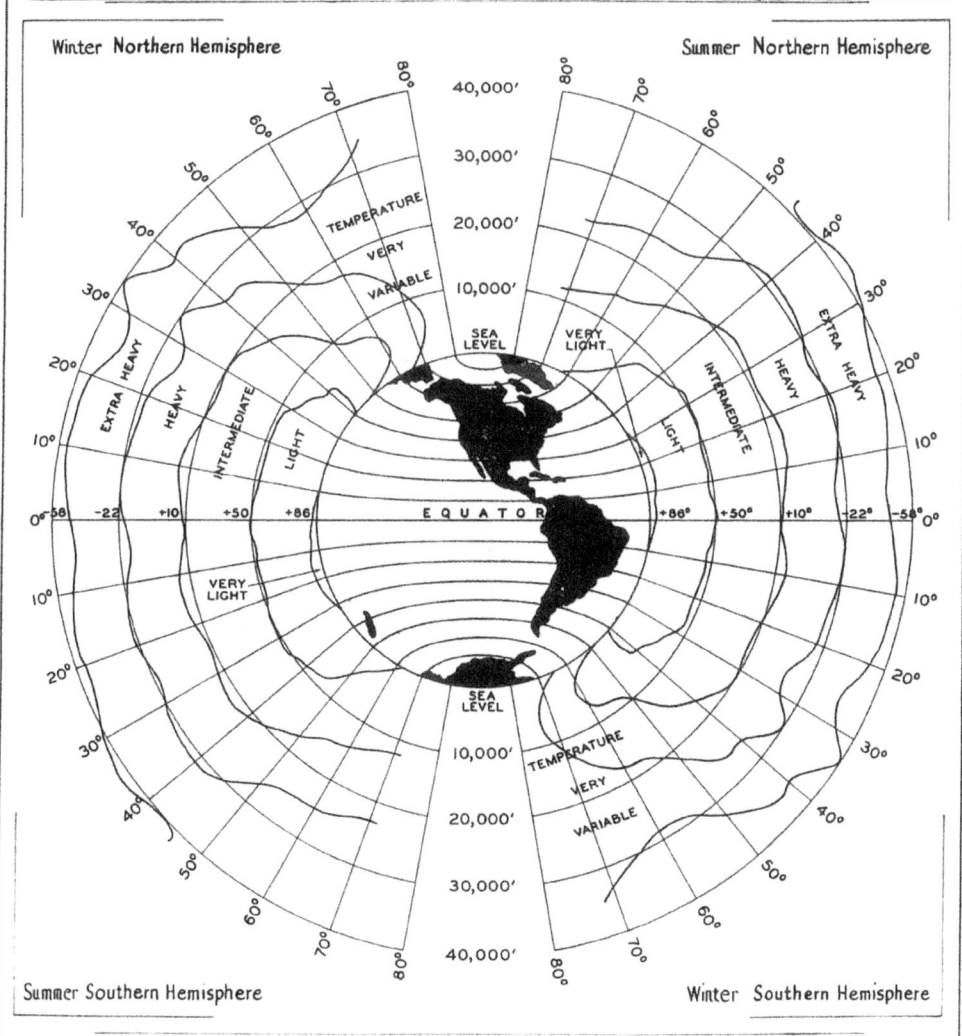

Reference Manual for Personal Equipment Officers, AAF Manual 55-0-1, Headquarters, Army Air Forces, Washington, D.C., June 1, 1945, p. 5-A-4. (SI Photo 81-335)

five zones covered a 36° F (or 20° C) range, with the progression being as follows:

"Very light" zone: 86° to 122° F, 30° to 50° C
"Light" zone: 50° to 86° F, 10° to 30° C
"Intermediate" zone: 14° to 50° F, -10° to 10° C
"Heavy" zone: -22° to 14° F, -30° to -10° C
"Extra-heavy" zone: -58° to -22° F, -50° to -30° C

But human response to thermal sensations varies greatly: comfort is related to humidity

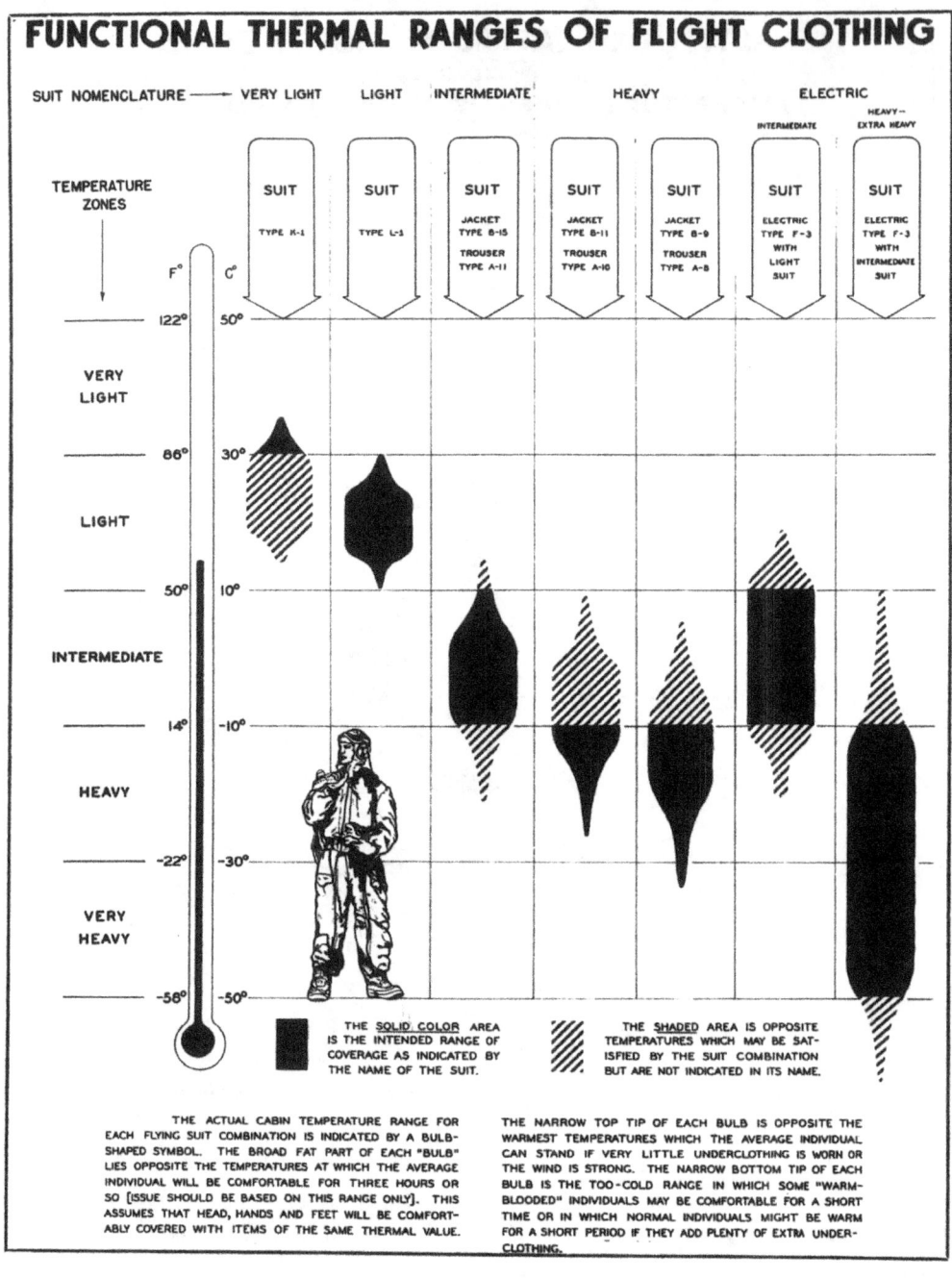

Reference Manual for Personal Equipment Officers, AAF Manual 55-0-1, Headquarters, Army Air Forces, Washington, D.C., June 1, 1945, p. 5-A-5. (SI Photo 81-334)

and temperature, and whether heat is being radiated or received also makes a considerable difference. For these reasons, such figures and classifications were only generalities. The temperature charts, therefore, could not have been expected to hold entirely true.

Still, a fairly intelligent estimate of the type of equipment needed for any single type of flying operation could be made by using weather records, clothing temperature-range charts, and altitude charts. (Two such charts from AAF Manual 55-0-1, "Functional Thermal Ranges of Flight Clothing" and "Altitude Latitude Isotherms," are reproduced in this chapter.) Items of body clothing, headgear, handwear and footwear having the same thermal nomenclature generally fitted well together. Except for the very light zone, it was assumed that a classification held true if the body clothing in question was worn over underwear and either a khaki or olive drab wool shirt and trousers. For most items, the nomenclatures adopted were based upon three-hour tolerance periods, so any given classification was subject to reclassification when time intervals were different. Electric clothing, however, served for an indefinite length of time over the intermediate, heavy, and extra-heavy zones. This more specialized clothing substantially improved the comfort, safety, and efficiency of aviators.

Label

The selection of the most appropriate items of flying clothing for a particular mission or operation had been comparatively simple when the garments were separated into "summer" and "winter" groups. Most of the items of summer flying clothing were originally given type numbers in the "A" series, and most winter garments were given type numbers in the "B" series (e.g., the Type A-2 summer flying jacket and the Type B-2 winter flying jacket). There were exceptions: winter flying boots, for instance, were given numbers in the "A" series. This was probably because there were no standard summer flying boots when the type numbers were first assigned to boots in the 1920s. Labels on such easily identifiable AAF garments usually listed only the type number (e.g., A-2, B-2), the drawing and contract numbers, the manufacturer, the size (40, 42, 44, etc.), and usually "Property of U.S. Army Air Forces." Labels were almost always black, with yellow or gold-color woven lettering.

With the new types of flying clothing introduced during 1943 and 1944 came labels listing the exact nomenclature of an item. This helped personnel select garments that were best suited to a particular mission or operation. For example, for a low-altitude mission in warm weather a lightweight flying suit, perhaps the Type L-1, might have been selected. It had a label containing the following information: "Suit, Flying, Light, Gabardine, Type L-1," followed by the specification number, the size—e.g., "Medium Long (38 to 40)"—the AAF stock number, the order number, and the manufacturer.

The labels on items made by different manufacturers during the war varied widely. Some remained black with woven yellow or gold lettering; others were black with woven white lettering or white with woven black or red lettering. Still other labels were white with printed black lettering. Occasionally, labels failed to give a garment type number. Label sizes were not uniform, and a few articles even had the nomenclature simply printed or stamped directly on the inside or outside with no actual label. (Items standardized for both Army and Navy use were, of course, identified by a label listing the specification number—e.g., "Spec. AN-H-15" on the summer flying helmet—and other basic information.)

Insignia

In addition to a label, most articles of flying clothing procured by the AAF in World War II were marked with the AAF insignia and

The AAF insignia was often printed or stamped on items of flying clothing made during World War II. (SI Photo 81–338)

1

2

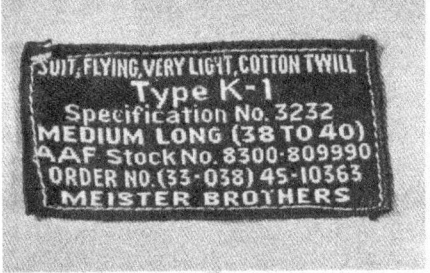

3

4

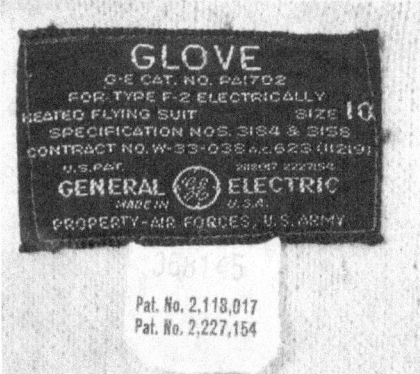

6

5

Examples of typical labels found on AAF flying clothing of World War II: 1. Black label with woven pale yellow-gold lettering for Type A-2 summer flying jacket (which was worn by Maj. Gen. Claire L. Chennault). This was a standard type of label used until late in the war. It did not include the nomenclature of the item since it was fairly obvious what it was. 2. White label with woven red lettering for the Type A-11 intermediate flying helmet introduced in August 1943. 3. Black label with woven white lettering for Type K-1 very light cotton-twill flying suit. Around 1944 labels began to include a description of the more specialized items of flying clothing. 4. White label with printed black lettering for Type Q-1 electric flying shoe. The "NE" stamped on the upper right-hand corner was a factory inspection mark. 5. Black label with woven yellow-gold lettering for electrically heated glove used with the Type F-2 electric flying suit. 6. Black label with woven yellow-gold lettering for Spec. AN-H-15 summer flying helmet standardized for use by both the Army and Navy. The AN indicates that the article is a standardized Army-Navy item, the H shows that it is a helmet, and the 15 stands for Type 15. (SI Photo 81–705)

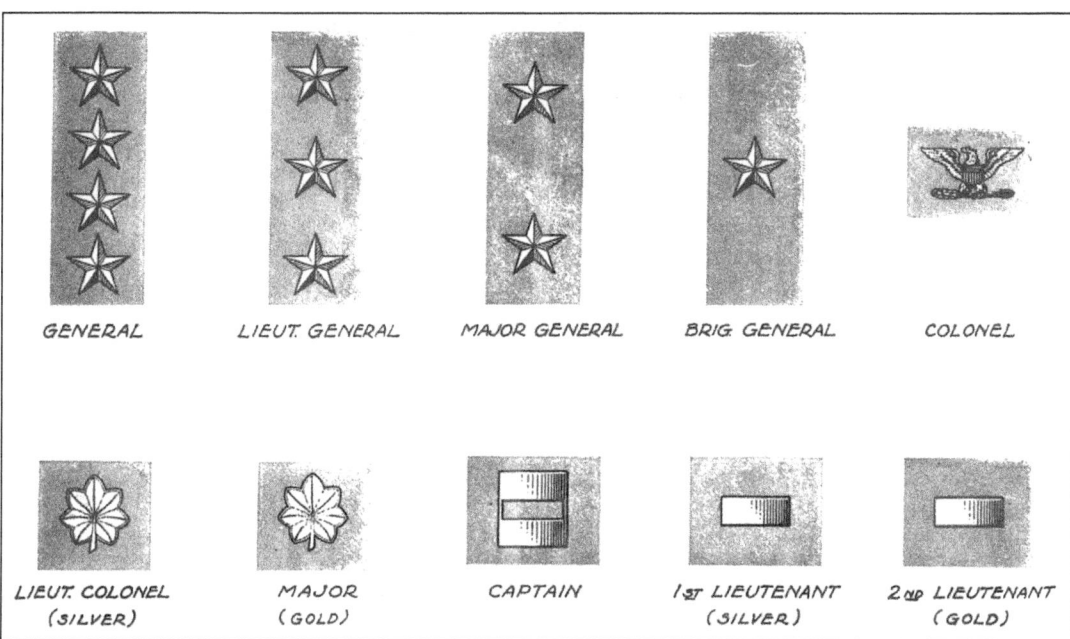

Officer's insignia of grade (rank), reproduced from Prescribed Service Uniforms, Army Regulation no. 600–35, War Department, Wash., D.C., Nov. 10, 1941. (SI Photo 80-20499)

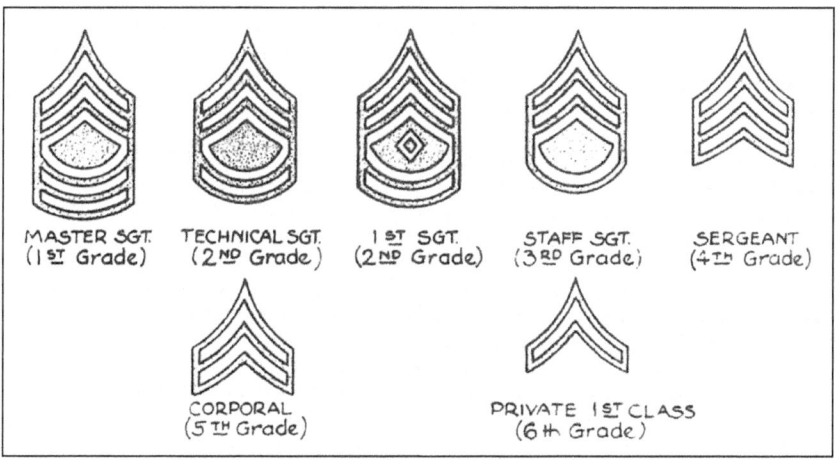

Enlisted grade insignia, reproduced from Prescribed Service Uniforms, Army Regulation no. 600–35, War Department, Washington, D.C., Nov. 10, 1941 (SI Photo 81-7852)

"Army Air Forces." This was usually accomplished either by a wet-process transfer or by stamping or printing in various sizes on the outside. Insignia could also be found on the inside of garments. Some flying suits had a more elaborate version of the AAF insignia printed on their upper left sleeves, just below the shoulder seams, either in full color or in black or white outline.

After issue, special insignia such as rank (grade) and unit were sometimes affixed to flying clothing. Insignia were most often worn on the Type A-2 leather flying jacket, which was occasionally decorated with "war art" in the form of painted pictures and was frequently worn as an outer garment with the service uniform while on the ground. (The A-2 and other jackets are discussed in detail in chapter 7.)

During the war personnel seldom wore grade insignia on any flying clothing other than the A-2 jacket and, occasionally, the "elastique" outer jacket of the F-2 electric suit. Officers sometimes wore their grade insignia on the shoulders of flying jackets and suits, but enlisted men almost never wore actual grade insignia. Neither was the use of metal devices (e.g., rank badges and wings) common, since they were potentially hazardous in forced landings. However, aircrewmen usually wore at least the semblance of a proper military uniform with insignia under flying clothing so that, if they were forced down in enemy territory, they would have the Geneva Convention protection afforded persons in uniform.

Sometimes, the name tags sewn on flying clothing included the wearer's grade. Officers' grade insignia, when worn, were of several different types. Silver or gold insignia were often printed or painted onto leather tabs, and plastic-like insignia might also be attached to such tabs. Cloth patches with woven grade insignia were sometimes used; an example of this was the Type K-1 flying suit with majors' leaves on the shoulders (shown in chapter 6). Embroidered insignia were occasionally sewed to the shoulders or shoulder straps (an example, the stars on General Claire Chennault's Type A-2 jacket, is illustrated in chapter 7).

Unit or organizational insignia were frequently worn on A-2 jackets and occasionally on other flying jackets and suits. The insignia were usually painted on five-inch leather disks that were sewed to a garment's left breast, but a few woven cloth or special leather patches were also used. Blank leather patches were available for issue through supply channels. The AAF patch, in woven cloth or leather, was frequently worn on the shoulder, especially on jackets, and the numbered air force patch was also worn on the shoulder by some flyers. Some leather jackets had all the insignia painted on them.[8]

Flags, Name Plates, and Wings

Some airmen sewed small U.S. flags on the shoulders and backs of their garments (as can be seen from the photos of A-2 jackets in chapter 7). But crewmen in some overseas areas also wore the so-called blood chits or escape flags, with appropriate texts, on the backs or insides of garments. This practice was especially common in the China-Burma-India Theater of operations and in Southeast Asia. Some of these cloth panels were the official, serial numbered types; others were locally procured. They promised rewards to natives who helped downed American flyers return to Allied lines. Leather blood chits (as well as other insignia) were made commercially in India during the war. (Examples of the escape flags are also shown on A-2 jackets illustrated in chapter 7.)

Leather name plates or tags were authorized and frequently sewed onto the jackets' upper left breasts. These tags usually measured five-eighths by four inches and were three thirty-seconds of an inch thick. Wearers' names, and sometimes their grades, were machine-stamped onto the tags by the units issuing the jackets. Flying cadets were sometimes provided with gold-colored metal name plates with attaching safety pins on the back. The overall dimensions were three-fourths by one and fifteen-sixteenths inches. Wearers' names were typed on thin cards and inserted into the frames of the name plates.

Aviation badges or "wings," printed on leather or woven on cloth, were also worn on the left breast by some flyers. J. Duncan Campbell's illustrated book on the history of U.S. Army aviation badges provides an excellent description of American wings through World War II.[9]

Colors

The traditional colors for Army clothing were khaki for summer or lightweight garments and olive drab, later forest green, for winter or heavy clothing. Many shades of olive drab occurred, however, especially with clothing manufactured during the war: tints varied from one manufacturer to another and also at

B-17 bomber crewman outfitted for a high-altitude combat mission. Over his Type B-15 jacket, A-11 trousers, electrically heated suit, and parachute, he is wearing the M-1 armored or "flak" vest with M-4 apron. A steel M-5 aviator's "flak" helmet is being worn over a standard flying helmet. He is also wearing a pair of B-8 goggles, an A-14 oxygen mask, and A-6A flying shoes. On his hands he appears to be wearing the electrically heated leather gloves usually worn over the rayon insert gloves. (SI Photo 80-20355)

different periods of the conflict. Some clothing was made in different brown and even gray hues. Constant washing and exposure to the elements under service conditions also affected the intensity of the color of garments.

A Typical Airman's Attire

The different items of flying clothing are described in the later chapters of this book. It may be appropriate at this point, however, to summarize what a fully equipped combat air-

A B-17 bomber crew of the 379th Bomb Group, Eighth Air Force, in England, March 12, 1945. A wide variety of flying clothing can be seen in this photograph. Items include Type B-4 life vests, RAF Type C leather helmets (top row, 2d and 4th from left), B-10 jackets, B-1 cap (bottom row, 4th from left), AN-S-31 flying suit (top row, 4th from left), and F-2 electric suits (bottom row, 3rd and 5th from left). The cap device of the man at top left is upside down. (SI Photo 80–20356)

man on a typical high-altitude mission might have worn during the later part of World War II.

A navigator on a B-17 bomber, for example, began by donning two-piece wool underwear and his ordinary wool uniform of shirt and trousers. On top of these he wore an electrically heated flying suit, probably a Type F-3—a two-piece garment with a bolero-style jacket and overall-style rayon trousers. Small, well-insulated wires ran through the suit to provide warmth without weight at extremely low temperatures. The airman could regulate his suit's temperature by turning a rheostat mounted at his station in the aircraft. He covered all that with a pile-lined B-15 jacket and A-11 trousers, each of which had a wind- and moisture-proof outer surface. A warm vest was also available as an optional item.

Protection against the cold was only the beginning. The navigator also wore a parachute, which often included a back pad survival kit attached to the harness. The B-2 survival kit contained items intended to help keep him alive if he bailed out or was forced down, though its contents naturally varied with the part of the world over which he was flying. His parachute, with harness, could have been a back, seat, or detachable-chest type, usually depending on his crew position. If he was going on an overwater flight, this flyer donned a B-4 or B-5 automatically inflatable life vest between his suit and his parachute. Finally, when entering combat, he shielded his body and accouterments with a canvas flak vest containing overlapping steel plates to prevent most 20mm aircraft and long-range anti-aircraft shell fragments from piercing his body. Armored vests produced in the later part of the war featured a single strap that, when pulled, detached the vest if a bailout was necessary.

Rayon gloves topped by electrically heated leather gloves took care of the airman's hands. The rayon gloves were provided so that, if he had to remove his outer gloves to repair or adjust some part of the plane, his hands would not freeze to the cold metal.

An AN-H-16 shearling winter flying helmet with headset or, more likely, a Type A-11 intermediate helmet; a pair of B-8 goggles; a steel flak helmet, probably a Type M3; and an oxygen mask such as the A-14, with microphone, protected his head and face. On his feet he wore wool socks, and over them he donned leather shoes. He then slipped his feet into electrically heated slippers, which he covered with A-6 or A-6A outer boots made of sheep shearling. The boots were also partially rubber-coated for protection against wind and moisture.

Flying clothing had to protect all members of a crew from extreme cold and heat, against enemy fire, and against all possible hazards that they might have encountered if they had to bail out or crash land and return to Allied lines. The airmen also had to have maximum freedom of action to perform efficiently the many tasks necessary in flying and fighting. For instance, the tail gunner had to be kept alive and comfortable at -60° F and still fit into his turret, the bombardier had to be warmed but left free to make his calculations and release his bombs, and so on through the crew. Beginning in late 1944 some fighter pilots were equipped with pneumatic anti-g garments, which minimized blackouts during maneuvers by automatically applying air pressure to the abdomen and legs during pullouts and turns. All this had to be done without adding too much to the total weight that could be carried in an aircraft of the period.

3

Research and Testing of Flying Clothing

The testing and evaluation of flying clothing goes back to World War I. Personnel at the equipment laboratories established at Mc-Cook and Wright Fields and other air bases tested clothing designed in their own facilities, as well as similar articles developed by the U.S. Navy and private industry.

During World War I U.S. attaches and other representatives began obtaining examples of military and civilian flying clothing and equipment for testing and evaluation by aviation personnel in the United States. Some items were also purchased for testing and trial, but in general it was found that the development of flying clothing in foreign countries had progressed little, if any, beyond the state of the art reached in the United States.[1] In addition, Army specialists carefully examined and tested Allied and captured enemy flying gear for new ideas and improved designs or materials. This practice was continued throughout World War II, and by the end of that war so much foreign flying clothing and equipment had been obtained by the AAF for examination that a classification system was established. Catalogs of loan items were published listing articles available for study by other agencies and private firms.[2]

During the 1920s and 1930s most items of flying clothing, especially those designed for winter use, were tested during altitude flights at Wright Field or in outdoor work on some air field chosen for that purpose because of cli-

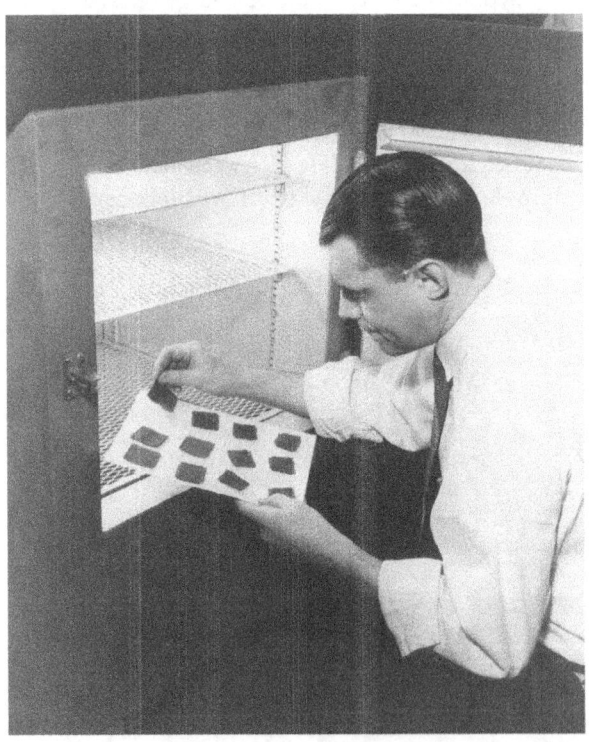

Drying test being performed on fabric samples in a special oven at the Materials Laboratory, Wright Field (SI Photo A4863D)

mate, mission, or other factors. Ladd Field, Alaska, was established in 1941 and soon became the site for both ground and flight testing of flying clothing and equipment. Testing was also conducted on Mount McKinley in 1942 at altitudes of 15,000 to 17,000 feet with -24° F temperatures and 50 mph winds. Tropical testing was centered at Eglin Field, Florida. Evaluation was also conducted by the Tactical Center and Equipment Board at Orlando, Florida.

Articles of flying clothing were given preliminary laboratory or field tests and, if they proved satisfactory, were standardized. Next, enough clothing was usually procured for service testing, accomplished by having each item used for a while in actual service at one or more air bases in the United States or overseas. After tests were completed, modifications or changes could be made before large-scale procurement was begun. An example of this was the controlled service testing conducted on the Type F-3 electrically heated flying suit at Gowen Field, Idaho, in 1944. As a result of these tests, a weakness was found in the electric cord connecting the suit to the aircraft's electrical system and was immediately remedied in production. Also during testing, the approximate "wear life" of an item of clothing was estimated by compiling detailed "chronological" records of wear.[3]

Sometimes, accelerated wear tests to meet immediate needs were conducted by subjecting an article of clothing to continuous use. For example, an item might be taken from a returning aviator and given to another one who was going out on a flight, with that process repeated for two or three weeks until the wear on the garment was equal to what would usually be received in a year of normal combat usage. Another accelerated test was the walking test, which determined the degree of fatigue that flyers would experience if

A laundering test, one of many performed on fabrics by technicians at the Materials Laboratory and the Personal Equipment Laboratory (SI Photo A4863E)

they were forced to make a long hike while wearing a complete outfit of winter flying clothing.

In 1944 the AAF adopted a carefully controlled method for determining the functional suitability of articles of clothing and equipment in simulated combat. It consisted of an opinion survey modeled after the Gallup Poll, in which items of clothing were issued to, and appraised by, aircrews at a selected training base. A proper ratio of pilots, bombardiers, navigators, and gunners was chosen for the sample group so that no one position would be overlooked when requirements for a garment were made.

After a few missions or a week of wear, each participant was interrogated with carefully worded questions concerning the garment. By tabulating several hundred answers, the AAF researchers could determine where pockets should be, whether closures were good or poor, and other factors. This procedure clearly indicated, for example, that gloves were sized too small, that the throat latch on the Type B-15 intermediate flying jacket was too short, and that the bailout oxygen bottle pocket on the Type A-11 flying trousers was too low.[4]

Not until late in World War II were adequate facilities available at Wright Field to perform all of the laboratory tests required on materials and articles of clothing being considered for use by the AAF. Instead, tests

 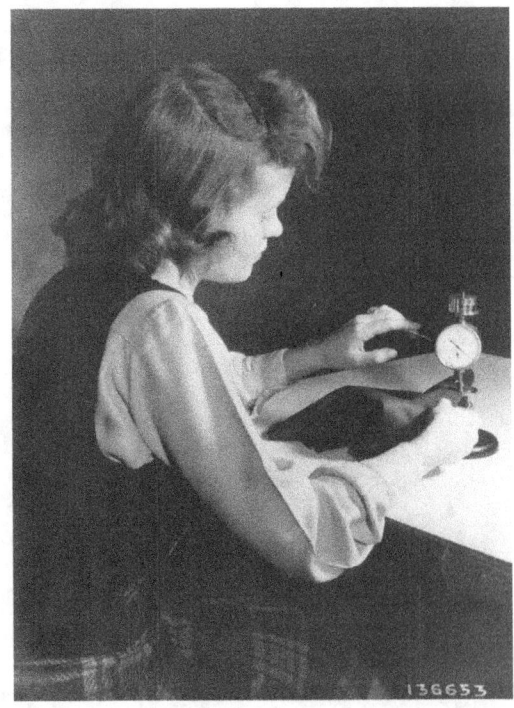

Left: Fabric undergoing a heat conductivity test. Studies disclosed that fibers are neither warm nor cool by themselves. Fabric structure largely determines whether heat is given off or retained. Fabric structure can also offer comfort in garments. For example, pile fabrics trap air, making them warm. It was learned that fabrics can be quilted and joined together to increase their insulating properties. The thicker the structure, the warmer the fabric will be. Down insulated and quilted fabrics can be formed in fabric construction to provide layers of insulating air, which increases their warming ability. Considerable experimentation with down-insulated clothing was done during World War II. (SI Photo A4863F)
Right: A thickness test being performed on a sample piece of fabric. Surprisingly, no one fiber is warmer than another. It was found that what is important is the thickness of the fabric. Some fibers weigh less and are good at retaining heat. Wool and silk weigh less than linen or cotton. Synthetics proved to be lighter in weight than natural fibers. (SI Photo A4863J)

were conducted through a cooperative agreement in the cold chamber at Yale University, the Harvard Fatigue Laboratory, the General Electric Cold Chamber, and the cold chamber at Monmouth Field, New Jersey. High-altitude tests were also made in the chamber at the Mayo Clinic, Rochester, Minnesota. Finally, in early 1943 the cold room in the Aero Medical Laboratory at Wright Field became ready for use, and a comparative test of shearling and electrically heated flying suits was performed.

By 1944 the low-pressure cold chamber in the Aero Medical Laboratory could be used to simulate the reduced air pressure present at an altitude of 80,000 feet and a temperature of -85° F. Thermocouples could be taped to the various parts of the bodies of test subjects to measure skin temperatures in cold-chamber tests. Wires from the thermocouples were connected to apparatus outside the cold chamber where an observer took readings. That procedure helped, for example, to ascertain whether the heating wires in an electrically heated flying suit were properly distributed. Conditions that could be found in the arctic, deserts, or tropics and on land or water were duplicated in the all-weather chamber, and about five hundred such tests were conducted by the end of 1944.

The relative thermal insulative values of various articles of clothing and other personal equipment were better determined by using the thermal or "Copper Man," which was constructed by the General Electric Company for use by the AML.[5] With that device the testing of clothing, sleeping bags, casualty blankets, and similar equipment was expedited and made more accurate. Shaped like a man 5-feet, 10½ inches tall, the thermal man had a "skin"

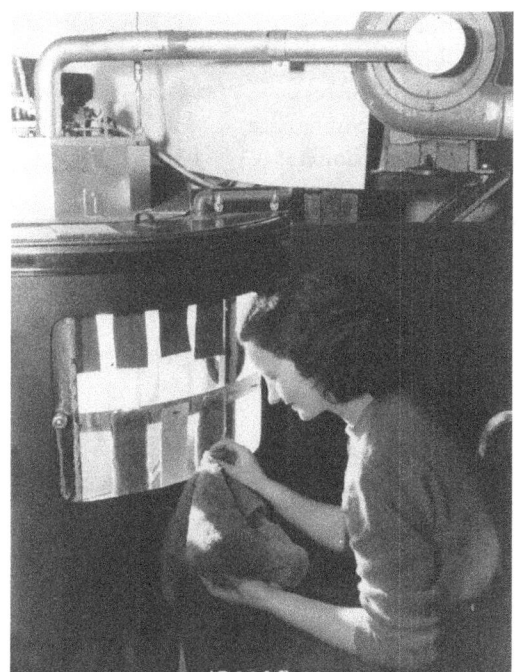

Left: Civilian technician preparing an accelerated weathering test at the Materials Laboratory, Wright Field. (SI Photo A4863A) *Right:* A proposed fabric for flying clothing undergoing an air porosity test. Moisture is given off by the body, and fibers and fabrics that can absorb this moisture and allow perspiration to evaporate from the skin are more comfortable to wear. Natural fibers such as cotton, linen, silk, and wool do a very good job of absorbing moisture from the skin. Man-made fibers, with the exception of rayon, do not. At very cold temperatures, perspiration that is not absorbed or allowed to escape from the clothing can cause frostbite. (SI Photo A4863G)

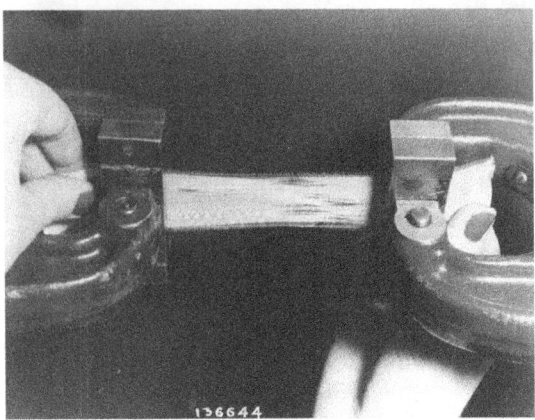 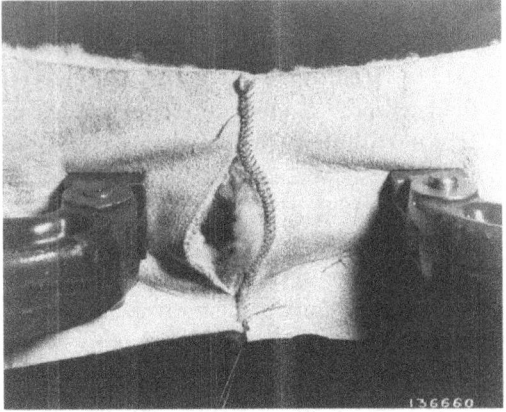

Left: **Testing the tensile strength of a fabric.** (SI Photo A4863C) *Right:* **A rip test performed on shearling.** (SI Photo A4863)

that was one-sixteenth of an inch thick and consisted of fifteen parts or areas, each of which had separate heat controls. Until the thermal man was developed, clothing testing was hindered by imprecision, because there were too many variables in any test on clothed human beings. Human physiological response was subject to considerable variation from one individual to another and even in the same individual from day to day, making it extremely difficult to measure the insulation value of an item of clothing. As a result, a long series of tests were necessary to obtain average values that could be considered characteristic of the human response. With the thermal man, however, the human variable was eliminated, and the protective value of the clothing was assessed with the precision typical of physical measurement.[6]

The then chief of the laboratory, Col. Otis O. Benson, Jr., in cooperation with Harvard professor Earnest A. Hooton, the noted physical anthropologist, directed another program at the AML. They studied 1,871 young men in the AAF to determine the average height, weight, dimensions, and physical characteristics of flyers and made their findings available to clothing, equipment, and aircraft designers and manufacturers. The typical American flyer in 1942 had the following measurements:

Height	5 ft., 9 in.
Weight	154.3 lbs.
Arm span	71½ in.
Reach	35 in.
Shoulders	17¾ in.
Chest diameter	8 in.
Waist diameter	8 in.
Chest circumference	36¼ in.
Waist circumference	30 in.
Head (7 1/8 hat)	22¼ in.
Biceps	11½ in.
Forearm	9½ in.
Thigh	20⅝ in.
Calf	14 in.
Height, seated	36¼ in.
Back to knee, seated	23⅜ in.
Knee to floor	21¾ in.
Breadth of seat	14 in.
Foot length	10½ in.
Hand length	7⅝ in.[7]

The first tangible results of that study were embodied in seven sculptured heads, representing precisely measured composites of all the types of faces found among the 1,871 subjects. Graduated from long to short, the seven heads presented a graphic demonstration of the broad range required in an item such as a satisfactory form-fitting oxygen mask. In 1942, after they were produced in plaster, the heads were furnished to firms

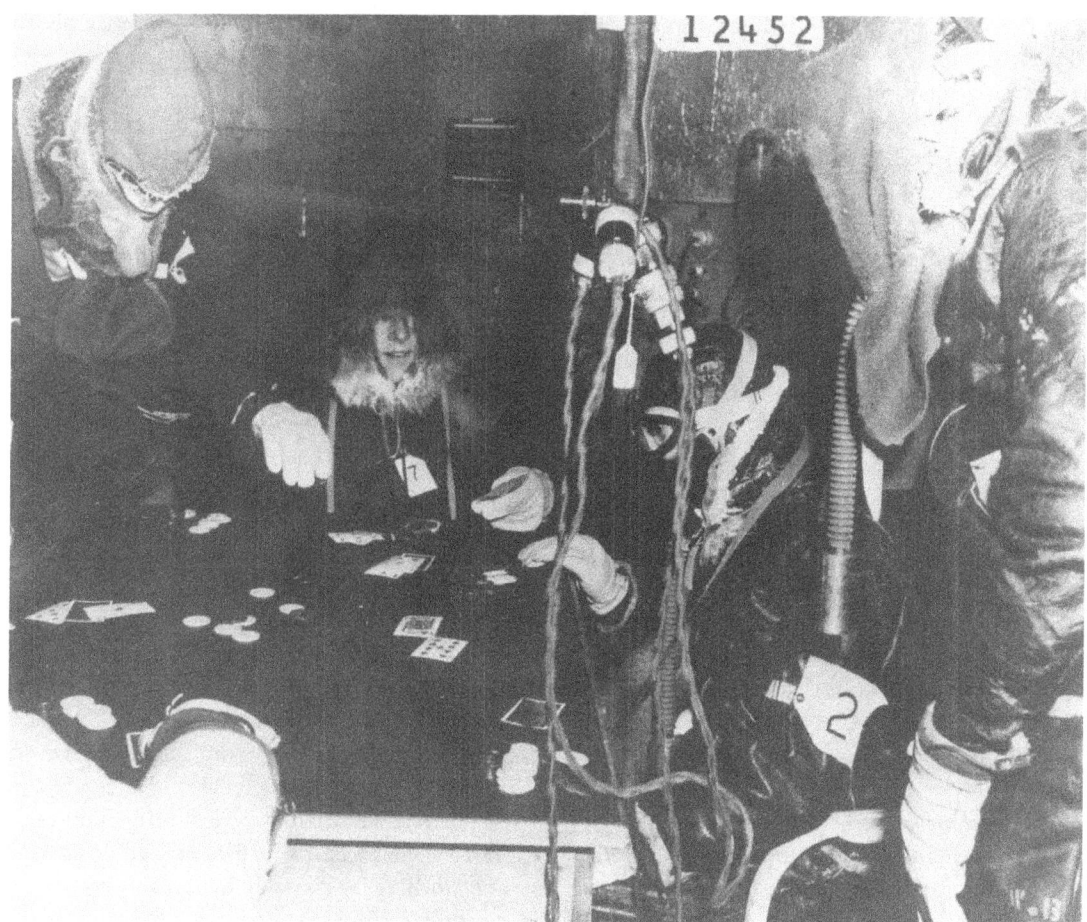

A cold-chamber test being performed to determine the relative comfort and efficiency of various types of clothing and personal equipment over an extended period of time. It was confirmed through testing that several layers of looser, lighter-weight clothing not only are more flexible and comfortable but also provide more warmth than one heavy layer because air is trapped between the lightweight layers. This air is heated by the body and acts as an insulator. Summer clothing on the other hand, should be loose and open to permit the heated air surrounding the body to escape. The air should also be allowed to get to the skin in warm weather to evaporate perspiration as it accumulates. (SI Photo A4866J)

making oxygen masks. They proved to be very helpful in designing masks that could be mass-produced in as few sizes as possible while fitting different facial types with a minimum of oxygen leakage.

The Materials Laboratory at Wright Field was responsible for testing fabrics to determine their tensile strength; their resistance to tear and mildew; their color fastness, air permeability, and water repellency. Gloves were tested by the Clothing Branch of the Personal Equipment Laboratory to ascertain their ease of donning, warmth, resistance to wear, and degree to which they reduced a flyer's manual dexterity in performing intricate work.

A human centrifuge was in active use at the Aero Medical Laboratory during the war. It was used mainly to study safely the occurrence and prevention of the effects of radial acceleration ("g" forces) in flying personnel.

At the direction of the chief of the Engineering Division, the Clothing Branch and the Biophysics Branch of the AML reached an agreement in October 1943 to cooperate in the cold-chamber and flight testing of all flying clothing. The cooperative testing arrangement was formalized by the creation of a Joint Research and Test Board to review and plan the development and testing of clothing and related personal equipment. The membership of the board was divided equally between the two laboratories. Its primary purpose was to determine the physiological feasibility of various flying clothing assemblies designed for use in all climates, including subzero, moderate, wet tropical, and desert. The precise study of clothing on AAF personnel exposed to temperatures and wind speeds characteristic of high-altitude operations under the most severe cooling stresses was considered essential to the development of the AAF flying clothing including hand-, head-, and footgear. Hundreds of separate tests were accomplished in the all-weather room and the refrigerated altitude chamber, as well as during flight.

The board emphasized clothing requirements for cold weather use and for hot climates, including fighter airplanes that experienced high cockpit temperatures. Tolerance curves, expressed in terms of dry bulb temperature, relative humidity, and duration were determined in hot room tests. In addition, studies of the added effect of direct solar radiation were conducted. The results of all these investigations were applied not only to clothing but also to ventilating requirements for aircraft.

Work on cold-protective clothing was accelerated, including a series of "clo" tests on experimental suits constructed of wool pile and on various types of lining and shell fabrics. Precise measurements were made of the effectiveness of infrared reflecting cloths in clothing and headgear. Miscellaneous projects included tests of an electrically heated casualty blanket for bomber aircraft, electric muffs, chamois covers for earphones, heated oversocks, and electric suits and gloves of improved design.

Although flyer's equipment developed by the Engineering Division received a final laboratory test for performance under simulated flight conditions in the low pressure chamber, it was essential that experimental items be subjected to preliminary flight tests before they were considered to have reached a stage of development that justified their submission for extensive service tests. The complex relationships between several conditions that could influence personnel in flight were difficult or impossible to duplicate in the low-pressure chamber. These conditions included propeller and engine noise, vibration, rough air, extreme changes in temperature within short intervals of time (+165° to -65° F), centrifugal force, glare, wind, movement in a limited space, emotional stress, and nervous fatigue.

In September 1943, to carry out systematic high-altitude flight tests with personnel at crew positions, the Engineering Division obtained a Boeing B-17E bomber that had formerly been used by the Boeing Aircraft Company for its high-altitude test flights. The plane was outfitted with special equipment that enabled it to reach exceptionally high altitudes (up to 43,000 feet) and ascend to 35,000 feet within thirty-five or forty minutes. Tests of many items of personal equipment and clothing used by bomber crews were successfully conducted aboard the B-17E. Similarly, personal equipment used by fighter pilots was tested in fighters; such as a Lockheed P-38, that had been modified into a two-place configuration.[8]

Not all research and development projects were successful. For instance, a program was initiated during the war to develop a method of flame-proofing fabrics used in flying clothing. Test garments were submitted by the three chemical companies involved in the experiments, and although the special substances applied to the fabrics raised their combustion point, flame-proofing was not adopted for a variety of reasons. In one test program at Eglin Field in 1944, several types of summer flying suits were treated with antimony oxide and were tested under controlled conditions. The tests indicated that the treated suits would not burst into flame and that the flame retardancy of the material was not diminished by sweat or by twelve launderings and dry cleanings. Still, they were warmer and more uncomfortable than untreated suits were. No suit, whether treated or not, would protect a person from the great heat of an intense fire of long duration. Since untreated summer flying suits offered adequate protection against short flash fires and were much more comfortable, it was recommended that flame-retardant material not be considered for general wear by flying personnel.[9]

By 1944 all of the technical facilities at Wright Field, including those of the newly organized Personal Equipment Laboratory, were performing the highly specialized laboratory work required to develop the complex assortment of AAF flying garments and equipment needed during the war.[10]

4

Heavy Winter Shearling Flying Suits

During the period from World War I through World War II, clothing designers probably expended more effort on the development of a satisfactory winter flying suit than on any other type of garment. With flying clothing a relatively new field for the clothing industry, early designs were logically based on clothing and equipment used by arctic explorers, trappers, motorcyclists, and Eskimos. Gradually, the designers set basic principles for the flying suits (e.g., the need for sleeves and pant legs to close tightly to keep warm air in and cold air out).

During 1917 and 1918 fur-lined and electrically heated one-piece flying suits made of leather, wool, and other heavy fabrics were developed and procured by the Aviation Clothing Board. Considerable attention was given to developing electrically heated clothing, but its undependability required that fur lining be retained. Unfortunately, however, a limited supply of good-quality fur in the United States

2d Lt. (later Brig. Gen.) Benjamin S. Kelsey wearing the Type B-1 winter flying suit at Mather Field, California, in 1931. Called the "Monkey Suit" because of its Chinese Nuchwang dog fur lining, it actually dated back to World War I and was designated as the Type B-1 during the 1920s. He is also carrying a pair of coney-fur "pocket" mittens and wearing the smooth "bare foot" moccasin-type flying boots. The goggles are probably Type B-6. (SI Photo 80–19095)

4. Heavy Winter Shearling Flying Suits

The Type B-2 winter flying suit was lined with nutria fur from a South American rodent. It was used as limited standard from 1926 until 1944. (SI Photo A4869G)

hindered the production of fur-lined garments. To relieve that shortage, the board imported Nuchwang dog fur mats from China. Suits containing these mats were used until 1931, when all Type B-1 "Monkey" suits lined with them were recalled because of their offensive odor, vermin infestation, tendency to shed, and problems with dyes that rubbed off on clothing and wearer's of the suits.[1]

Other types of flying suits were tested with varying results during the 1920s and early 1930s. As early as 1923, sheepskin was considered as a substitute for fur lining in test suits. The sheepskin was used not for the entire garment, as was later done with the shearlings, but only for the lining. One example of this type of construction was the Type B-1 jacket, A-1 trouser combination of 1931.

Another tested suit featured an outer shell of leather or Bedford cord and a lining of nutria fur, which comes from a South American rodent. Designated the Type B-2 but also known as the Type A-3, this suit remained in the inventory as limited standard from 1926 until March 14, 1944, when its stocks were exhausted. In addition, some "modified" B-2 suits were made with blanket lining, while experimental suits made during the 1920s were designated Types B-3 through B-6.

In February 1927 it was recommended that

calfskin suits be standardized and procured since they were less expensive than the nutria-lined Bedford cloth suits and required no inner lining or outer shell. And on May 12, 1928, the Air Corps adopted the leather suit with blanket lining as standard, designating it the Type B-7. (That suit is covered in more detail, along with the Types B-8 and B-9 winter suits, in chapter 6.) Blanket lining was also used during that period in suits made from corduroy and Bedford cloth.

Although new materials or combinations of materials sometimes seemed, at the time of their initial tests by the Equipment Branch at Wright Field, to be superior to the clothing in production, they frequently proved to be unsatisfactory or disappointing in actual use. For example, all of the leather and cloth suits with fur lining procured during that period were too heavy, bulky, and cumbersome, while the blanket-lined Type B-7 suits were not sufficiently warm.

In April 1934 Maj. Malcolm C. Grow, flight surgeon, recommended using Alaskan reindeer skin in flying clothing, and test suits were constructed.[2] However, Maj. E.L. Hoffman, chief of the Equipment Branch, soon recommended that the study of reindeer clothing be discontinued and that flying clothing be constructed of sheep shearling instead.[3] Major Hoffman based his recommendation on several factors, including the availability, comfort, and thermal-value similarity of lamb shearling and reindeer skin. Shearling's noncompressibility and its resistance to rain and, especially, wind made it well suited for the open-cockpit or unheated aircraft of that period.

Major Hoffman and the other advocates of shearling garments succeeded in winning their acceptance. The first shearling winter flying garments were developed during a two- or three-year period. Because the Air Corps needed new, improved flying suits to wear while carrying the air mail, however, they were standardized rather hurriedly after short service tests during the winters of 1933 and 1934 at Wright Field and Chanute Field.

The first shearling winter flying outfit in 1934: the Type B-3 jacket, with collar turned up; the Type A-3 trousers; probably the Type B-5 helmet; Type A-5 shoes; and Type A-9 gloves. The suit was separated into two parts for better sizing and comfort. (SI Photo A4864F)

On May 8, 1934, the two parts of the first flying suit constructed of shearling were standardized as the Type B-3 winter flying jacket and the Type A-3 winter flying trousers and placed on procurement. The jacket and trousers were made separately to aid comfort, convenience, and sizing.[4] Adjustable suspenders were provided for the trousers. The jacket had a gusset under each arm and a bellows at the shoulders. A zipper extended the full length of the front, and the trouser legs, with a pocket below each knee, had full-length zippers, as well. The flesh side of the pelt served as the outside shell for the garments, while the wool was, of course, worn on their inside.

The shearling garments, constructed of pelts from young sheep, were called "electrified lamb skin" by the clothing industry. The pelts' smooth, fur-like appearance was achieved by submerging the curly wool in acid, oiling it, and then alternately combing and ironing the wool fiber until it had been straightened. Finally, the pile, or fiber, was clipped to a desired length and smoothness. Originally, the fiber for each garment was five-eighths of an inch long. In July 1935 the length of the fiber on new jackets was increased to one and one-fourth inches for the body and three-fourths of an inch for the sleeves.[5] Most suits manufactured during World War II had a one half-inch pile.

Another winter jacket, the Type B-4, was designed in the form of an Alaskan parka. Service tests on it officially began on August 9, 1934, and it was adopted as standard on November 7, 1935. The B-4 jacket's classification was changed to limited standard on April 29, 1941, and it was declared obsolete on March 27, 1944. The B-4, which had a zipper front, was intended to be worn not only by pilots over their winter flying suits but also by mechanics who had to work in arctic temperatures. Shearling winter clothing was also developed over a period of several years specifically for mechanics and maintenance personnel and was standardized in 1937.

Unfortunately, the introduction of shearling garments did not resolve the serious dissatisfaction with winter flying clothing that had existed for a number of years. As soon as the suits entered general use, both flying and maintenance personnel severely criticized them for being too heavy, inflexible, and cumbersome. The suits were considered to be warm and windproof, but they did not allow perspiration to escape from the underclothing of an active wearer. They were so bulky that some Army flyers involved in forced landings had to discard their shearling suits in order to make long treks out of wilderness areas.[6]

As new aircraft with enclosed cockpits and gun turrets entered service between 1935 and 1940, a lighter-weight winter flying suit became necessary. No extensive effort was made to develop any other type of winter suit, although some attention was given to developing electrically heated suits (which are discussed in chapter 5). The general assumption seemed to be that, despite the shortcomings of the shearling suits, the costs and availability of raw materials made them the most desirable garments. After all, funds for the Air Corps were very limited during the Depression years.

During this period the Air Corps conducted many experiments to discover how to make the leather more pliable, moth resistant, and less absorbent of water, oil, and dirt. The natural flesh side (or outside) of the shearling clothing made during the first few years of manufacture had been rather soft and absorbent. In the late 1930s a new finishing process, called the Korsseal Waterproofing Treatment, was introduced. The flesh side was coated first, with a polyacrylate leather dye, and then with a top finish lacquer. The resulting smooth, seal-brown leather was more resistant to moisture, gasoline, oil, and dirt. It tended, however, to be stiffer, slightly heavier, and often flaked with normal use. Fortunately, the flaking problem was reduced during the war as the process for coating shearling was improved.[7] In addition, ordinary leather garments in the Air Corps were maintained by periodically applying saddle soap.

The Air Corps's efforts to provide winter

Shearling clothing consisting of the Types B-3 jacket and A-3 trousers, August 2, 1939. The outsides of the two suits at left are still in the "raw," while the suit at right has been weatherproofed through the application of brown polyacrylate leather dye and lacquer as a top finish. The three pilots (left to right), Capt. Pearl Robey, Capt. C.S. Irvine, and Lt. R.P. Swofford, flying from Patterson Field, Ohio, had just set a new international altitude record of 33,400 ft. with payload of 5,000 kg (11,023 lbs.) in a Boeing B-17A. (SI Photo 81–329)

flying clothing of proper weight during the 1930s by utilizing available stocks were reflected in the Class 13 Stock Lists of that period. The B-1, A-1 and the B-2, A-2 winter outfits were issued at stations in southern areas while the B-3, A-3 outfit was retained for use at northern stations. Combat crews received priority on the issuance of two-piece suits. In addition, to consume older garments first, one-piece winter suits such as the B-2, B-7, and B-9 were issued to enlisted personnel on flying status. When they were available, these suits were also issued to ground-crew personnel in extremely cold climates.

In the spring of 1939 the Air Corps finally attempted to meet the need for a lighter and less cumbersome winter flying suit by completing the development of an intermediate (or lightweight) shearling outfit. Designated the Type B-6 jacket and A-5 trousers, the new outfit was standardized on June 12, 1939; became available for use during the summer of 1940; and saw service throughout the war. The shearling pelts had a seal-brown finish and a pile that was only one-fourth of an inch long. The B-6 jacket could be quickly differentiated from the older B-3 jacket by the location of its pockets: the B-3 had one large patch pocket, cut at an angle, on its lower right front, while the B-6 had a slash pocket on each side of the zipper on its lower front. Pictures will occasionally be found painted on the backs of both the B-3 and B-6 jackets. The A-5 trousers had a zipper on the fly and on the full length of

Crewmen of Curtiss C-46 transport, about 1942. The man at left is wearing a Type B-6 shearling jacket and a white silk scarf, while men at center and on right are wearing Type B-3 shearling jackets. Man at right has a T-30 throat microphone and an HS-33 headset with ANB-H-1 receivers. All appear to be wearing Type B-1 flying caps. (SI Photo 77-5816)

each leg, as did the A-3 trousers. Both types of trousers also had a pocket below each knee, and adjustable suspenders were attached.

One other intermediate outfit—the Type B-5 jacket, A-4 trousers combination—was developed during this period. Intended for wear in aircraft with enclosed cabins or turrets, this unlined outfit was made of wool fabric and warp knit. The jacket had a sheep shearling collar. Service testing of the suit began July 11, 1938, and the trousers and jacket were designated limited standard on June 12 and 15, 1939, respectively. They were procured in limited quantities only, since the outfit did not fully meet the requirements for either an intermediate or a winter flying suit. The jacket was declared obsolete on March 27, 1944, followed by the trousers four days later.

During 1940 and 1941, manufacturers submitted proposals that new suits be made of pile-woven fabric and other materials, but the Air Corps never approved them because sheep shearling was still considered the best all-around material for winter flying suits. Cold-chamber tests conducted during the summer of 1940 demonstrated, however, that the bulk necessary for shearling clothing to provide adequate warmth at temperatures between -30° and -50° F would seriously impair a pilot's freedom of movement and contribute toward dangerous fatigue. As a result of these tests, it was recommended that lightweight electrically heated clothing be developed.[8]

At a conference held on September 20, 1941, at the Office of Production Management in Washington, the Air Corps decided that it would need sixteen million square feet of shearling material for 1942 and another twelve million square feet for 1943. The bombing of Pearl Harbor, however, changed that almost immediately, and the AAF and Navy expanded immensely during 1942. That growth was studied by representatives of both the AAF and the Aeronautics Board of the Navy during a conference in April 1942, and the massively increased requirements for shearling were determined for the period between July 1, 1942, and June 30, 1944:

Army—
  plane crews   47,100,000 square feet
  ground crews   40,060,000   "   "
  Subtotal: 87,160,000   "   "
Navy—
  plane crews   16,790,000 square feet
  ground crews   14,250,000   "   "
  Subtotal: 31,040,000   "   "
  TOTAL: 118,200,000 square feet

The conference report added that each new suit would require 75 square feet of material.[9]

The tremendous requirements for shearling material led to a serious situation in the shearling market. The War Production Board (WPB) froze all stocks of shearling, and efforts were made to increase its production. Because of the critical situation, several more conferences were held during the spring and summer of 1942. During May, for example, a conference and exhibit of flying clothing was held in Washington at the instigation of Gen. Henry H. Arnold. The conference resulted in a recommendation that the number of types of flying clothing be reduced. It was also urged that multilayer garments be developed so that the warmth of flyers could be better regulated in accordance with their needs.

According to (then Capt.) A.P. Gagge of the AML, who attended that conference, all of the then standard items of flying clothing were laid out on a long table for inspection. General Arnold examined each item and said that he would throw onto the floor all types of clothing that he wanted removed from the inventory and replaced by substitute or improved items. After tossing down the old, "classic" Type A-2 leather flying jacket and the shearling clothing, General Arnold said: "We don't need leather. Get something better." Discarding the Type A-2 jacket and other favorite items caused considerable surprise and dismay among those present, including Paul Manson, civilian chief of the Clothing Branch at Wright Field at the time.[10]

General Arnold's desire to replace leather clothing in AAF service was based in part on the anticipated shortage of leather caused by the tremendous wartime demand. For their part, the British stopped manufacturing leather and shearling clothing, except for some helmets and gloves. Improved types of fabric clothing were eventually developed by the AAF, but stocks of the leather garments continued to be used through the end of the war.

As reports of the development of fabric garments (e.g., the Royal Canadian Air Force's Type E suit) became known, it caused serious concern to the WPB and other agencies and individuals involved in the shearling expansion

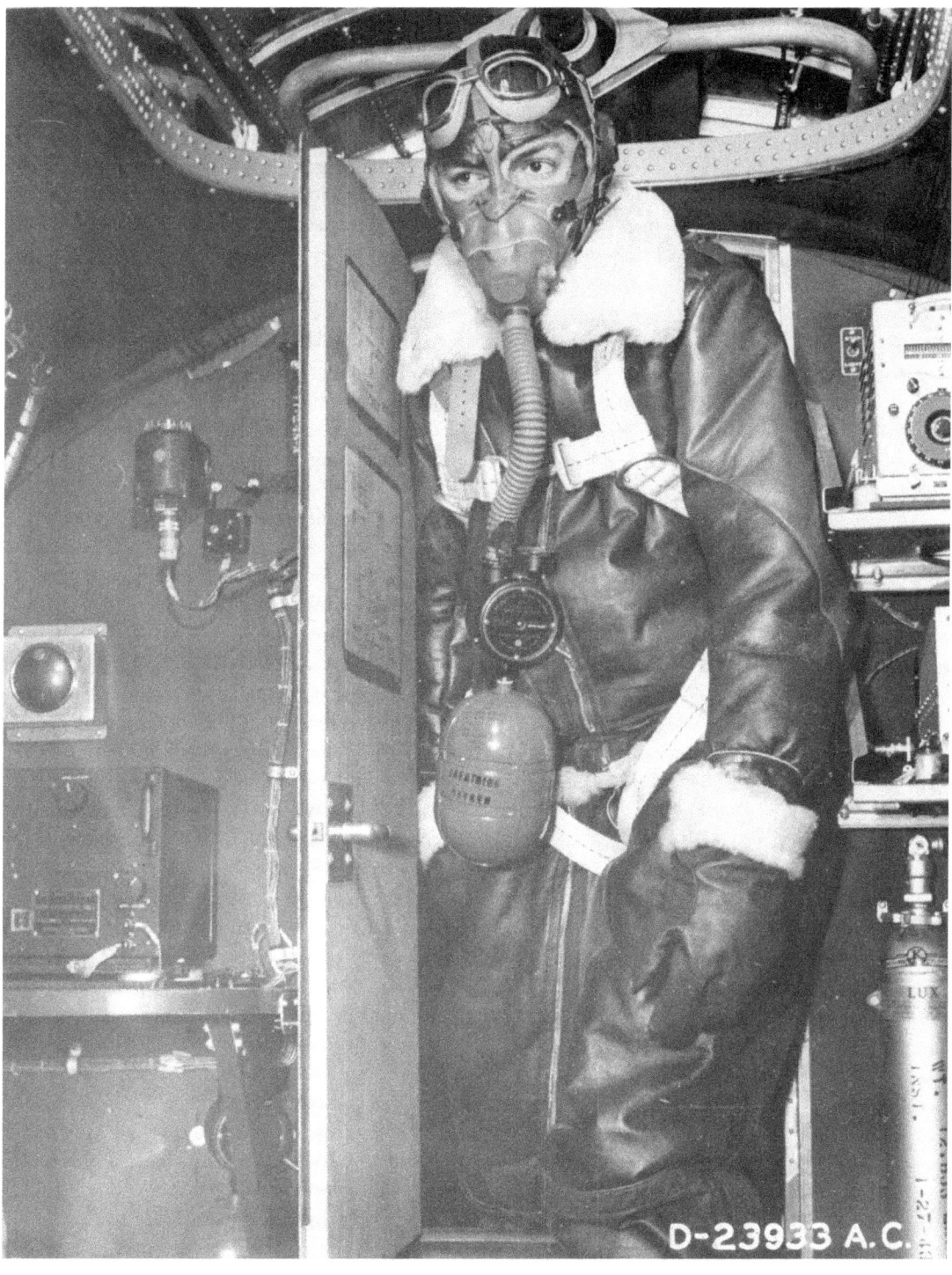

Shearling clothing, as worn by a crewman aboard a Boeing B-17, showing its bulk. Although warm, shearling had a reputation for being heavy, inflexible, and cumbersome. This man is using a portable oxygen unit, known as the walk-around bottle, while moving about the plane at high altitude. Used here with the A-10 mask, it provided a four to eight minute supply of oxygen, depending on the altitude and the activity of the user. He is also wearing Type A-9 gloves and B-7 goggles. (SI Photo 80–20357)

program. Any severe reduction in the production of shearling would seriously upset trade and cause great financial loss to packers, skin dealers, and sheep growers, who had responded patriotically to the government's efforts to increase production. On November 17, 1942, the chief of the Experimental Engineering Section at Wright Field responded to inquiries about plans for the new developments by stating that the AAF did not intend to discontinue using shearling as a material used for its clothing and that any other types of clothing developed would only be used in limited quantities for special purposes.

The opposition to shearling clothing continued to increase, however, and General Arnold called another conference in January 1943 to study the progress that had been made in flying clothing. The result was a recommendation that the development of more suitable flying clothing be expedited.[11]

Tests made in Alaska during the winter of 1942-43 confirmed the protection against extreme cold provided by the shearling "Alaskan Suit." Composed of the Type B-7 jacket and A-6 trousers, this outfit had been service tested for about three years before it was standardized on June 12, 1941. The jacket was eight inches longer than the Type B-3 and had a one-inch pile body, five-eighths-inch pile sleeves, and one-fourth-inch shearling hood. The trousers were made of five-eighths-inch pile, and had knit cuffs cut in the style of plus-four knickers. The first B-7 jackets probably had a plain zipper front. Later production jackets, however, had an overlapping front opening with a zipper inside and braided cotton cord loops and buttons outside.[12] A strip of wolf fur was also added around the face opening of the hood. Type A10 shoes were intended to be worn with this outfit.

After these Alaskan winter tests, the opponents of shearling clothing again stated that it was too bulky and not suited for walking and that it should be replaced by less bulky material that would not become stiff in cold weather. From the tests it was concluded that "a combination of garments of a warm material

The "Alaskan Suit" of 1941 consisted of the Type B-7 jacket and A-6 trousers. This flyer is wearing an early version of the suit with a Type B-2 cap, A-10 shoes, and probably A-6 gloves. (SI Photo A4864G)

such as wool or alpaca with wind-resisting alternates, covered with a hooded wind breaker (parka), proved to be the warmest and most flexible body covering for severe temperatures."[13]

By May 1943 combat reports from overseas and other unfavorable information on shearling clothing prompted the AAF Equipment Board in Orlando, Florida, to recommend that the shearling garments on procurement be supplanted by other types of clothing under development at Wright Field. These types included the new quilted down (buoyancy) suits and the multiple-layer-pile fabric suits. The

Type A-6 shearling winter trousers cut to style of plus-four knickers for the "Alaskan Suit," 1941. This example has the outside of the shearling in the "raw," without weatherproofing. (SI Photo A4864J)

B-17 crewman wearing shearling winter flying clothing consisting of an AN-H-16 helmet, AN-J-4 jacket, AN-T-35 trousers, A-9 gloves, and A-6A shoes. (SI Photo A4861E)

board also urged that the new garments be procured and issued as quickly as possible to all combat crew members going overseas and that the stocks of flying clothing then on hand be issued to personnel of ground crews and training units.[14]

Despite all the valid reasons for discontinuing the production of shearling clothing, the government felt bound by moral, legal, political, production, and financial obligations to continue procuring shearling material in large quantities during fiscal year 1944. In July 1943 it ordered fifteen million square feet of shearling. Only after that, when no additional requirements for shearling beyond fiscal year 1944 could be seen, did the WPB and Department of Agriculture initiate measures to decelerate the production of raw shearlings.

In 1943 shearling clothing similar to the AAF issue was standardized for use by both the Army and the Navy and then placed in production. An example was the winter flying jacket, Spec. AN-J-4, sometimes marked AN6553 or 6553-AN-J4. This jacket was made of three-fourths-inch shearling with the usual brown or dark brown leather finish outside, a zipper front, and two lower patch pockets. It was worn with the AN-T-35 shearling trousers with suspenders. These trousers had a zipper on the outseam of each leg, on each outseam at the waist, and at the front center. Pockets were located below each knee, and one was above the left knee. Like earlier shearling clothing, the outfit was stiff, bulky, and heavy.

The development of new, improved types of multilayer fabric flying clothing (discussed in chapter 6) essentially eliminated the future use of shearling. Production of the new types of clothing began in time to meet the requirements of 1944. And, though some types of shearling clothing remained in stock for use as limited standard until the end of the war, the production of shearling finally came to an end.[15]

Other nations also used sheep shearling clothing. This German Luftwaffe second lieutenant, winner of the Knight's Cross of the Iron Cross, is wearing a shearling flying coat over his uniform while standing in front of his Bf-109E fighter, about 1941. (SI Photo 74–3058)

5

Electrically Heated Flying Suits

The first electrically heated flying suits were developed by the French during World War I, and the earliest American types were based on French samples. These suits were of heavy construction and fur lined to protect flyers when the electric heating units failed (a frequent occurrence). Instead of being completely wired with heating units as were the suits used during World War II, the "Electric Suits" of 1918 consisted primarily of a wire "harness" attached to the suits and connected both to copper heating units in the gloves, shoes, and helmet and to heating pads on the knees, elbows, shoulders, etc. The first suits used in airplanes were battery-heated, but later suits were connected by copper wires to an electric generator on a plane's engine.[1] By the time of the Armistice a suit with a rheostat temperature regulator had been tested and had been called a considerable improvement over suits in which heat could be controlled only by plugging in and unplugging the suits.[2]

Some experiments with electrically heated clothing, such as the old type

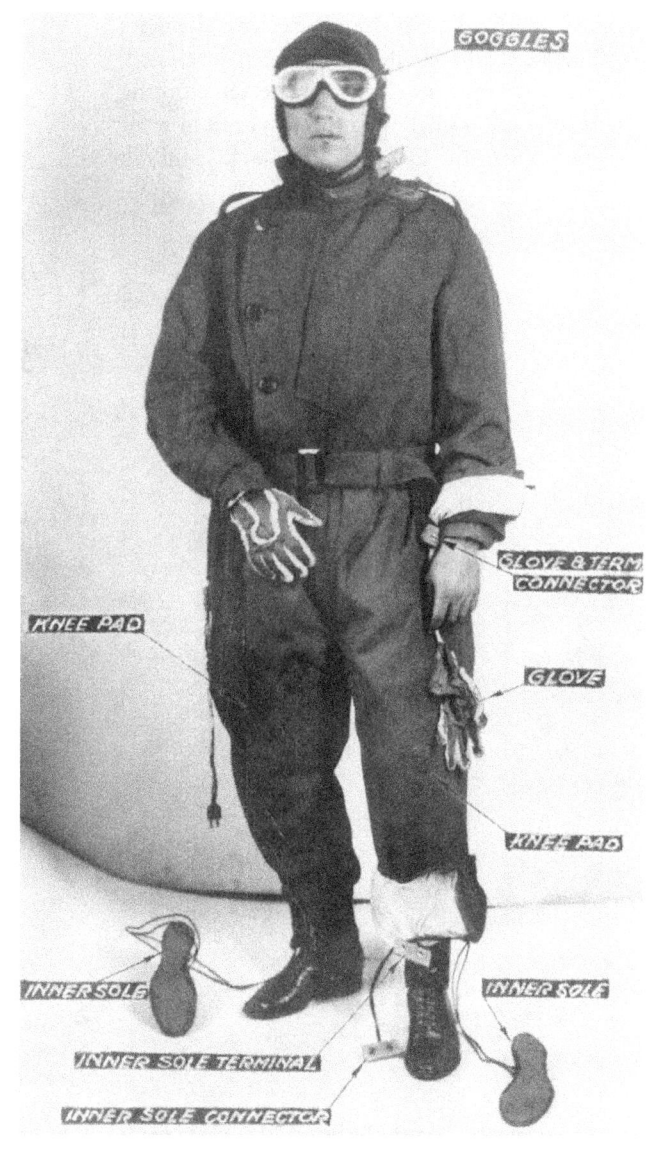

Experimental electrically heated flying suit and accessories, 1921. Only specific parts of the early suits were wired with electrical heating units. (SI Photo 80-20366)

B-3 suit, were made during the 1920s and 1930s. Since the planes used during most of that period had open cockpits, however, the Air Corps stressed the development of clothing with natural insulative and wind-resistant characteristics (e.g., the sheep shearling suits), rather than fabric materials. Adequate electrical systems for completely wired clothing were absent on most light planes of that era and could not be added because of their extra weight and cost of installation. Moreover, neither adequate insulation nor satisfactory materials for creating flexible heating elements and wiring in the suits had yet been developed. Still, two types of electrically heated clothing were used in small quantities as limited standard during the 1920s: electric "socks" and silk inner gloves. They were still listed in the Air Corps Class 13 Stock Catalog of March 1929 but had been discontinued by the time the June 1, 1934, issue was published.

The introduction in the late 1930s of modern, long-range bombers such as the Boeing B-17 stimulated a renewed interest in the development of electrically heated flying clothing.

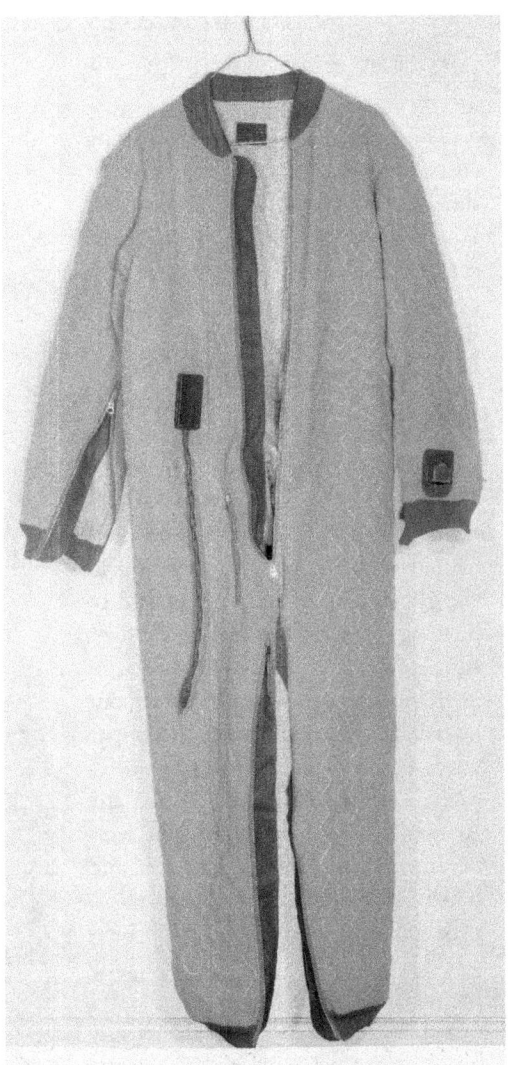

Type F-1 electrically heated flying suit, often called the "Blue Bunny" or "Bunny Rabbit" suit. Standardized on April 4, 1941, it was intended to be worn under a winter or other flying suit along with electric gloves and shoes. The F-1 proved to be unreliable like all earlier suits because of recurrent breakage of the heating elements while in use. (SI Photo 81-336)

Experimental electrically heated flying suit made by the U.S. Rubber Company being tested at Ladd Field, Alaska, in 1942 (SI Photo A4865E)

Military planners recognized the need to provide flyers with comfort and freedom of movement during extended missions while they were operating in turrets and other confining parts of their aircraft.

During 1938 and 1939 a twelve-volt, three-amp, electrically heated vest was developed and procured for service testing. It was described as having "wool felt metal core yarn" and was made by Colvinex. (The vest was still listed in service-test status in the Stock List dated September 30, 1942.)

In the summer of 1940 the General Electric (G.E.) and U.S. Rubber companies prepared sixteen complete outfits consisting of suits, gloves, and shoes for service testing. After high-altitude tests at Ladd Field, Alaska, and Selfridge Field, Michigan, were completed, G.E.'s one-piece suits proved to be more satisfactory than U.S. Rubber's garments and were designated the Type E-1 for twelve volts and Type F-1 for twenty-four volts.[3] Each type was constructed of the same wool material that G.E. had been using in its electric blankets and was to be worn as an undergarment under a light- or medium-weight flying suit.[4] The wires used for the heating elements could not withstand the repeated flexings that they received during testing, and considerable trouble with breakage consequently developed. Minor modifications were made in the wiring and control mechanisms of the suits during the winter of 1940-41, after which specifications were prepared in March 1941 for the gray-fabric Type E-1 suit, with Type C-6 gloves and Type C-1 shoes, and the light blue Type F-1 suit, with Type E-1 gloves and Type D-1 shoes. Short cords with plugs connected the electrical wiring of the suits to the gloves and shoes. On April 4, 1941, all items were standardized, and contracts were let for their production.

For several years many people had been presenting valid arguments against the development and use of electrically heated flying suits. As far back as World War I, reports had been made about electrically heated suits failing and pilots being burned by the breakage of the wires. Other arguments centered on the electrically heated suits' inability to provide adequate protection against the cold when an aircraft's electrical system failed or a bailout was necessary. The problems with the flexible heating units and the temperature-control mechanisms still had to be resolved before the Air Corps could depend upon electric clothing under operational conditions.

The development of electrically heated clothing continued to receive the highest priority despite objections, and by the summer of 1941, electric connectors were being installed for the tail and turret gunners on B-17, B-24, B-25, and B-26 aircraft. A special rheostat for temperature control, the Q-1A, which was mounted in the aircraft, was designed for use with the new E-1 and F-1 suits and accessories.[5] Unfortunately, the "underwear" type suit proved to be unreliable because the heating elements repeatedly broke when they were in use. By March 1943 eighty thousand E-1 and F-1 "Bunny Rabbit" suits had been procured, but many of them were still stored

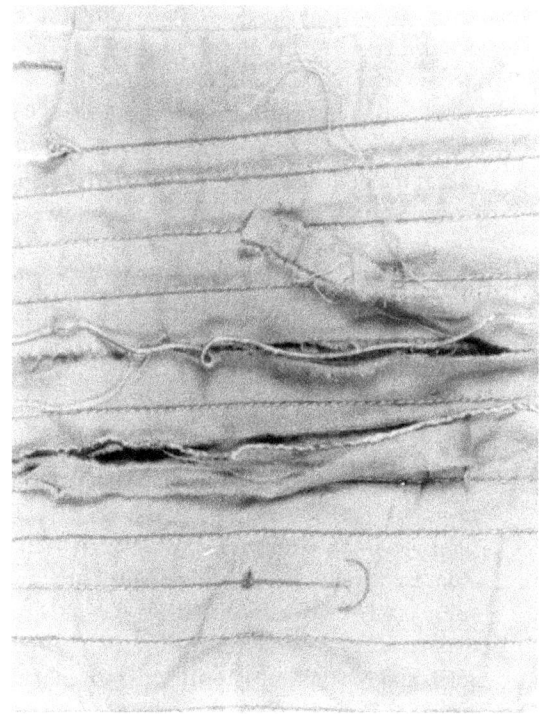

Defective wiring in an electric suit. (SI Photo A4865F)

at depots, despite the shortage of suits in Europe. That situation was primarily due to delays in modifying aircraft, but it may also have been due to a desire to modify the suits to eliminate their deficiencies before they were sent overseas for combat use. Late in the war F-1 suits were modified for use as rescue or warming suits for downed flyers or medical patients.

During this time development proceeded on other types of electric suits with the intention of overcoming the difficulties encountered with the E-1 and F-1 types. In the latter part of 1942 tests were made on wool fabric, blanket-lined suits that were to be worn over regulation underclothing and shirts and underneath fabric or shearling outer garments. The improved type of two-piece suit that emerged from those tests featured more flexible wiring and was eventually standardized on August 13, 1943, as the Type F-2.[6] The F-2 was placed on procurement, and sixty thousand outfits were purchased.[7]

Unlike the older E-1 and F-1 suits, the new twenty-four volt Type F-2 suit was categorized as a "uniform," not as underclothing. Its outer shell of brown "elastique" wool could be separated and used as normal wearing apparel by flyers forced down in enemy territory. Some jackets had a fleece collar, while others had a conventional uniform collar. Insignia were sometimes worn on the outer jacket. A small electrical connection was mounted on each jacket's chest to accept the cord for the oxygen mask heater or the heated lens that could be used with the B-8 goggle. Electrically heated gloves and shoe inserts were provided for use with the suit and were connected by snap fasteners on tabs at the cuffs of the jacket and trousers.

As inevitably happened, problems were encountered with the new F-2 outfit, but they were largely matters of tailoring and fit. For instance, the opening at the bottom was too small, making the trousers difficult to remove; the lining was not tailored for sitting; and the shoulder construction gave insufficient freedom for arm movements. A more basic problem was that the suit was too bulky. In addition, if the suit was not getting electric current, it did not provide sufficient protection in very low temperatures. On February 19, 1944, a slight modification of the F-2 suit, the Type F-2A, was designated as substitute standard at the same time as the F-2. It was similar to the F-2 except for the incorporation of thermostats into the wiring for controlling heat.[8] But, even though the F-2 and F-2A suits were improvements over previous suits, they were still not the final answer.[9]

In March 1943 the first mass test of flying clothing was made in the new cold chamber in the G.E. Laboratory at Bridgeport, Connecticut. Eight men wearing a variety of cold-weather suits were exposed to a temperature of -60° F for eight hours or as much of that period as they could endure without danger of serious injury. One man, wearing the heaviest available shearling suit, was forced to withdraw from the test after only two hours. The other seven, who were wearing electrically heated suits with a variety of outer garments including pile-lined and experimental coveralls, were able to end the test without serious discomfort.[10]

A third type of electrically heated flying suit designed and used during the war, the Type F-3, was developed by the Flying Clothing Branch at Wright Field during the latter part of 1943. Standardized on February 19, 1944,[11] It included a bolero-style, zipper-front jacket and bib-type overall trousers made of olive drab or greenish cotton-and-rayon twill, and it was accompanied by electric gloves and shoes. The outfit was intended to be worn over a standard uniform shirt, trousers, and underwear and under a cotton-twill intermediate flying suit lined with alpaca pile. A small receptacle was mounted on the chest to accept the cord for the electrically heated lens, which could be used with the B-8 goggle or the oxygen mask heater when one was used.

The F-3 outfit was the first electric suit to enable flying personnel to work safely, comfortably, and efficiently at temperatures of -60° F.[12] It was better insulated than its predecessors

Waist gunner aboard a Boeing B-17G bomber wearing the Type F-2 electric suit, standardized on August 13, 1943. It was considered to be in the category of a uniform and not underclothing as was the case with the F-1 suit. The two-piece, two-layer suit had a brown "elastique" wool outer shell. The inner, heated layer connected with electric gloves and electric inserts worn in black felt shoes for the F-2 suit. The gunner is wearing an AN-H-16 winter flying helmet. (SI Photo A4865H)

had been and, when worn with appropriate outer garments, provided much more protection during a power failure. The suit's temperature could be adjusted with a rheostat at the crewman's station in the aircraft.

The complete F-3 outfit utilized a twenty-four volt, multi-circuit arrangement that included two independent parallel electric circuits for the jacket, three circuits for the trousers, and two circuits each for the accompanying shoes and gloves. This system, which was also used in the F-2 suit, provided for a partial operation of the outfit in case one or more of the circuits failed. As is mentioned in chapter 2, an improved series of wires capable of 250,000 flexings was developed in the spring of 1944 from three alloys composed of silver, beraloy, and BB bronze. Those wires were produced in both flat and round form for use as heating elements and helped immensely in solving the long-standing problem of breakage due to flexing. The new wires were incorporated into the F-3 suits then in production.

When the F-3 suit was designed, provisions (such as more fullness in the knees) were made to provide better fit and increased comfort when a wearer was sitting. The suit also provided strain relief by maintaining slackness in its wiring even after its cloth had been bent or flexed to the maximum degree experienced in active use. The sizes of the jacket and trousers could be individually selected to meet each flyer's personal needs. And, if part of the outfit was damaged, the rest of it could still be used.

Finding a satisfactory means of connecting the wiring in the suits with the heating elements in the gloves and shoes caused considerable concern to the AAF designers. One problem was with the snap fasteners first used on the F-2 and F-3 suits: fusing and burning of the metal caused by incomplete electrical

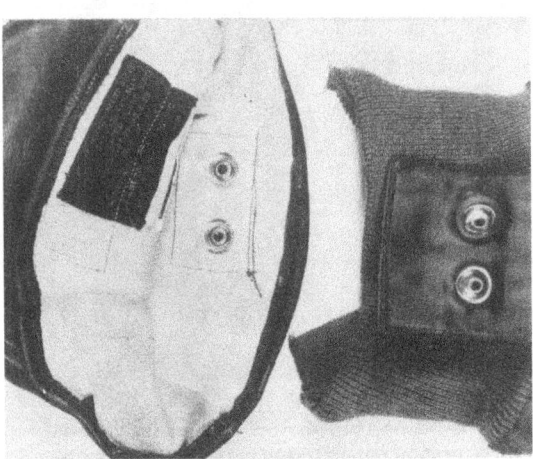

Above: View showing snap or press-stud type of connection on electrically heated glove for F-2 suit. (SI Photo A48668)

Right: The Type F-3 electrically heated flying suit. This outfit was intended to be worn over a uniform and under an intermediate flying suit. The F-3 featured a short jacket with zipper front closure connected to trousers that were of the bib-overall type and had knit wool anklets, adjustable suspenders, and an eighteen-inch "pigtail" for connection to an extension cord. The electric shoe or slipper was worn in a felt or A-6 shoe. Suits made after May 1944 used the new, more flexible wire, which made them much more dependable. (SI Photo A4866)

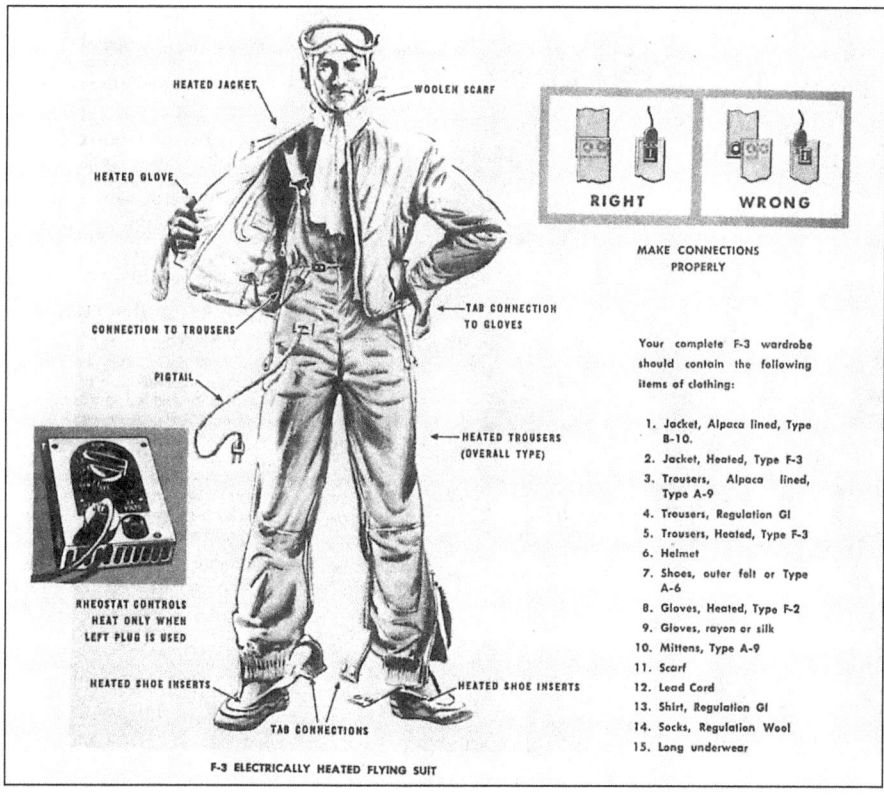

Top: The production version of the Type F-2 electrically heated flying outfit. (SI Photo 82–1332) *Bottom:* The Type F-3 electrically heated flying outfit. (SI Photo 82–1331)

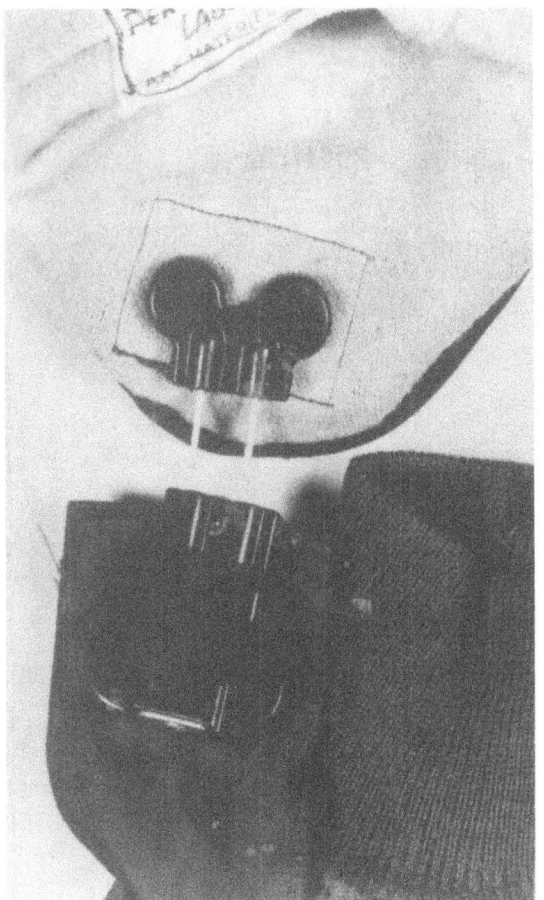

contacts sometimes distorted the snap fasteners so seriously that they could not function satisfactorily. The dilemma was resolved by developing a positive locking-bayonet-type fastener, which was incorporated into the F-3 suit. The modified outfit was designated the Type F-3A and standardized on October 21, 1944. Also on that day, the original F-3 suit was reclassified as substitute standard, but with the new fastener it could easily be modified into the F-3A configuration.[13] The Clothing Branch of the Personal Equipment Laboratory at Wright Field regularly encountered similar engineering problems as it worked to devise adequate, comfortable, and attractive clothing for the flying personnel of the AAF.

In the May 1944 issue of the *Air Surgeon's Bulletin,* the editor commented on electric suits:

> The electrically heated flying suit has long held the promise of becoming the ideal clothing for military aviation. It supplies heat when needed, is light in weight, comfortable to wear, and allows ease of movement. The shortcomings of the earlier designs have been overcome in the F-2 and F-3 suits. Overheating of certain areas in the suit has been eliminated by the scientific determination of the heat requirements of various parts of the body, and failure has been reduced by revision of construction.[14]

Details of electrically heated gloves are found in chapter 9; electrically heated shoes are described in chapter 10.

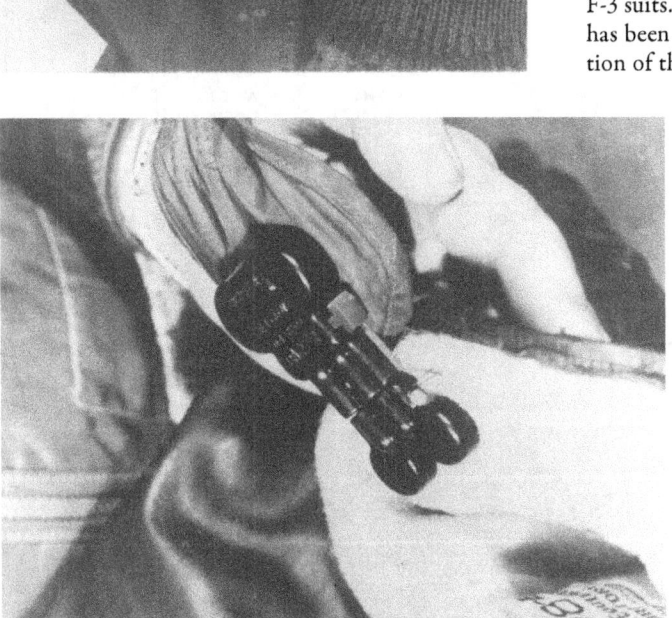

Top: Connector-adapter featuring positive locking bayonet-type fastener installed on snap or press-stud connectors for electrically heated glove for F-3A suit. (SI Photo A4866C) *Bottom:* Method of making glove connection with positive locking bayonet-type fastener. (SI Photo A4866D)

6

Other Types of Flying Suits

The early leather and fabric winter flying suits with fur or felt lining, the shearling suits discussed in chapter 4, and the electrically heated suits studied in chapter 5 were not the only suits developed for use by Army aviators. Clothing designers used a wide variety of linings and shell fabrics in their quest to meet the flyer's widely varied needs.

One-piece winter flying suits in 1932: the Type B-7 (left), standardized for use in 1928; the Type B-8 experimental suit, which received service testing (center); and the Type B-9 (right), adopted as limited standard in 1931. The B-7 and B-9 suits saw limited service until 1944. (SI Photo 43694)

Blanket-Lined Suits

Blanket material was used for lining flying clothing as early as World War I, and experiments continued during the 1920s. Wool, for example, was used during this period for blanket lining in suits made of leather, corduroy, and Bedford cloth. In the winter of 1925-26 a leather, blanket-lined, one-piece winter suit was tested in temperatures as low as -30° F at an altitude of 20,000 feet by Lt. J.A. Macready, chief of the Flying Section at McCook Field, Ohio. Lieutenant Macready reported that he

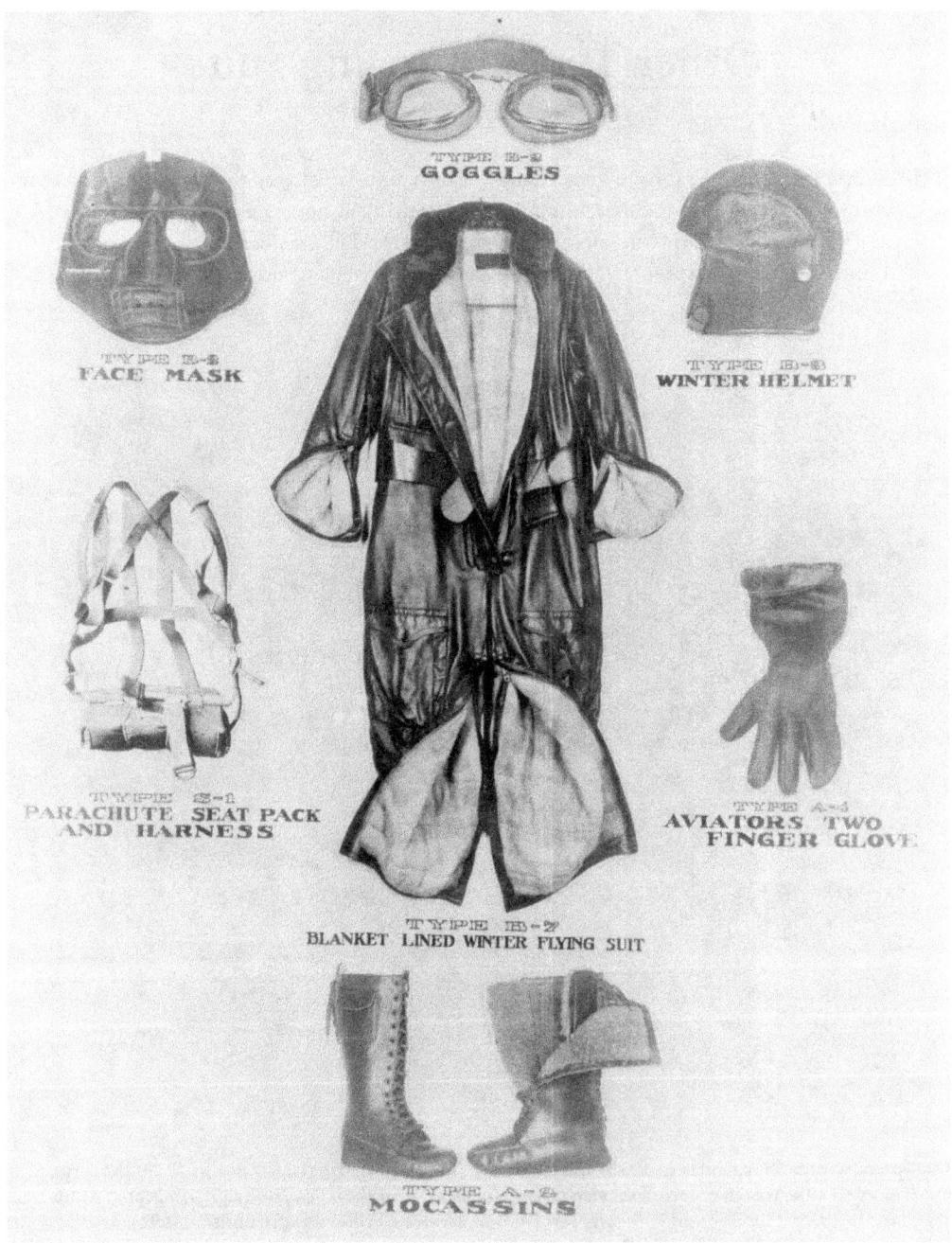

Flying clothing used by the Army Air Corps in 1928. (SI Photo A4868E)

found the suit to be very comfortable and less bulky and cumbersome than the standard fur-lined suits in use at that time.[1]

After considerable testing, a leather, blanket-lined suit designated the Type B-7 was adopted as standard on May 12, 1928. It was changed to substitute standard on June 12, 1931, and although the B-7 was called "stiff and bundlesome" by many flyers and was not considered sufficiently warm, some were continued in use until the outfit was finally declared obsolete on March 27, 1944.[2] Variations of the B-7 suit were also made including suits made with fur lining. Some B-7 one-piece suits were divided in the late 1930s and listed as separate jacket and trousers in the Air Corps Class 13 Stock Lists issued between 1938 and 1943. (This jacket should not be confused with the Type B-7 winter flying jacket of 1941, which was made of shearling.)

Fabric- and Sheepskin-Lined Suits

A joint Army and Navy conference on flying clothing was held at Wright Field in February 1931, and reports were made on various fabric- and sheepskin-lined winter flying suits that

Winter flying suit (left) consisting of the Type B-1 jacket and A-1 trousers. Light winter flying suit (right), with Type B-2 jacket and A-2 trousers. Both outfits were standardized in 1931 and remained in the inventory until 1944. Two-piece winter suits were introduced to ensure the wearer a better fit. (SI Photo A4864D)

had been tested during that winter as replacements for the old, fur-lined Type B-1 "Monkey" winter flying suit, which had proved to be particularly drafty, bulky, and heavy—up to sixteen pounds depending on size. Alpaca- and llama-pile-lined garments had been tested by the Navy, and the Army had tested a one-piece suit of calfskin, lined with detachable silk-pile material, a one-piece horsehide suit lined with lamb shearling, and a two-piece horsehide suit lined with lamb shearling. The participants at the conference decided that the one-piece horsehide suit lined with lamb shearling was the warmest, most flexible, easiest to don, and most desirable of those tested. It was standardized as the Type B-10 on June 12, 1931, and one thousand one-piece B-10 suits were procured in 1932. The B-10 suit was used, but its design was soon modified to separate it into two parts to permit sizes to be interchanged and provide closer fit when issued. Both the jacket and the trousers could be worn with lighter garments. This two-piece development was adopted as standard on December 15, 1931, and was procured as the B-1 winter jacket and the A-1 winter trousers. Both were changed to limited standard on May 8, 1934, when the shearling B-3, A-3 outfit was standardized. The B-1, A-1 continued to be used until September 29, 1944, when its components were declared obsolete after their stocks had been exhausted.[3] According to one newspaper article, the A-1 trousers were unique. When the zipper leg fasteners were open, they lay flat and blanket-like upon a table. A wearer donned them by putting his arms through suspender straps and zipping up the legs. In addition, the trousers' cuffs and other openings had improved closures to make them less drafty.[4] Lt. (later Brig. Gen.) Benjamin S. Kelsey, who wore this suit, said, however, that "the horsehide suits were the stiffest, most uncomfortable damned outfits to fly in of any that I ever encountered."[5]

Pile-Lined Suits

Two winter suits similar to the blanket-lined B-7 were the Types B-8 and B-9 one-piece suits, with detachable silk-pile linings. Service testing began in 1930 on the B-8, an experimental calf-leather suit, but it was never standardized for use. Still, some size 44 B-8 suits were stock-listed as nonstandard issue until about 1938. The B-9, made of horsehide, was more flexible and lighter than either the B-7 or the B-8. It was accepted as limited standard on June 12, 1931, and not declared obsolete until March 21, 1944.

The type B-11 light winter suit, standardized as one unit on June 12, 1931, was very much like the shearling lined B-10 suit, except for the B-11's silk-pile lining. The two suit's classification histories were almost identical: like the B-10, the B-11 was separated and standardized—as the B-2 jacket and A-2 trousers—on December 15, 1931; changed to limited standard on May 8, 1934; and declared obsolete on September 29, 1944, after its stocks were exhausted.

While pile-lined suits such as the B-9, the B-11, and the B-2, A-2 combination remained in the inventory as limited standard during the 1930s, attention was focused during this period on the development of the shearling winter suits discussed in chapter 4. In June 1940 the Materiel Division at Wright Field received an inquiry from the Continental Textile Mills in Philadelphia, Pennsylvania, concerning the Air Corps's possible interest in pile woven fabric for lining either electric or nonelectric flying suits. This material was proposed as a more flexible substitute for shearling garments. Continental Mills was advised that the Air Corps believed that shearling was the best available material for use in winter flying clothing, and since there was no shortage of shearling, no change in the present winter flying clothing was contemplated at that time. The same textile mills inquired again in November 1941 and received a similar reply from the Experimental Engineering Section, which also mentioned that "inasmuch as shearling consists of a leather backing with the natural sheep pile, no lining materials are necessary."[6]

By 1942 increasing attention was finally being given to the possibilities of alpaca- and wool-pile fabrics in the construction of intermediate and winter flying suits. This came about partly, at least, from the possible wartime shortage of shearling material and partly from the increasing reports being received from overseas of the unsatisfactory characteristics of the shearling garments. There were almost inexhaustible quantities of alpaca-pile material available, according to the Willis and Geiger Company of New York, which certainly must have made an impression on AAF officials since the United States was by then in the war. Material made from the hair of the alpaca, a domesticated South American mammal related to the llama, had been used in modern times mainly for lining winter clothing.

Comparative tests with shearling and pile garments were conducted during December 1942 by the Fabrics Research Laboratory in Boston under the direction of the AML. The researchers found that:

1. Shearling had the highest insulative qualities but the lowest permeability.
2. The insulative qualities of shearling could be duplicated with a double layer of alpaca pile fabric with less than a third of the bulk.
3. A closely woven fabric like gabardine or airplane cloth would reduce very considerably the air permeability of loosely woven fabric like alpaca or wool pile.
4. Air permeability of a layer clothing combination is a desirable factor since it aids in preventing water vapor from freezing in the clothing.[7]

Flight tests made in Alaska by the Cold Weather Test Detachment during 1942 and 1943 indicated that the multiple-layer alpaca-pile garments then under development could be satisfactorily worn in temperatures of -35° F for between four and six hours. That report was confirmed by tests conducted at Ladd Field, Alaska, during the same period, which found that:

A combination of garments of a warm material such as wool or alpaca with wind resistant alternates proved to be the warmest and most flexible body covering for severe temperatures. The shearling suits tested were less warm than the layer fabric suits and less flexible and more cumbersome.[8]

During this period Sir Hubert Wilkins, noted Australian polar explorer, was called in as a temporary consultant from the OQMG for duty with the Cold Weather Test Detachment. In an effort to satisfy their urgent requirements for cold weather clothing and emergency equipment for use in the arctic, Air Transport Command (ATC) directly contacted the QMC. During the winter of 1942-43 several thousand of the new Army arctic pile suits were procured by the ATC through the QMC.

In January 1943 a fabric knitted-pile jacket, the type B-8, was standardized for use as an Alaskan inner jacket with the Type A-7 inner trousers of the same construction. These garments were intended to be worn under other flying clothing for additional warmth.

Development began at Wright Field in October 1942 on an intermediate alpaca- and wool-pile flying suit, designated the Type B-10 jacket and Type A-9 trousers, and a heavy alpaca-and-wool-pile suit, the Type B-11 jacket and A-10 trousers. All of these garments were standardized on July 22, 1943.[9] The B-10 jacket and A-9 trousers were changed to substitute standard on April 7, 1944, when the B-15 jacket and A-11 trousers were standardized, and to limited standard on February 7, 1945. The intermediate suit was constructed of an olive drab cotton twill outer shell that was wind and moisture resistant and was lined with a 50/50 alpaca-and-wool-pile fabric. The B-10 jacket had a low mouton collar, knitted wristlets and waistband, a zipper front closure, and a large pocket with flap on each side just above the waistband. The A-9 trousers had three leg and two hip pockets and a false pocket opening on each side seam at the hip. Suspenders were provided. This suit was intended to provide adequate protection down to about 15° F and could be worn over an F-3 electrically heated suit for protection against a much lower temperature.

The B-11 jacket of the heavy, or winter, suit was made of gabardine with take-up straps at its wrists and had a lining that consisted of a heavy grade of deep single-face alpaca and wool-pile fabric. Although it was somewhat similar in appearance to the intermediate B-10 jacket, the B-11 jacket had a mouton-fur-lined hood instead of a collar and was mackinaw- rather than jacket-length. Its front closure had a zipper inside and buttons outside. The pockets included two slash pockets for the hands and two lower pockets with flaps. The matching A-10 trousers were made of cotton twill and had three leg pockets and two hip pockets, an access slit and side pocket in each side seam of the hip, and a take-up strap at the bottom of each leg. They were also lined with alpaca and wool fabric, and suspenders were included.

Further tests and actual usage proved that these suits were generally satisfactory but that certain changes would probably be advantageous:

1. Change in cut at elbow, knee, and seat to allow greater freedom of movement.
2. Double-face alpaca pile instead of single face for greater warmth.
3. Rayon lining would add to cleanliness and ease of donning.
4. Slash style pockets.
5. Full length zipper openings on legs of trousers.[10]

These recommendations were incorporated into the suits' design to produce a modified intermediate suit—the Type B-15 jacket, A-11 trousers combination. This outfit was standardized on April 7, 1944.[11] A few other minor improvements, including a higher collar and greater overlap between the jacket and trousers than were found in the B-10, A-9 combination, were also added to the new suit. The B-15, A-11 outfit, however, used the same materials and

The Type B-10 intermediate jacket and B-1 cap being worn by T/Sgt. Joe Urbanoski, a Martin B-26 radio operator of the 322d Bomb Group, Ninth Air Force, about September 1944. The Type A-9 trousers were usually worn with the B-10 jacket. (SI Photo 81–332)

The heavy winter alpaca-pile flying suit of 1943 included the Type B-11 jacket and the A-10 trousers. (SI Photo A4866F)

6. Other Types of Flying Suits

had the same general appearance as the B-10, A-9 combination. In addition, the same type of adjustable suspenders could be used with the A-9, A-10, and A-11 trousers: they were each made in accordance with Spec. 3221 of olive drab cotton-elastic webbing, one and one-half inches wide; and all metal parts were zinc-plated and lacquered black.

In late 1944 a few additional, minor changes were made in the B-15, A-11 outfit, and it was redesignated and standardized as the Type B-15A jacket and Type A-11A trousers on November 4, 1944.[12] Small triangular tabs were added to the upper right and left chest area of the jacket as attachment points for the clamps

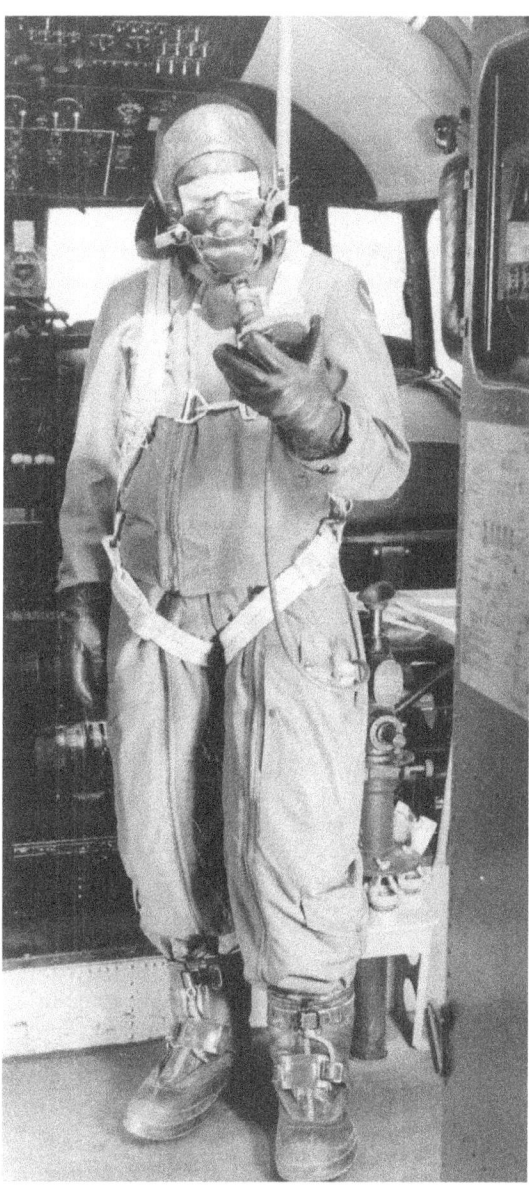

The heavy alpaca-lined flying suit, consisting of the Type B-11 jacket and A-10 trousers, being worn over the B-10 jacket, A-9 trousers intermediate suit. The shoes are probably the A-14 mukluk. The AN-H-16 helmet and B-8 goggles complete the winter outfit. (SI Photo A4866G)

Intermediate flying suit, 1944. The Type B-15 jacket and A-11 trousers are worn here by a C-54 navigator squinting at a plotter. Other items include an AN-H-15 helmet, A-14 oxygen mask, A-11 gloves, and A-6A boots. (SI Photo A4866H)

on the "demand" type of oxygen hose. A communication-wire lead tab was also attached to the left chest, and a bellows, box-shaped pocket with flaps was added to the left thigh part of the trousers to act as a hose container for the bail-out oxygen assembly. The location of the bailout oxygen-bottle pocket was also moved up approximately three inches as a precaution against injury to the knee when making a parachute jump.

The final changes in this suit were made after additional experience in action and included the incorporation of rayon lining over the alpaca interlining. On May 21, 1945, the improved jacket, the Type B-15B, was designated as standard, with the B-15A redesignated as substitute standard. The trousers were also slightly modified and designated as the

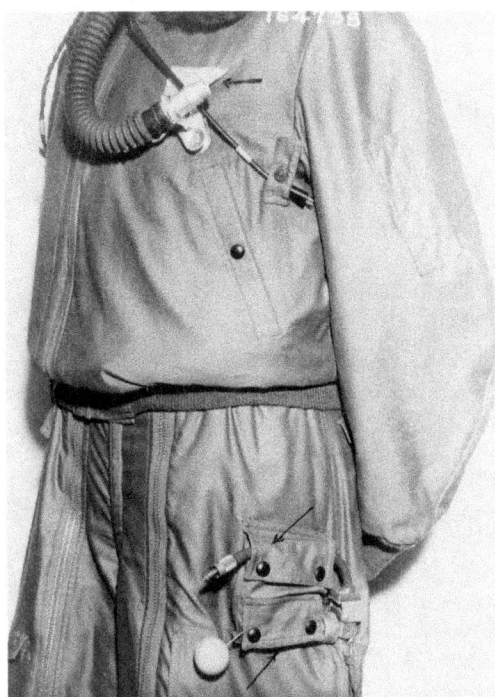

The Type B-15A intermediate jacket and A-11A trousers, showing modifications made in the fall of 1944. The improvements included a communication-wire lead tab and small triangular tabs. The latter were added to the upper right and left chest area of the jacket as attachment points for the clamps on the "demand" type oxygen hose. A box-shaped pocket with flaps was included on the left thigh of the trousers, to act as a hose container for the bailout oxygen assembly. The ball in the photograph, sometimes called the "Green Apple," was used to activate the oxygen for high-altitude bailout. (SI Photo A4867)

Another view of the successful Type B-15 intermediate jacket and A-11 trousers combination, with A-11 intermediate helmet, B-8 goggle, A-14 oxygen mask, A-11 gloves, A-6 shoes, and B-4 life vest. (SI Photo A4861H)

Type A-11B on June 4, 1945.¹³ Most of these pile-lined garments remained in use with the AAF and the USAF for many years after the war.

The use of manufactured pile body clothing marked a great advance over shearling. It was less bulky than shearling, and its greater strength enabled it to resist crushing and subsequent loss of warmth in a surprisingly effective manner. By using outer jackets that could be donned over others, the degree of insulation could be controlled by the demands of a situation in a way that was hardly possible with a single, heavy leather, shearling garment.¹⁴

The greatest development and use of the pile fabric suits was in conjunction with the progress made in the electrically heated suits. The use of the two types, either in combination or separately, provided adequate protection with lightness of weight and freedom of motion for any low temperature encountered while flying during World War II.¹⁵

Quilted Down and Feather Suits

Among the earliest types of flying suits to be considered were those constructed with an outer shell of wind-resistant material and a lin-

Lt. J.A. Macready in a quilted-down high altitude flying suit used in a flight to 40,800 feet in 1921. This experimental suit proved to be warm and lightweight, but the materials from which it was constructed were not sufficiently serviceable for general use. The oxygen mask and fur mittens should be noted. (SI Photo A48678)

ing of quilted down or feathers. Down-filled and quilted suits were constructed and tested during the early years of work at the Air Service Clothing and Parachute Branch at McCook Field, Ohio. The tests convinced Maj. E.L. Hoffman, chief of the Equipment Section, that quilted suits, although warm, were too bulky and cumbersome. He suggested the substitution of kapok and also the possibility of lining the legs and sleeves of the suit with fur instead of quilted down. Major Hoffman felt that this arrangement would allow the wearer increased freedom of motion and also enable him to float in an upright position if he was forced down while flying over water. The possibilities of using the down-filled garments as flotation suits had always furnished a strong argument in their favor. (Flotation suits are discussed in chapter 7.) The possibility of modifying the thickness of the garment to meet the varying needs of the different parts of the body was another point that had been presented in favor of the quilted suits.

Lt. J.A. Macready, chief of the Flying Section at Wright Field, wore a quilted down suit on some of his well-known high-altitude flights in 1921, and during one of these flights he reached an altitude of 40,800 feet. He found that, although the suit provided satisfactory warmth and lightness, its materials were insufficiently serviceable.[16] The possibility of combining lightness and warmth in suits of quilted down, feather, or kapok was never entirely forgotten by the designers of aviation clothing, however, and variations of these types of garments were used to a limited degree during the 1920s and 1930s.[17]

Not until September 1942 did the Clothing Branch begin serious development work on a modern quilted down winter flying suit. The flexibility, porosity, and design of the down test suit that resulted favorably impressed the AAF School of Applied Tactics and the Equipment Board at Orlando, Florida, when it was compared with the older shearling suits. As a result, both agencies recommended that the suit be standardized and procured as soon as was possible for issuance to combat crews being sent overseas. The outfit was standardized on July 22, 1943, with the outfit designated the Type B-9 jacket and Type A-8 trousers.[18] This jacket was made of olive drab gabardine with a quilted, down-filled satin lining. A zipper was inside the front opening with buttons outside, and a lined hood bordered

A crewman aboard a B-17 wearing the heavy, quilted, down-filled winter suit. The Type B-9 jacket and A-8 trousers were standardized in 1943. The mittens are the Type A-12; the shoes Type A-6A. (SI Photo A4867F)

with mouton was provided. The trousers were made with an olive drab cotton-twill outer covering with quilted lining. They had three leg and two hip pockets, and adjustable suspenders were included.

Fifty thousand of the B-9, A-8 outfits were procured. In actual use, however, the suit proved to be excessively clumsy because huge procurement contracts for sleeping bags by both the QMC and the AAF made it impossible to secure 100 percent eider-down filling for its construction. The 40 percent down, 60 percent feathers combination that was actually used tended to stiffen the suit to a point where it did not much resemble the beautifully light and flexible earlier models of pure down.[19] Production was discontinued by early 1944.

Summer Flying Suits

Lightweight flying suits or coveralls were originally developed to protect the clothing of

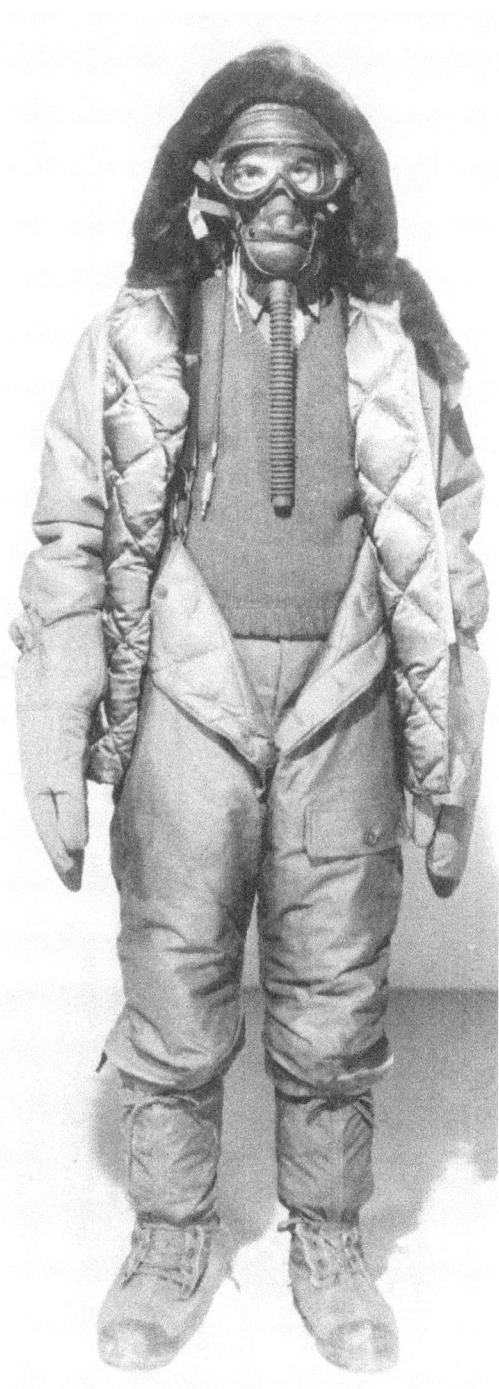

The quilted, down-filled winter flying suit showing the B-9 jacket and A-8 trousers open. Other garments include the AN-H-16 helmet, B-8 goggle, A-14 oxygen mask, A-12 mittens, olive drab knit sweater, and A-14 mukluks. (SI Photo A4867E)

The Type A-3 summer flying suit in 1928, with zippers on the front, sleeves, and ankles. The A-3 suit continued in limited use until 1944. (SI Photo A4867J)

Left: A Type A-4 summer flying suit manufactured during World War II. Although officially superseded by the AN-S-31 Army-Navy suit in 1943, the A-4 continued in wide use through the end of World War II and could still be found in service with the USAF during the Korean War. The helmet is the AN-H-15, with AN-6530 goggle. The parachute is the S-1 or AN6510–1 seat pack. All specimens from NASM collection. (SI Photo 81–313) *Right:* The Type A-4 summer flying suit in 1930. The A-4 was a comfortable suit made of olive drab gabardine material; it saw service from the days of the open cockpit well into the jet age. (SI Photo A4868)

6. Other Types of Flying Suits

Maj. Gust Lundquist (left) and Maj. Frederick Borsodi, assigned as test pilots for this captured German Focke Wulf Fw-190 fighter in April 1944. Both are believed to be wearing the Type A-5 summer flying suit. Except for its zippers on the breast and leg pockets, the A-5 was very similar to the A-4 suit in construction. The special sun shade on the B-8 goggle is noteworthy. (SI Photo 80–20359)

an aviator from oil and dirt and to provide some wind protection. With tight closures at the wrists and ankles, a flying suit kept out cold drafts and also helped prevent the snagging of clothing on switches or other exposed parts of an aircraft.

During World War I Air Service aviators had available a lightweight, unlined, one-piece flying suit similar to a mechanic's coverall. However, many Army flyers preferred to wear the service uniform with helmet, goggles, gloves, and perhaps a leather flying coat for flights in warm weather at low altitudes.

This practice continued after the war even though lightweight or summer one-piece flying suits were procured in limited quantities during the 1920s. The Type A1 and A-2 suits, developed and procured in the mid–1920s, were made of gabardine and olive drab cotton, respectively. The A-2 was used only for service tests. The A-1, however, was used into the 1930s, and two sizes of this obsolete design were still listed as available for issue in the Air Corps Stock List as late as September 30, 1942. Both suits were officially replaced by the Type A-3, which was made of olive drab cotton material. It had a bellows back, a zipper front closure, and two breast and two knee pockets.

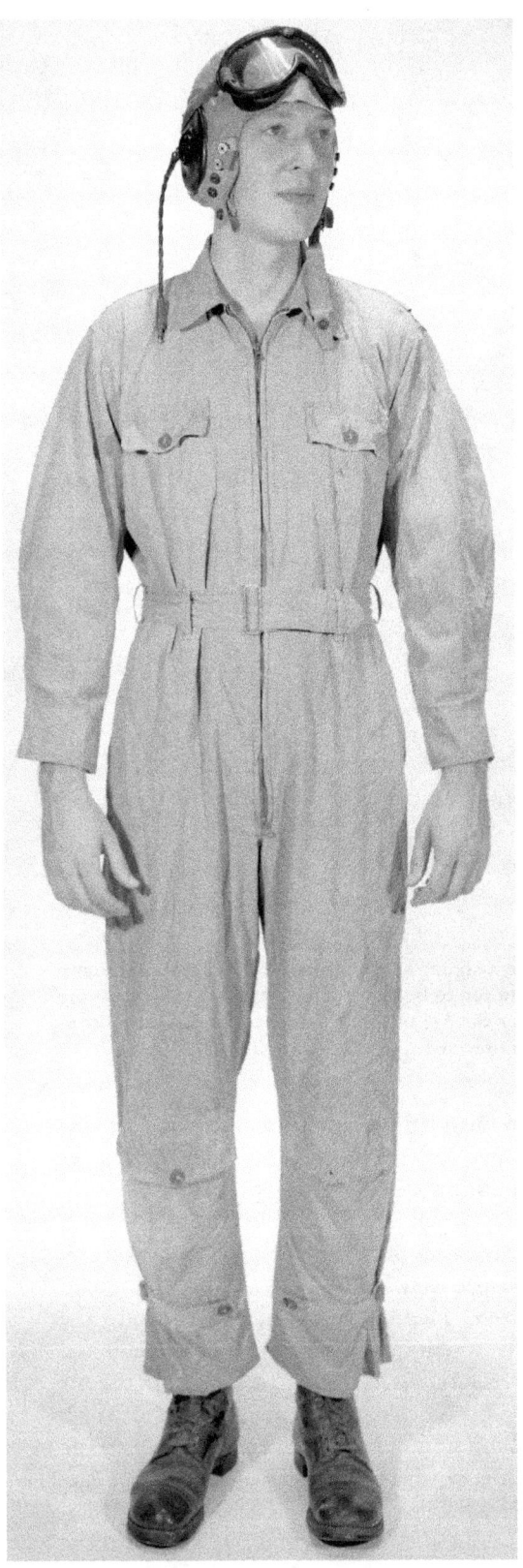

The A-3 suit continued in limited use until it was finally declared obsolete on March 21, 1944.

The well-known Type A-4 summer suit was similar to the A-3 but was made of olive drab gabardine. It was standardized on March 18, 1930, and saw extensive service, in slightly modified form, through and after World War II. The typical wartime A-4 had a zipper front closure, an open pocket at an angle on the right breast, and an open pocket on the lower right leg just below the knee. The Type A-5 suit was the same as the wartime A-4, except for its slate-blue color and zippers on the breast and leg pockets. The A-5 was standardized on June 23, 1937, but saw only limited service use.

A summer flying suit of moleskin was listed as nonstandard issue in the Stock Lists published during the late 1930s through September 30, 1942. Only three sizes were available.

The Type A-6 suit was standardized from July 18 to October 16, 1944, before it was declared inactive.[20] This suit was redesignated the Type K-1 and was standardized on November 3, 1944. The A-6 was procured in limited quantities in both cotton twill and gabardine and was similar to the AN-S-31 Army-Navy suit, standardized for joint use by both services on April 23, 1943.

The general criticism of summer flying suits was the exact opposite of what was said about winter flying suits: the summer suits were considered to be too warm for use in hot weather. Some personnel improvised; for example, during the war crewmen in some hot, overseas areas such as China were known to cut off the sleeves of their summer flying suits in an effort to make them more comfortable. Others often flew in khaki uniforms without wearing a protective suit.

The AN-S-31 summer flying suit was standardized in 1943 for use by aviators of both the Army and the Navy. This example, in lightweight khaki cloth, is labeled "Suit, Summer, Flying, AN-S-31A." This type of suit was produced in quantity and was made in a variety of fabrics. The helmet is the AN-H-15, and the goggle the B-8. Specimens from NASM collection. (SI Photo 81-321)

During the summer of 1942 a survey was conducted among crew members at a Hawaiian air base. It showed what they considered to be the desired characteristics in a summer flying suit:

1. Flexibility was considered of prime importance.
2. Flame proofing was much desired.
3. Flotation protection was requested.
4. Cooler and lighter clothing for ground use was needed.
5. Better fitting suits were suggested so as to reduce the danger of snagging inside of planes and to give a neater appearance on the ground.
6. No problem of cold discomfort was indicated.[21]

Through mutual agreement between the Army and Navy, the Spec. AN-S-31 summer flying suit was developed as an improved summer suit and was standardized for use by both services on April 23, 1943. The procurement of the same suit for both services was intended to expedite production. A quarter million of these improved suits were procured during 1943 for use by the AAF as a proposed replacement for the Type A-4 suit. The AN-S-31 remained in service with the AAF and USAF long after the end of the war.

The suits were originally made in two weights—one, a fabric composed of 50 percent cotton and 50 percent wool, and the other, a cotton twill material. They were considered to be generally satisfactory, but minor changes were recommended. The alterations were generally for better fit, although closure of the cuffs for protection against wind and a zippered front closure to the crotch seam were also suggested. These recommendations were incorporated into later models of this suit, and a surprising number of variations, especially in type of fabric and color, were produced. For example, a very light suit was constructed of poplin or Byrd cloth and was produced to meet the need for cooler flying clothing and mosquito protection in the tropics. These suits in both weights had the added advantages of pockets with zippers,

The AN-S-31 Army and Navy summer flying suit proved to be a popular garment and was used by the AAF and later the USAF for several years after the end of World War II. This P-47 pilot is wearing the experimental Type E-2 "escape" shoe tested during 1944, and the standard AN-H-15 summer flying helmet with either a B-7 or AN-6530 goggle. (SI Photo A4868C)

openings over knees for more comfort and coolness, and ventilated arm pits.

The standardized Army-Navy summer suit was frequently made of khaki or olive drab fabric with a label marked AN-6550 or AN 6550-AN-S-31, or of a lightweight greenish fabric labeled AN-S-31A, which probably indicated a modified suit. Another variation in gray-green fabric was marked AN-S-31-M44. A one-piece, zipper-front summer flying suit, with belt, was also made in greenish cloth and was labeled AN-6550-M34. The *M44* and *M34* indicated the size—e.g., Medium size 44 and Medium size 34.

A typical AN-S-31 or AN-6550 suit had the following characteristics: a one-piece unlined coverall made of light gabardine wool or cotton twill, a zipper closure, a take-up strap at the bottom of each leg at the ankle and at each hip along the outseam, and access slits next to the side pockets. Pockets with buttons and flaps were located on each side of the breast and on the lower legs. A fabric belt was also provided and attached to the suit. A bellows-pleated back allowed freedom of movement. The front collar terminated in pointed tabs, which differed from the rounded Type A-4 collar. The front zipper had a keeper at both ends.

A modified form of the Army and Navy AN-S-31 summer suit and the A-6 suit was developed during 1944 for the AAF's use. This suit was made either of khaki-shade, very light cotton twill (Byrd cloth), which was designated the Type K-1, or of olive drab, worsted-warp, cotton-fill gabardine, designated the Type L-1. Both were standardized on November 3, 1944, and placed on limited procurement. The K-1 very light suit and the L-1 light suit featured a bloused-over and pleated back, which gave greater freedom of arm movement; a zipper front opening to the crotch seam; and

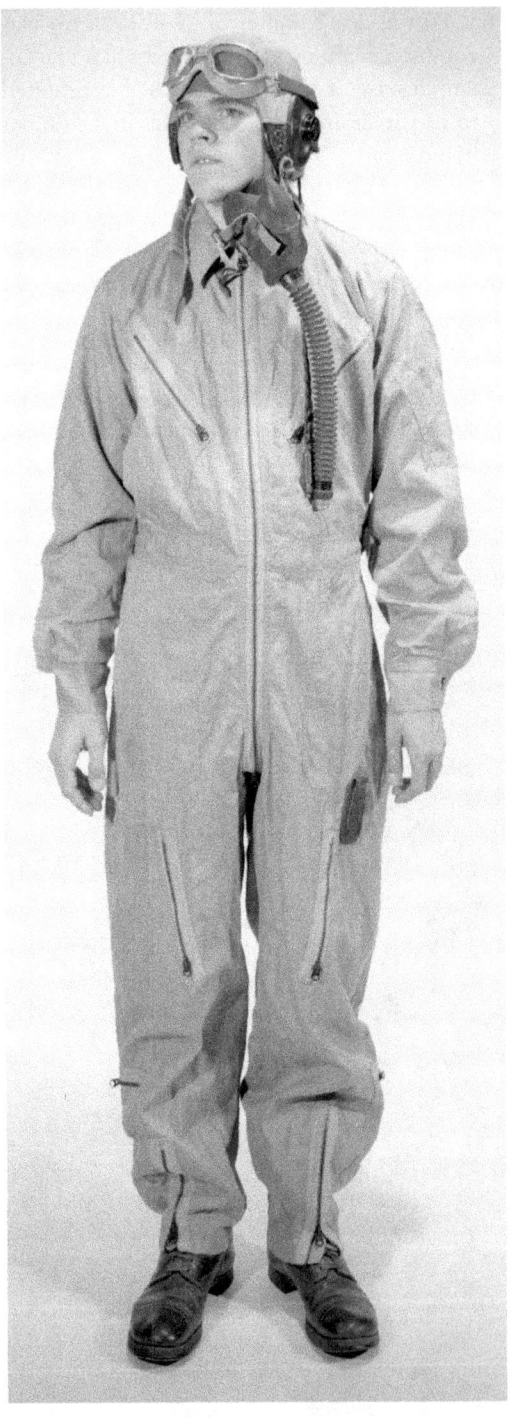

"Suit, Flying, Very Light, Cotton Twill, Type K-1," is the official designation found on the nomenclature label of this summer suit. It was developed in 1944 for wear by AAF flying personnel in tropical areas or during very hot weather. The K-1 was similar in style to the L-1 light suit and the AN-S-31 suit. The leather-covered clamp on the left thigh for holding maps and check lists should be noted. An AN-H-15 summer helmet, AN-6530 goggle, A-10A oxygen mask, and GI high-top shoes complete the outfit. All items from NASM collection. (SI Photo 81-319)

a zipper closure at the bottom of the trouser legs for easier donning and removal. The pockets were also more adequate: both suits had diagonal breast pockets and two leg and two thigh pockets, all with zipper closures. A leather-covered map holder was attached on the left thigh of most suits, and a pencil pocket was located on the left upper sleeve.

The Type K-1A suit, although similar to the K-1, had modifications to the cuffs and belt and used snap fasteners. The Type K-2 was also similar to the K-1 but was made of loosely woven nylon material. It was probably issued along with the L-1A suit after the war. Development of the K-2 suit continued in the USAF, and the K-2B was a standard USAF issue well into the Vietnam War period.

The L-1A suit was the same as the L-1, except for the same modifications that were made for the K-1A suit. There was also an L-1B suit in sage green, which was probably a postwar issue. The L-2 suit featured a cotton-twill outer shell with a rayon-wool lining and had an attached hood.[22]

As is mentioned above, all of these summer suits, with the exception of the Type L-2, remained in use with the AAF and the USAF for many years after the end of World War II.

7

Other Items of Body Clothing

Summer Flying Jackets

Leather coats were among the first items of special flying clothing purchased for use by Army aviators before World War I. Leather coats were also listed along with all other standard items of flying clothing in the official Army aviator's clothing and equipment list published in early 1918.[1] Short and long leather flying coats were gradually phased out of general use during the 1920s, although the Air Corps Stock Lists still carried them in several sizes as a nonstandard item as late as September 30, 1942. Those coats were replaced for normal wear by the olive drab cape leather Type A-1 summer flying jacket, standardized for use on November 7, 1927. This jacket had a knitted collar and cuffs. It could still be found in limited use in World War II and was finally declared obsolete on September 29, 1944, after stocks were exhausted.[2]

On September 29, 1930, service tests began on another, improved summer jacket, the Type A-2 flying jacket. It also replaced the short and long leather flying coats and became one of the "classic" garments of the Army Air Corps. It was standardized on May 9, 1931, and was used steadily through the 1930s and World War II. The A2 jacket, like the "50-mission crush" cap

The Type A-2 summer flying jacket was one of the most popular garments ever issued to aviators. First standardized in 1931, it became a "classic" during its long service life and remained in use in every theater until after World War II. The example in this recent NASM photo was originally worn during the war by Lt. Col. (later Brig. Gen.) Robert W Waltz, 390th Bomb Group, Eighth Air Force. The 390th Group insignia is on the left breast. The helmet is the AN-H-15 with AN-6530 goggle. (SI Photo 81–322)

of World War II, became a status symbol as well as a practical garment for flyers. It was, however, among the items of leather clothing that Gen. H.H. Arnold ordered replaced by a substitute or improved garment during a conference in Washington in 1942. But even though the Spec. AN-J-3 flying jacket was officially adopted as a replacement in 1943 for use by not only the AAF but also the Navy, the good old A-2 remained a favorite garment for aviators and served throughout the war on every air base and on every fighting front.

The A-2 jacket was made of seal-brown horsehide leather and lined with light brown spun silk. It had a leather collar, zipper front, and brown knitted cuffs and waistband. The AAF or numbered air force patch was sometimes worn on the shoulder. Unit insignia and a name tag, sometimes with the appropriate type of aviator's badge, were often sewed to the left breast. Officers frequently wore their rank insignia on the shoulder straps. The back of the jacket was sometimes decorated during World War II with elaborate art work painted directly on the smooth leather. The picture could be a reproduction of the aircraft insignia on the nose of the man's plane or perhaps a sweetheart, a pinup girl, or even a patriotic scene. This practice seemed innocent enough until November 26, 1943, when a B-17F bomber of the 351st Bomb Group, Eighth Air Force, was shot down near Eggese, Germany. Three of the crewmen were wearing A-2 jackets with "Murder Incorporated" and the AAF aircraft insignia painted on the back. The German press carried photographs of Lt. Kenneth Williams wearing such a jacket and claimed that the saying was an official slogan carried by all members of bomber squadrons. The Germans declared it tantamount to a U.S. admission that its air forces deliberately engaged in terror bombing of residential areas. The embarrassment caused the United States by the Nazi propaganda prompted AAF commanders to look for, and eliminate, any similar ill-chosen inscriptions or pictures on jackets and aircraft.[3]

Rear view of the A-2 summer flying jacket worn during World War II by Lt. Col. (later Brig. Gen.) Robert W. Waltz, 390th Bomb Group. The excellent "war art" was painted directly on the horsehide leather jacket. Each bomb indicates a bombing mission over enemy territory. Each swastika represents an enemy aircraft shot down in combat. The flour sack and POW illustration at left indicate an air supply mission for Prisoners of War at the end of World War II. The helmet is the AN-H-15 summer helmet. (SI Photo 81–325)

The Fourteenth Air Force "blood chit" identification patch, sometimes called an "escape flag," was often worn on the A-2 jacket by personnel in the China-Burma-India Theater of operations (CBI). It included a pledge of reward from the U.S. government to anyone who helped downed American airmen return to Allied lines. The blood chit also featured the Chinese Nationalist flag on the panel and was originally worn sewed to the jacket's back. Crewmen, however, began concealing the patch inside the jacket after a few flyers landed among the Communist Chinese and learned that it was dangerous to display the Nationalist Chinese flag in Red-held territory. Allied airmen in other theaters of operation carried or wore other types of blood chits, which usually came as part of a survival-escape kit.

Another special embellishment worn on the A-2 jacket was a special red lining that was installed, instead of the normal light brown lining, for aces of the 56th and 479th Fighter Groups flying out of England during the war. Aces in these units also wore red linings in their regular uniforms.[4]

Jackets such as these, worn on dangerous combat missions, through thick and thin, made a splendid souvenir upon discharge at the end of the war. Even today, the old A-2 jackets are sought-after collector's items and command high prices when they are in good condition. Reproductions of the Types A-2 and B-3 jackets are now being offered for sale by commercial firms and even come complete with authentic looking labels. For everyday use, a modern copy is more practical than a valuable original jacket, but collectors of authentic flying clothing must make sure that they are not accidentally buying reproductions.

In the late 1930s development began on a whipcord flying jacket intended to replace the leather jacket. The results were the Type A-3, a commercial flying jacket of whipcord with a wool fabric lining, and the Type A-4, which was similar to the A-3 except that it was unlined. Both were designated as limited standard on August 20, 1940, and were procured in limited quantities. They proved, however, to be both less satisfactory than the leather A-2 jacket in design, durability, and cleaning and less popular with aircrew personnel. The Types A-5, A-6, and A-7 were all commercial fabric jackets. Each was service tested beginning in 1941 and declared obsolete on July 1, 1943.[5] The A-5, made by the General Athletic Company as Model no. 31, was a conventional windbreaker-type jacket with a zipper front, snap cuffs, and normal collar.

1st Lt. Richard Morris, 92nd Bomb Group, Eighth Air Force, wearing his "50-mission crush" cap and beautifully painted A-2 jacket in 1945. Morris was the pilot of the B-17 illustrated on the back of his jacket. The U.S. flag shoulder patch is also noteworthy. Morris's cap is on exhibit in the National Air and Space Museum. (SI Photo 81–328)

Type A-2 flying jackets being worn by P-40 pilots of the Fourteenth Air Force in the CBI. The U.S. flag over the Fourteenth's "blood chit," which was originally worn by the "Flying Tigers" of the American Volunteer Group should be noted. The officer at right has his squadron insignia sewed to his upper left breast. (SI Photo A103255)

It had a large, semicircular patch pocket on the lower left and right side of the front.

The Spec. AN-J-3 intermediate flying jacket was standardized on April 27, 1943, and was used in limited quantities by both the Army and Navy during the latter half of the war. Quite similar to the A-2 jacket, the AN-J-3 was made of brown leather, including the collar, had knitted cuffs and waist band, and a zipper-fly front.

Little is known about the Type B-12 jacket. It was intended for wear as an alternate to the regulation officer's blouse or coat. Made of olive drab wool, it was procured in small numbers by the AAF late in 1943 and was resold to flying officers as an optional item. The B-12 was standardized on October 30, 1943, but it was classified as inactive less than a month later on November 22. On February 2, 1944, its status was changed to substitute standard, and the jacket was finally declared obsolete on September 29, 1944, after its stocks were exhausted. The B-12 was listed in the Type Designation Sheets as a winter flying jacket, but it was apparently considered more as an intermediate flight jacket since its discontinuation was probably due to the development of the Type B-13 jacket.

By the end of the war, the Type B-15B intermediate jacket (discussed in chapter 6) had officially replaced all of the above garments as the standard jacket of issue.[6]

Type A-2 flying jacket worn during World War II by Maj. Gen. Claire L. Chennault. General Chennault was the commander of the famous "Flying Tigers," the American Volunteer Group, and later the U.S. Fourteenth Air Force. He wore his "blood chit" as a pocket sewed inside the right side of his jacket. Under his name tag on the left breast is a painted leather disk with the original form of the Fourteenth's insignia designed by M.Sgt. Howard Aregard at Kunming, China. The insignia officially approved by the War Department on August 6, 1943, had the tiger reversed to face in the opposite direction so that it could be "advancing" on the shoulder patch, which was usually worn on the left shoulder of the uniform. The CBI patch was often worn on the right. Other insignia include two embroidered silver stars sewed to each shoulder strap, the CBI patch on the left shoulder, and the AAF patch on the right shoulder. Both of these patches were made of leather and are typical of insignia made commercially in India during World War II. This jacket is in the NASM collection. (SI Photo 81–317)

Flight Jackets

The origin of the AAF flight jackets, Types B-13 for officers and B-14 for enlisted men, can be traced to the battle jacket in Great Britain (part of the "battle-dress" uniform there) and to the Royal Canadian Air Force (RCAF) "aircrew suit." This type of short, light jacket was first tested and modified for American use by Army QMC personnel in England. The early "ETO" (European Theater of Operations) or "Eisenhower" jackets, as they were called, were made of olive drab wool and featured two vertical "slash" pockets on the front. Many were issued to AAF personnel in late 1943. The

Army QMC later developed this popular jacket design into the standard M-1944 Eisenhower or "Ike" jacket that was issued to the entire Army and had two upper patch pockets instead of the slash pockets. The main reason for developing this type of jacket was the need to provide a garment that was suitable for both combat and service, or "Class A," use. It was constructed without the skirt found on other standard blouses and coats so that it could be worn under the M-1943 field jacket with less unnecessary bulk around the hips.

The B-13 and B-14 flight jackets emerged as the AAF further modified the original Eisenhower jacket. The main difference between the new flight jackets and the early ETO jackets was the supplementation of the original large vertical slash pockets on the front with two concealed, flapped upper-breast pockets. The slash pockets allowed better integration with the parachute harness. The B-13 and B-14 were similar to each other, except for the types of wool used. Cloth for officers' clothing was usually of a higher quality than that used for enlisted men's wear. Both jackets had concealed buttons on their front fly. Like the M-1944, they had no skirt and could be worn comfortably under a heavy flying suit. Full insignia, including shoulder patches and rank insignia, were usually worn on these jackets.

Left: The AN-J-3 intermediate flying jacket was introduced in 1943 for use by both Army and Navy aviators. It was very similar to the popular A-2 leather flying jacket worn by Army aviators since 1931. (SI Photo A4868G) *Right:* The Type B-13 flight jacket being worn by an AAF major in 1944. Insignia was usually worn on the lapel. (SI Photo A4868J)

The B-13 and B-14 flight jackets were standardized on March 14, 1944, and about five hundred thousand of them were placed on procurement during 1944. They were changed to limited standard on January 8, 1945, and were declared obsolete on March 14, 1946. After that time all personnel used the regular QMC Ike jackets.[7]

Light Utility Flying Jacket

On May 21, 1945, the "Jacket, Flying, Light, Utility, Type L-2" entered service-test status with the AAF. (The Type L-1 was a nurse's flying jacket and is discussed later in this chapter with other women's flying clothing.) The L-2 was standardized and placed on procurement after the end of the war as a replacement for the A-2 jacket. It remained in service with the AAF and later the USAF for several years.

The L-2 was made of a moisture- and mildew-resistant cotton-twill outer shell and was lined with rayon-faced wool-backed material. The jacket was produced in olive drab no. 7 shade (leaf green). It had a knitted collar, wristlets and waistband, a zipper front closure, and a leather tab on the breast for attaching the oxygen hose clip.

Flotation and Exposure Garments

In 1912 an advertisement appeared in *Aeronautics* magazine for a kapok-filled life jacket for flyers, similar to the life jackets or vests then carried aboard ships. In 1917 the Navy and Coast Guard began developing flotation suits for their aviators' use. And during the winter of 1918-19, the Air Service tested a commercially designed one-piece flotation garment called the "Dreadnaught Safety Suit." Invented by an I.V. Keviczky, this suit was made of rubberized material and was padded with kapok.[8] Its rubber wristlets and collar were elasticized to help make it watertight. Several of these suits were said to be in use at the Naval Air Station at Pensacola, Florida, during the 1918-19 winter. Dreadnaught suits were also apparently ordered by the U.S. Navy for the crews of the Curtiss NC flying boats it used in the transatlantic flight in 1919.[9] Other early flotation garments included the Spalding "ATC Non-Sink Coat," with quilted kapok lining, and the "Ever-Warm Safety Suit." All of these suits could float for a considerable period of time, but despite their seemingly auspicious beginning, they all proved during use to be too heavy, bulky, and cold when worn for any but the shortest length of time.

Experiments with flotation suits continued, and during the 1920s two designs received Air Corps type designations. The Type C-1, an experimental suit made by the Marshall-Field Company of Chicago, was tested during the mid–1920s. The Air Corps, however, did not standardize and procure the suit. The Type C-2 was a redesigned, lightweight, one-piece "nonsinkable" fabric suit made with "Chicago" foam pads in its chest and collar. Service testing on the C-2 began in 1925, and the suit was standardized on October 23, 1928. Its status was changed to limited standard on March 6, 1936, but the C-2 was retained in use until its stocks were exhausted and it was declared obsolete on March 13, 1944. (By then, during World War II the RAF in Britain was using the Taylor Buoyant suit, a one-piece, yellow fabric winter suit with built-in kapok pads around the chest and collar for flotation.)

Although the Air Corps and the AAF never standardized any other suits specifically for flotation in the years preceding and including World War II, these were not the only flotation suits developed. Over the years, patents were issued for many rather impractical flotation suits, including pneumatic types.

The Air Corps shifted instead to life vests. In 1921 the U.S. Air Service had begun testing a khaki duck, quilted-kapok "nonsinkable" garment. Standardized as the Type A-1 coat on September 30, 1931, it was redesignated the Type A-1 life preserver vest in the mid–1930s.[10] Service testing of an improved kapok life preserver vest, the Type A-2, began on August 15, 1934, and on March 27, 1936, the A-2 was designated limited standard. The Air Corps used both vests until they were declared obsolete on March 21, 1944. The A-1 and A-2 were very dependable, but they were bulky

The Type C-2 flotation suit, called a "life preserver" suit by the Air Corps, was made with foam pads in the chest and collar. It was used in limited numbers from 1928 until 1944. (SI Photo A4869G)

when worn over flying clothing inside an airplane.

The Air Corps had little opportunity in the years between the wars to benefit from actual experience with different types of life preservers. The Navy, however, was continuously experimenting with and service testing various flotation devices. By the late 1920s compact life vests of kapok or cork construction had replaced suits and coats as the preferred flotation garments of most military and civilian airmen making overwater flights.

During the 1930s the more compact pneumatic life preserver vests of the "B" series were introduced. Many people in the Air Corps did not consider these automatically inflated carbon dioxide (CO_2) vests to be as safe as the kapok types, but the new vests gradually gained favor as they were perfected. The Type B-1 pneumatic life preserver vest of yellow rubberized drill was adopted as substitute standard on April 11, 1932. It was followed by the improved Types B-2 and B-3 pneumatic vests, which were standardized on May 16, 1933, and January 8, 1936, respectively. During World War II the AAF adopted the well-known B-4 vest, developed by the Navy, and often called the "Square Bottom" or "Mae West." It closely resembled the B-3 and was standardized on May 6, 1942. The B-4 and the Spec. AN-V-18, AN6519-1 vest were both widely used during the war and proved to be very satisfactory. On December 12, 1944, the AAF standardized a more buoyant vest, the

Type B-5, that was used into the postwar period. It featured an improved "collar" that could better support the head in the water, an important factor in the case of a wounded, exhausted, or unconscious person.

The increased flying over the icy North Atlantic and Aleutian areas during the early part of the war greatly emphasized the need for adequate flotation and exposure suits. Maj. M.P. Kelsey, a flight surgeon of the Eleventh Fighter Command, pointed out in 1944 that lifesaving equipment then was inadequate and that action should be taken as soon as possible to provide flying clothing that could sustain life in water temperatures of 65° to 35° F. Maj. Kelsey warned that, with existing equipment, "Some patients survived immersion for as long as an hour while others died after half an hour's exposure."[11]

The down-filled quilted suits that were developed for cold-weather wear had some of the characteristics of flotation and exposure suits and were occasionally suggested as possible solutions to this problem. They were, however, too permeable to protect an individual from the frigid water for any great length of time, even though they did maintain their buoyancy characteristics.

In 1942 experimental suits filled with milkweed "batt" were tested, and by 1943 various suits undergoing testing at Eglin Field, Florida, could keep individuals afloat for as long as seven hours. Unfortunately, they could seriously handicap an exhausted man trying to swim to shore or climb onto a life raft since they absorbed sufficient water to weigh as much as fifty pounds.[12]

It became obvious that for flights over frigid water a flotation garment had to perform the function of, or be used in combination with, an exposure suit. Unfortunately, no suitable exposure suit that could perform this dual function was developed before the end of World War II, although the one anti-exposure suit standardized by the AAF during the war—the Type R-1—did provide some buoyancy with the air trapped inside it.

The R-1, standardized by the AAF on January 29, 1945, was actually developed by the U.S. Navy, which used it extensively for many years. The suit consisted of a yellow two-ply, rip-stop nylon coverall that had been water- and airproofed

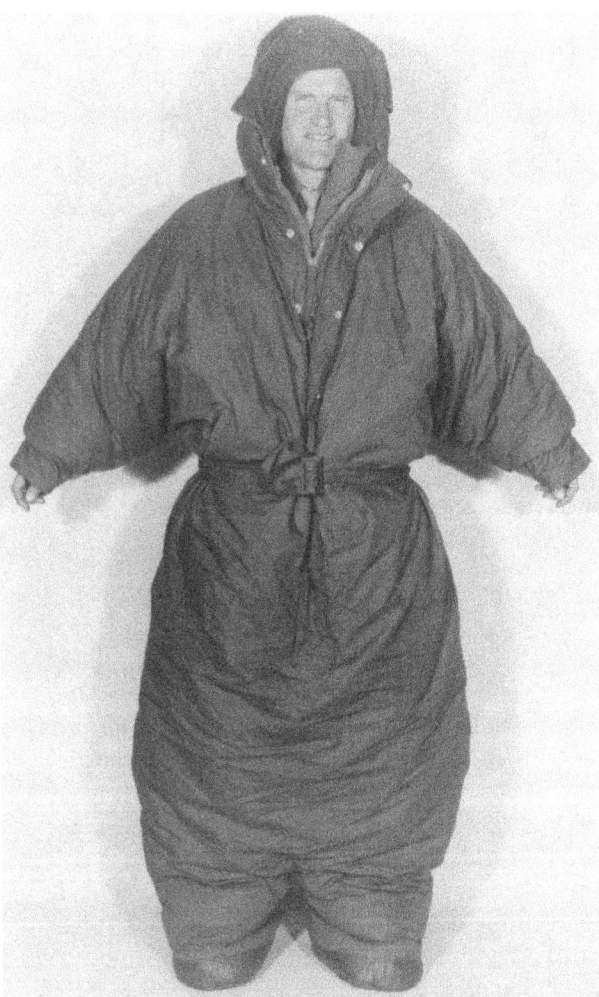

Experimental walk-around sleeping bag, also called the "Penguin Suit," which could be considered a type of exposure suit if used on land. It is shown being tested by Norman Bright, one of the cold-weather experts at the Personal Equipment Laboratory during World War II. It was not adopted because the bulk made movement almost impossible. (SI Photo A4869J)

with a neoprene coating. Boots and a hood were attached as integral parts of the suit, and drawstring closures provided seals at the wrists and neck.[13] The suit came with the F-1 anti-exposure gloves in a zippered yellow carrying case and could be donned in about one minute. It was intended to be worn mainly by personnel flying aboard bomber, patrol, and transport aircraft. The suit was made large enough to fit over practically any size man wearing flying clothing. It reportedly provided protection for up to an hour if its wearer were in water where the temperatures were as low as 28° F and for a longer period if he were aboard a life raft. The time could be extended still further if the user's head and hands were kept dry.

Electrically Heated Rescue Suit

Late in World War II a heated warming, or rescue, suit was devised through a field modification of the F-1 electrically heated flying suit. The F-1's chest and leg zippers were lengthened so that they met at the crotch, and longer arm zippers were usually added. The new design allowed the whole suit, except for the arms, to be laid out as a sheet and then wrapped around a rescued airman or medical patient who was chilled or in shock and needed mild external warmth applied. Heated gloves and shoes were optional for use with the modified F-1, which could be used in air- or watercraft as well as on land.[14]

An electrically heated blanket, or casualty bag, was placed in production by the AAF and introduced for use in 1943. It had been designed (Project no. 127) by the Eighth Air Force Central Medical Establishment in England in collaboration with personal equipment officers in the field and a group flight surgeon. In addition to its heating abilities, the bag possessed sufficient buoyancy to keep a wounded man afloat for fifteen or twenty minutes if a forced landing were made at sea. This item was, of course, classified as equipment rather than clothing.

The "Suit, Flying, Anti-Exposure, Quick Donning, Type R-1." This gear was intended for quick donning (approximately one minute) by crew members of heavy bombers and cargo planes before an emergency ditching of the aircraft at sea. It protected the wearer from exposure while floating in cold waters and from exposure to wind, spray, and rain when marooned in a life raft. It was sized to fit a large man dressed in heavy, bulky flying gear but was provided with take-up bands to adjust it for smaller men. (SI Photo 80–19516)

Sweaters

Sweaters were among the first items worn by early civilian and military aviators during cold weather. They were an excellent source of warmth, and because of the inefficiency of standard flying clothing over the years, they remained popular. Sweaters also absorbed perspiration and protected the flyer's more expensive outer garments.

The use of sweaters by Army aviators is rather confusing. Only one sweater was given a type number and listed in the Type Designation Sheets, and it was the old Type A-1 *mechanics* sweater—a knitted wool, vee-neck, pullover style that was standardized on March 20, 1926. The A-1 was finally declared obsolete, with stocks of it turned over to the QMC, on August 9, 1944. Some aviators may have worn this sweater.

No sweater was listed as part of the regular issue of GI clothing in Army Regulation 600-

35 and changes, *Prescribed Service Uniform*. However, the Quartermaster Supply Catalog no. 3-1, *Enlisted Men's Clothing and Equipment*, dated April 1944, listed two sweaters as special-issue items: an olive drab, all-worsted, slipover type with a high-collar, buttoned neck; and an olive drab sleeveless sweater. Both were intended for troops on special duty, such as those serving in the Arctic, and mountain troops. Flyers may have obtained and worn some of them, too. The Air Corps added a "Sweater, Aviators, Size 40," as nonstandard issue to its June 1, 1940, stock list. This sweater had no type number, but it was still available in the list published on September 30, 1943.

According to Donald Huxley, civilian chief of the Clothing Branch at Wright Field from World War II until 1975, many sweaters and similar items were locally procured and used by aviators.[15] In addition, both sleeveless and long-sleeve olive drab sweaters could be purchased in the Army Post Exchanges, and many others were furnished by the Red Cross as well as by relatives and friends in the States.

The venerable Type A-1 mechanics sweater, which was used from 1926 until 1944. This olive drab shaker-knit sweater was typical of the type worn by many Army aviators through World War II. (SI Photo A4868D)

Vests

What many people think was a sweater was actually the "Vest, Flying, Winter, Type C-2"—a sweater-type vest, made of olive drab worsted yarns, that had raglan sleeves with rib-knit cuffs and a rib-knit vee-type collar. The C-2 also had a tubular rib-knit waistband, a pocket on the lower left side, and a zipper front closure. The vest was standardized on June 18, 1934, changed to limited standard on

A vest made during the latter part of World War II without a nomenclature label. It was constructed of fabric with a pile lining and a zipper front. Specimen from NASM collection. (SI Photo 81-323)

1st Lt. (later Lt. Col.) Donald S. Lopez of the 75th Fighter Squadron (5 victories), in the cockpit of his P-51C "Lope's Hope" at Chikkiang, China, in November 1944. He is wearing a long-sleeve, olive drab Type C-2 sweater-vest with a zipper front under his leather A-2 flying jacket. The CBI patch on his left shoulder, B-7 goggles, A-14 oxygen mask, and RAF Type C leather helmet should be noted. Lt. Lopez obtained the helmet in India from an RAF pilot in exchange for a pair of AAF sunglasses. U.S. earphones were installed in the British helmet to make it compatible with the radio equipment in the P-40 and P-51 aircraft flown by the 23rd Fighter Group. (SI Photo 81–331)

June 2, 1942, and finally declared obsolete in 1946.[16]

The first vest to be officially adopted by the Air Corps was the Type C-1. It was originally called a "Jacket, Aircraft, Pilot's (Vest)," but this was changed to "Vest, Flying, Winter, Type C-1." This vest was constructed of a mercerized-cotton fabric shell and padded with paperback kapok fiber. It had no collar or sleeves, and was retained by two tie strings located on each side of the front. Placed on limited-standard status on June 18, 1934, the C-1 was procured and used as a nonstandard item during the 1930s and the early years of World War II.

Unlike the C-2, the Type C-3 vest was fabricated of three-eighths-inch lamb shearling and was made without sleeves. This vest had a zipper front closure and usually had an elastic-knit panel on each side to increase its flexibility. The C-3 was standardized on May 28, 1936, and was declared obsolete in 1946. Both the C-2 and C3 vests were originally developed and issued to be worn under the shearling flying suits for additional warmth.[17]

Other vests included a twelve-volt, three-amp electrically heated type that was service tested from around 1939 until 1943 and a fur-lined flying vest that was listed as nonstandard in the September 25, 1941, issue of the Class 13 Stock List. A fabric, wool-lined vest with zipper front closure but no label was also produced and used during the later part of World War II.

Underwear

Underwear, like ordinary Army uniforms, was developed by the QMC and was classified as individual, not flying, clothing. It is mentioned here, however, because of its importance to aviators.

Aircrew personnel on long missions required underwear that provided sufficient warmth without unduly increasing discomfort. Developments in wool, rayon, and nylon fabrics during the war—as well as special designs for elbows, knees, and crotches—added to both the warmth and the comfort of undergarments. The wool content in some winter underwear was reduced to 50 percent and 35 percent without reducing its insulative qualities, and shrinkage was lowered from about 30 percent to 5 percent.

Most GI underwear, especially that provided overseas, was olive drab, but AAF personnel sometimes received white undergarments such as cotton undershirts, T-shirts, and shorts. Buff-color two-piece long underwear of wool knit was also issued to flying personnel, and even today former wearers remember how itchy it was.

Pilots and aircrew members also complained from time to time about the unattractiveness of the underclothing issued to them, particularly the "long-john" type of long wool underwear. They requested lighter and dressier undergarments for wear on leave and "trips to town." The color preferred by those stationed in England was reported to be "robin's egg blue."[18]

Scarves and Mufflers

Scarves proved very useful to aviators flying in open cockpits because they not only kept the neck warm and prevented drafts but also protected the neck from chafing. In addition, scarves could be used by flyers to wipe off goggles, windscreens, and instruments. They remained popular long after the closed-cockpit aircraft was introduced.

Scarves were often made of white silk from discarded parachutes. One such model was listed without type number as standard issue in the Air Corps Stock Lists that were published during the late 1930s and the early World War II years. Those lists also included an unnumbered nonstandard-issue flying scarf made of wool. Another scarf developed during the war for flyers' use was listed in the Type Designation Sheets as the Type N-1. It was a circular knitted wool band designed to protect the neck and throat from low temperatures and was standardized for limited procurement on November 9, 1944.

Mufflers were among the standard items of issue developed by the QMC. Army Regulation 600-35, *Prescribed Service Uniform,* published during the war, listed an olive drab, wool muffler with a commercial pattern for issue to officers, warrant officers, and flight officers. Another muffler was authorized for enlisted men.

Scarves and mufflers, like sweaters, were often purchased by individual airmen or obtained from friends, relatives, or the Red Cross.

Miscellaneous Flying Clothing

A heavy, olive drab, wool shirt and trousers were available to aviators during the war. These garments, whose Type Designation Sheets have not been found but specimens of which are included in the NASM collection, were normally worn under a regular flying suit. Insignia may have been worn on the shirt, which was marked "Shirt, Flying, Heavy, Type A-1." The shirt had an ordinary button fly and two upper and two lower patch pockets. It was normally not tucked into the trousers. The pants that probably were worn with the A-1 shirt had knitted cuffs and oval pads reinforcing the seat and knees. They were marked "Trousers, Flying, Inner, Type E-1." (The NASM examples vary slightly in color.)

Nonstandard Items

The Air Corps centralized its procurement during the 1920s. Standard flight materiel items were stocked in depots and were requisitioned by units and stations through supply channels, usually on an annual basis. However, some nonstandard items without type numbers—including flying helmets, gloves and shoes, and even summer and winter flying coats and suits—were also procured and used.

A severe shortage of many items of clothing and personal equipment accompanied the great expansion of the armed forces that followed the United States' entry into World War II in December 1941. Flying clothing and equipment were often pooled or shared to help overcome the shortages. In addition, obsolescent and even service-test equipment was brought out of storage and re-issued; and many improvised, locally procured, and nonstandard items were pressed into use, particularly by training units. As AAF units began arriving overseas in 1942, they found that some of their standard-issue garments and accessories for aviators were inadequate, as well as unavailable in sufficient quantities and sizes. As a result, flyers purchased or obtained nonregulation and custom-made garments including boots, hats, helmets, and similar items wherever they could and then used them to fill their requirements. This included both garments intended for Army ground forces personnel and Navy flying clothing and personal equipment. RAF flight matériel was particularly welcome when it could be obtained. For example, RAF flying helmets were especially popular and were often modified to accommodate AAF earphones. RCAF winter clothing was also held in high esteem by American flyers.

Authorized garments were sometimes altered to suit the wearer, and this, too, was often tolerated during the war. For instance, service caps were frequently converted to "50-mission crush" caps by removing the grommets, giving them a jaunty look like caps that had been crushed down by earphones on many combat missions. In addition, insignia and pictures were painted on leather jackets, and all types of insignia were worn. It was simply human nature for most people to want to wear something special or distinctive.

As the war progressed, new and improved types of clothing and personal equipment began arriving in quantity for U.S. airmen. The items used by flyers became more standardized, and regulations were more carefully enforced. Still, old and odd items continued to be used by flyers through the end of the war, and they may still be found in collections of wartime clothing and equipment.

Service Uniforms

A detailed description of the U.S. Army service uniforms developed by the QMC and worn by AAF personnel during World War II is outside the scope of this study. Mention must be made, however, of the principal service uniforms since airmen normally wore a uniform of some type under their flying clothing, especially when they were participating in operational missions overseas. If an airman was forced down in enemy territory, an official uniform with grade insignia was important in order for him to have the protection afforded to a soldier in uniform by the Geneva Convention. A captured airman without a recognized uniform could be executed as a spy. Moreover, if he was confined in a prisoner of war camp, it was desirable for him to have a regular uniform to wear, instead of just bulky flying clothing.

During World War II the uniform was worn in accordance with prescribed directives, including AR 600-40.[19] Although the service coat was not always worn under flying clothing, the rest of the winter or summer uniform was usually worn, including the shirt (with insignia), trousers, and identification tags (dog tags). The best-known uniform worn by officers was the "Pinks and Greens," actually a forest green coat and pinkish-beige trousers. (It is still considered by many people to be the most attractive uniform ever worn by personnel of the U.S. Army.) The Type B-13 olive drab wool jacket and trousers combination for

Typical AAF service uniforms worn during and after World War II. Flyers normally wore a regulation military uniform, with grade insignia, under their flying clothing so that if they were forced down in enemy territory they would have the protection of the Geneva Convention. Left to right: Col. A.D. Olson, B-29 pilot, wearing the famous "Pinks and Greens," one of the best looking American uniforms, 1945; Lt. Col. D.C. Shilling, well-known ace with 22½ victories, wearing the olive drab wool "Ike" jacket, c.1946; unidentified major and B-17 pilot in tan gabardine summer uniform, 1942; M/Sgt. J.A. Graham, crewman on XB-29, wearing the olive drab winter enlisted service uniform, 1944; and M/Sgt. E.H. Dibble, aircrewman, wearing the popular olive drab "Ike" jacket outfit, c. 1946. Khaki cotton summer uniforms were also frequently worn by both officers and enlisted men while flying in warm climates during World War II. (SI Photo 81-7379)

officers on flying status and the B-14 jacket outfit for enlisted men were very similar to the M-1944 "Ike" jacket and trousers that became standard issue for the entire Army in 1944. These jackets were more practical for flying than the officer and enlisted service coats, which had a skirt that was bulky when worn under a flying suit.

Tan gabardine, and khaki cotton "chino" summer shirt and trouser combinations were frequently worn under flying clothing by officers and enlisted crewmen when the weather and mission permitted. Crewmen flying aboard transport aircraft often dispensed with flying clothing altogether and wore just the service uniform. In hot areas, such as Panama, the South Pacific, and China, airmen frequently flew in their summer uniform, which was much cooler and more comfortable than a flying suit.

The standard service cap (usually with the grommet removed) and the garrison or "overseas" cap of olive drab wool, gabardine, or khaki material were normally worn with the service uniform but also were often worn while flying, especially in transport or bomber aircraft.

Generally speaking, the uniforms worn by U.S. Army personnel during World War II were considered equal to, and in many cases superior in cut and material to, those worn by the soldiers and airmen of other nations.

Flying Clothing for Women

Army flight nurses and Women's Airforce Service Pilot (WASP) personnel were required to wear male flying clothing during the early part of the war, but that proved to be rather unsatisfactory. Even the smallest men's sizes were too large for many women, and male clothing often did not fit properly.

Eventually, special items of flying clothing were developed for flight nurses. Among this clothing was a blue woolen flight uniform, which consisted of the waist-length Type F-1 nurses' flying jacket, the Type A-1 nurses' aviation slacks, and the Type A-1 nurses' aviation skirt, all standardized on June 7, 1943. Early in 1944 the color of this uniform was changed from blue to olive drab. A Type C-1 nurses' aviation "overseas" style cap (also standardized on June 7, 1943) was worn with this outfit.

An intermediate winter alpaca-pile flying suit, the Type A-1, was designed for use by flight nurses. It consisted of an outer shell and insert for winter flying but could be worn as a summer suit by eliminating the insert. This suit was standardized, probably in 1944, but apparently it was quickly replaced by a new combination—the Type B-17 jacket and A-13 trousers.

That new B-17, A-13 intermediate nurses' flying suit similar to the flyers' intermediate suit was also issued in 1944, with the jacket standardized on May 4 and the trousers standardized May 15. This outfit was intended for use over the olive drab wool suit or uniform and was made of a water- and mildew-resistant olive drab cotton-twill outer shell, lined throughout with alpaca- and wool-pile fabric.

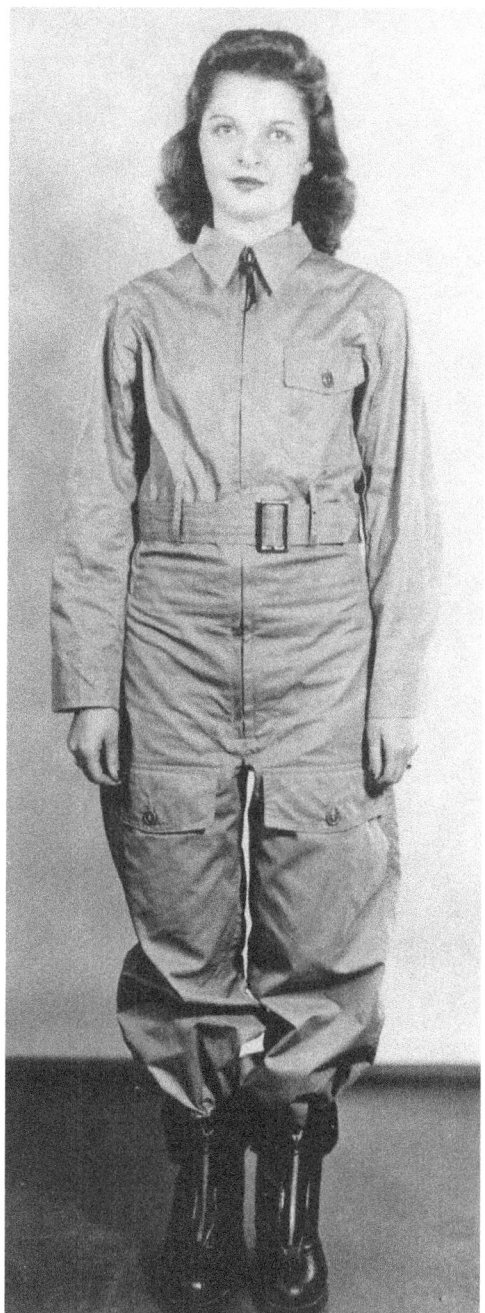

Proposed nurse's one-piece winter flying suit tested during 1943. The shoes are probably the Type A-9. (SI Photo A4869C)

The jacket had a mouton collar, knitted wristlets and waistband, and a zipper front closure, while the trousers had knitted cuffs with a zipper running the entire length on each leg. One

WASP pilot of an AT-6 trainer wearing the intermediate flying suit standardized in May 1944. The Type B-16 jacket and A-12 trousers for WASPs resembled the flight nurse's outfit and the intermediate suit worn by male personnel. The shoes are the Type A-16 for WASPs and nurses. (SI Photo A4869F)

pocket was located on each thigh, and one oxygen-bottle pocket with zipper in the outseam was above the left knee. The trousers had two side openings with zippers, and suspenders were included. To accompany this intermediate suit, flyers' standard intermediate helmets were authorized for flight nurses' use. Because the nurses' hair provided thermal insulation, summer or light helmets usually were sufficient. Many nurses preferred to wear the caps provided with the basic light suit, even in intermediate temperatures.

7. Other Items of Body Clothing

The flight nurse's intermediate flying suit consisting of the Type B-17 jacket and A-13 trousers, standardized in May 1944. This outfit was very similar to the standard B-15 jacket, A-11 trousers combination for male personnel, which was lined with alpaca pile material. (SI Photo A4869E)

On January 10, 1945, a new light suit with improved tailoring and design was standardized as the Type L-1 jacket and the Type L-1 slacks. The skirt was discarded since it had not proven useful in flight. Both the jacket and the slacks were made of olive drab worsted-wool gabardine, and the jacket was provided with adjustable waist straps, shoulder pads, two breast pockets, and a pencil pocket on the left sleeve. The slacks had a zipper closure on the left side, an adjustable front waistband strap, and two side pockets. A Type L-1 "overseas"-

type cap was provided for this suit. It was made of the same material as the suit but was lined with rayon and trimmed with gold-and-black braid, the designation of an officer. (All nurses were commissioned officers.)

A very light flying suit made of lightweight but tightly woven insect-resistant khaki cotton twill was added to this clothing series on January 22, 1945, as the Type K-1 jacket and Type K-1 slacks. Both were similar to the L-1 garments in appearance. The K-1 jacket included adjustable waist straps, detachable shoulder pads, two breast pockets, and a pencil pocket on its left sleeve. The slacks had a zipper closure on the left side, an adjustable front waistband strap, and two side pockets. An "overseas" type cap was also provided for wear with this outfit and was standardized as the Type K-1 cap, also on January 22, 1945. It was made of a khaki-shade tropical worsted cotton twill outer shell, lined with rayon and trimmed with the gold-and-black braid of an officer.

An intermediate shearling overshoe, the Type A-16, was standardized for use by flight nurses and WASP personnel on May 2, 1944. It was very similar to the Type A-6 men's shoe but was smaller in size. The A-16 had rubber soles, removable felt insoles, and a zipper front closure. It fitted over the women's field shoes or over low service shoes. Flight nurses also were issued smaller sizes of the standard flyers' handwear. The light Type B-3A glove and the intermediate Type A-11 glove were usually worn.

An intermediate flying suit very similar to the nurses' outfit was developed for wear by the WASP personnel during the early part of 1944. It consisted of the Type B-16 jacket, standardized on May 4, and the A-12 trousers, standardized on May 15. The WASP organization was discontinued at the end of 1944, however, and this suit was placed on limited-standard classification on March 1, 1945.[20]

8

Headgear

Flying Helmets

Football helmets were the first protective head coverings for aviators to be procured by the U.S. Army before World War I. Flyers needed them during the early days of flying in case they were in an accident, and students and instructors continued to wear hard helmets until shortly after the war. But when U.S. airmen reached France, they learned quickly that the helmets did not allow the freedom of head movement that was so important in combat flying. As a result, Allied aviators usually wore soft helmets at the front, although many German flyers preferred to wear hard-leather crash helmets, even in combat. The soft helmet, however, provided little crash protection. Meanwhile, the hard helmet was discontinued by the Army Air Service after World War I and was not re-introduced by the AAF until jet aircraft were developed at the end of World War II.

Flying helmets were also needed to reduce the engine-noise interference with radio reception and to protect the aviators' heads and, especially, their ears from propeller blasts and the cold. The helmets also provided some protection against flash burns if there was a fire.

Many types of commercial and experimental helmets were tested between the wars, and several types of nonstandard helmets were occasionally procured in small quantities to fill limited and special requirements. These included a soft chamois flying helmet; a special fawn reindeer–lined helmet; a summer helmet with visor, Spec. 3016; and a high altitude helmet with venturi-type mask and an oxygen

The Roold protective aviators helmet was widely used before and during World War I in Europe and the United States. Made of cork, rubber, and metallic fibers and covered with painted fabric, it offered considerable protection to the head. Allied military flyers wore hard helmets mainly for training during the war. Specimen from NASM collection. (SI Photo A43695)

U.S. Army Air Service pilot in 1918 wearing an improved helmet with radio headset, probably the Type 1-A made by Western Electric. This captain is also wearing a face mask, oxygen mask, and Meyrowitz Luxor–type goggles. Goggles with a large face pad were also worn in cold weather to provide a complete covering for the face. Note the lacing on top of the leather helmet for adjusting the size for a better fit. (SI Photo 80-20360)

Typical soft flying helmet of the World War I period, also used during the 1920s. Usually made of leather and lined with fabric or fur, this type of helmet protected the wearer from the wind, rain, and cold, as well as engine noise. The military generally discontinued the use by aviators of Resistal safety goggles such as these during the 1920s, but they could still be purchased from civilian firms, such as Karl Ort, until 1941. Specimens from NASM collection. (SI Photo 18473F)

connection. None of these helmets received type numbers; although some remained in the inventory for years and were listed in the Air Corps Class 13 Stock Lists.

Electrically heated helmets were studied and tested at various times, but it was found as early as 1921 that the additional heat furnished by electricity was not really necessary for head comfort or protection. (Some experts estimate that at least 40 percent of the total body heat escapes from the head.) Electrically heated helmets were discontinued in the early 1930s, but a twelve-volt electric cloth insert for wear under the regular winter helmet was produced in limited numbers early in World War II.

The traditional soft cloth and leather helmets worn during 1918, with or without earphones, received minor improvements during the 1920s and 1930s. By the mid-1920s helmets were generally classified as either "A" (summer) or "B" (winter) series.[1]

Summer Flying Helmets

For several years after World War I, the Air Service utilized stocks of lightweight flying helmets that had been procured during 1917 and 1918. The first three summer flying helmets standardized in the 1920s under the then new supply system—the Types A-1, A-2, and A-3—were used in limited quantities and gradually phased out of service. The A-2, however, was carried in the stock lists as limited standard issue until 1940. The Type A-4 helmet, of chamois-lined cape leather, was standardized in the mid-1920s. It was reclassified

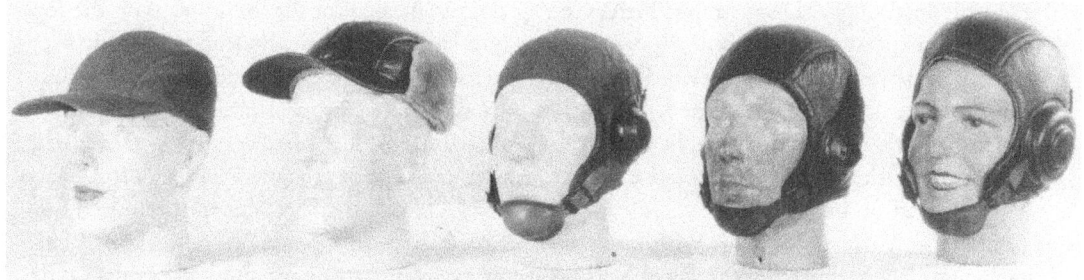

Headgear for airmen, 1940. According to the original caption, left to right: pilot's summer flying cap, Type B-1; pilot's winter cap, Type B-2; summer helmet, Type A-8; intermediate helmet, Type A-7; winter helmet, Type B-5. (This B-5 must have been an experimental variation.) (SI Photo 81–326)

as limited standard on June 13, 1933, and retained in use until it was finally declared obsolete on April 10, 1944. The Type A-5, standardized on November 27, 1924, was provided with goggles and a face mask but was placed in inactive status on October 11, 1929.

The Type A-6 helmet and all of the summer flying helmets that followed it saw long service, including during World War II. The A-6, a tan or olive drab lightweight cloth helmet with a silk lining was standardized on March 13, 1931, and declared obsolete on March 24, 1944. It was intended for wear in southern and tropical areas. The Type A-7 was actually an intermediate helmet and had a horsehide outer shell with chamois lining cemented to it. It had a chin strap with cup and was very similar in style to the Types B-4 and B-5 winter helmets. The A-7 was standardized on May 3, 1933, changed to limited standard status on March 24, 1941, and declared obsolete on September 29, 1944.

The Type A-8 helmet, standardized on October 12, 1933, was constructed of tan gabardine fabric. A silk sun mask originally was attached to the inside; it could be drawn across the face and fastened with a leather strap that fitted over the chin. The helmet also had a

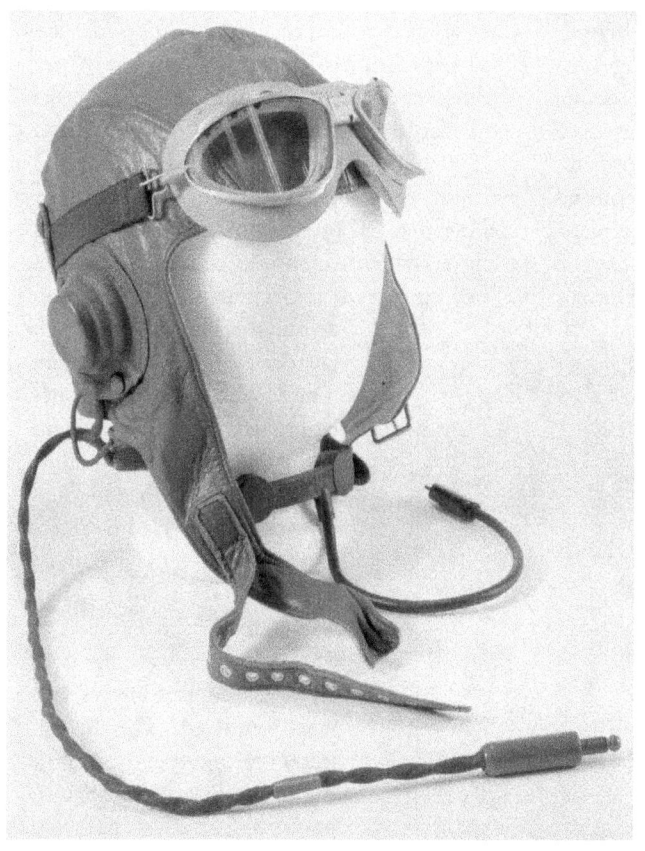

The Type A-4 summer flying helmet was standardized during the 1920s and was issued as limited standard from 1933 until 1944. It was made of brown cape leather with chamois lining. This example is equipped with an ANB-H-1 headset. A throat microphone made by Western Electric, marked "T-30-Q," and an AN-6530 goggle are shown in this NASM specimen photograph. (SI Photo 81–312)

chin cup instead of a throat strap. The A-8 remained in the system in limited quantities until World War II and was declared obsolete on September 29, 1944. The Type A-9, similar to the A-8, was constructed of light olive drab gabardine without lining and had a throat strap instead of a cup. Standardized on December 24, 1941, it was made with hook attachments to accommodate the Types A-9 and A-10 oxygen masks. This helmet was made with a cord that could be adjusted around the face and neck for a closer fit, an important feature for flights in an open cockpit or crew position.

As early as 1935 tests were conducted in the Equipment Laboratory at Wright Field to find more effective soundproofing materials and improved methods for construction of helmets. It was determined that one-half to two-thirds of the noise that reached a helmet wearer entered under the headgear's edge. Attempts were made to devise means of sealing the edge of the helmet, but this caused so much discomfort that the idea was dropped.[2]

New and improved oxygen masks required adjustments in the construction of helmets. The then new Types A-9 and A-10 oxygen masks required helmets with attachment points (hooks) for the mask straps on the top and sides, and both the summer and winter helmets were changed to accommodate these masks in late 1941 and early 1942. The introduction in 1942 of the Type A-10 Revised demand-type oxygen mask (Type A-10R, later A-10A), with snap attachments, required further base modifications to helmets. All helmets for flight use procured after the middle of 1943 included studs for oxygen mask snap-attachment and retaining straps for goggle headbands as standard equipment. During the war helmets were procured in four sizes: small, medium, large, and extra large.

Most criticism of helmets during the early part of World War II, and the subsequent need for modifications, concerned the earphone sockets, the face and neck fit, the chin or throat strap, and their integration with other articles of personal equipment. (The Alaskan Test Expedition of 1942 found that the winter helmets then in use were not liked by the flyers and that they preferred the RCAF helmets.)

Until 1943 flying helmets were procured without provision for earphones. Cotton ear pads, Spec. 3121, were available for use with helmets when earphones were not utilized. They consisted of circular pieces of cotton velour stitched together with cotton batting between them. They were three and one-eighth inches in diameter and one-half inch thick. In addition, some flyers used ladies' powder puffs. Headset kits were available and were fitted at the bases to the users' needs. Variations of the leather earphone retainers were also used and were requisitioned as they were required. The brown leather earphone cup used during the early years of the war, part no. 34B2029, had two snaps and was three inches in diameter.

The Type A-9 summer flying helmet, which had a drawstring for adjustment around face and neck for a closer fit. The hooks are for attaching the Types A-9 and A-10 oxygen masks. (SI Photo A4854G)

As a result of wartime experiments, considerable success was achieved in increasing the noise-exclusion qualities of the earphone receptacles or "donuts" and in adding to the receptacles' comfort by shaping them to fit more closely around the ears, thereby reducing the air spaces at those points. Neoprene was used to make the receptacles until the rubber shortage in 1943 forced the use of wool fiber and kapok. Beginning with the Spec. AN-H-15 helmet, the new earphone receptacles were built into helmets at the factory. Among the helmets using the improved type of sound-insulated earphone mountings were the AN-H-15, AN-H-16, and the Type A-11. They were also used on several variations of Navy helmets and radio headsets. The concept remained in use through the Vietnam War as a component in the Combat Vehicle Crewman (CVC) helmet.

The Spec. AN-H-15 summer flying helmet was standardized on April 23, 1943, as a replacement for the Type A-9. It was intended for both Army and Navy use as a part of the clothing and equipment standardization program. Made of khaki Byrd cloth, it featured the large, black rubber, acoustically insulated receptacles for the ANB-H-1 earphones, similar to those that were later used on the Type A-11 intermediate helmet and the AN-H-16 winter helmet.

The Type A-10 helmet, similar to the AN-H-15, was standardized by the AAF for limited procurement on July 18, 1944, a year after the Type A-11 was introduced. The A-10 was made of khaki cotton-twill cloth and was designed to accommodate the Howard design 5-C earphone mounting socket. After a slight modification the helmet was re-designated the Type A-10A, but the specification number, 3230, remained the same. In 1945 the A-10A replaced the AN-H-15 as the standard AAF summer flying helmet, and the AN-H-15 became substitute standard.

The last helmet in the "A" series developed during the war was the Type A-11 intermediate helmet. The A-11 was standardized on August 6, 1943, and by the end of the year, 207,000 had been placed on procurement. Made of brown cape leather and lined with chamois skin, it had the black rubber, kapok-filled cushioned earphone mountings that were designed

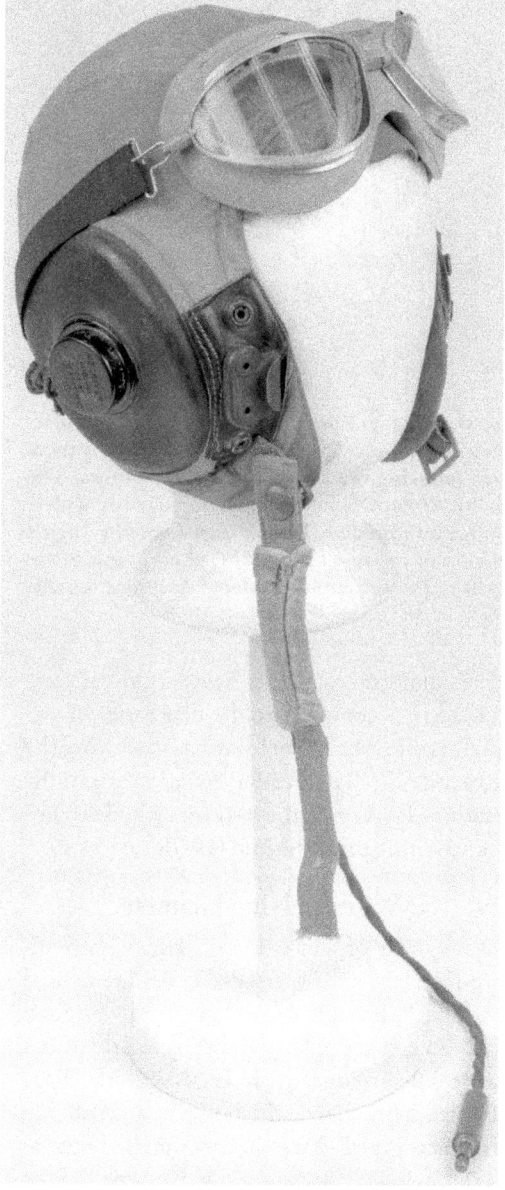

The AN-H-15 summer flying helmet and AN-6530 goggles introduced in 1943 for use by both Army and Navy aviators. The snap attachments are for the Types A-10, A-13, and A-14 oxygen masks. The earphones are the standard Type ANB-H-1, which were installed in the improved black rubber low-frequency sound-insulated headset mountings. Specimens from NASM collection. (SI Photo 80–15152)

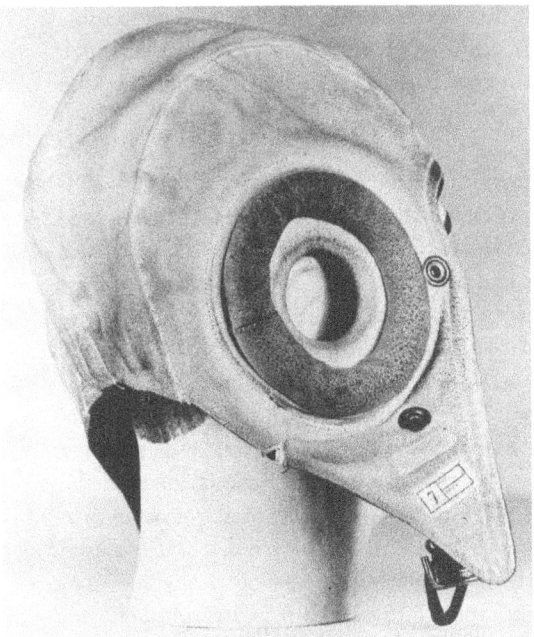 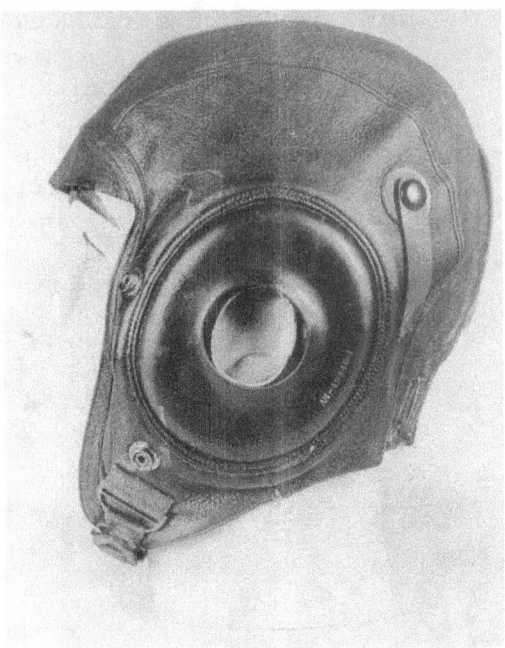

Left: Inside view of the Type A-11 intermediate helmet showing its lining. During the war the noise-exclusion qualities and comfort of the earphone receptacles or "donuts" were improved by shaping them to fit more closely around and in back of the ears, thus reducing the air spaces at these points. The headset is not installed in this helmet. (SI Photo A4861D) *Right:* One of the most popular and widely used flying helmets of World War II was the Type A-11. An intermediate helmet introduced in August 1943, it was made of cape leather with either a chamois-skin or doeskin lining. This photograph shows an early A-11 with the ANB-H-1 headset removed from the improved sound-insulated earphone mountings. (SI Photo A4861C)

for the ANB-H-1 radio receivers and that were insulated for low frequency sound. It also had a quick-release chin-strap buckle. In late 1943 doeskin, made from the pelts of South African or Brazilian hair sheep, was substituted for chamois as a helmet lining after being found more uniform in thickness. The helmet's outer shell was later made of earth-brown sheepskin leather.

The A-11 helmet was found to be generally satisfactory in service but received small modifications because of minor criticisms, such as the need for a softer chin strap and for a buckle and strap at the base of the neck to allow better adjustment. The type designation was unchanged. Combat crews stationed in England were very satisfied with the A-11, and it eventually replaced the RAF Type C flying helmet that they had frequently been using. The AAF and USAF continued to use the A-11 for many years. For example, after new earphones were added to accommodate the new series of aircraft radios, the helmet saw service during the Korean War. The Federal Aviation Administration (FAA) used the A-11 for altitude chamber training until the mid–1970s.

Winter Flying Helmets

A variety of winter flying helmets were introduced over the years, and several remained in service through World War II. The original fur-lined types procured during World War I were replaced during the 1920s with the Type B-1 leather helmet, which was lined with dog fur. The Type B-2 was an experimental nutria-lined helmet, also known as the Type B. The Type B-3 helmet was made of cape leather and was fur lined. It was standardized on August 2, 1925, and continued in limited use for many years, until it was officially declared

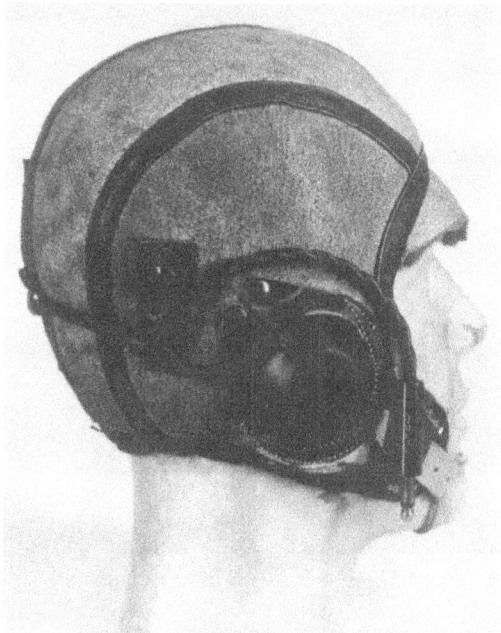 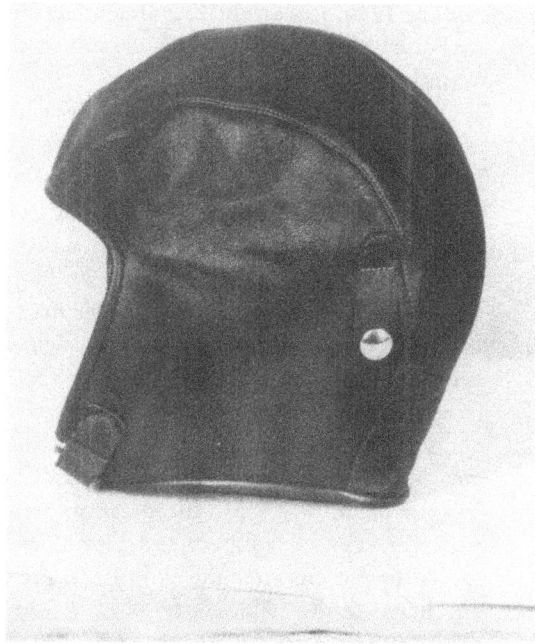

Left: Another helmet that saw extensive service was the Type B-5. This winter helmet was made of shearling and was worn from 1933 until 1944. Early B-5 helmets, such as the example in this 1936 photograph, were made with horsehide leather used only as a covering for the seams. From the late 1930s the B-5 was made with a full horsehide outer shell. (SI Photo A4854F) *Right:* The Type B-3 was in use longer than any other winter flying helmet. Standardized in 1925, it saw limited service until 1944. The B-3 was made of cape leather and was fur lined. (SI Photo A4854D)

obsolete on March 31, 1944. The B-4 winter helmet, standardized on July 28, 1930, was similar to the Type A-3 except that the lining was constructed of silk-pile fabric. The outer shell was made of cape leather, and the helmet fit closely around the face and neck. The B-4 was declared obsolete on September 29, 1944, after its stocks were exhausted.

The next development in winter helmets was the Type B-5 shearling. Apparently, this helmet, made of one-fourth-inch pile shearling, was originally made with horsehide leather used only as a covering for the seams; it was later made with a full horsehide outer shell. A chamois-lined chin strap with cup was used instead of the previously preferred throat strap. The B-5 was standardized on May 2, 1933, and declared obsolete at the same time as the B-4. As with the other helmets of that period, earphone receptacles, if required, were fitted to the user at his base.

The Type B-6 winter helmet, standardized on December 15, 1941, had a shearling construction and a brown finish. It was originally made with hook attachments for the A-9 oxygen mask, but was modified about 1942 to take the A-10R or A-10A oxygen mask with snap attachments. Many helmets manufactured earlier were modified to later specifications. The B-6 was officially replaced by the AN-H-16 helmet in 1943.

The Type B-7 helmet was a hood type that consisted of a one-fourth-inch shearling body and a two-inch double-thickness wolfskin facestrip. It was standardized on August 17, 1942, and declared obsolete on March 14, 1944, when its stocks were exhausted. The helmet was evidently procured in very limited numbers, and no specimen is known to exist today.

The "Helmet, Flying, Winter, Spec. AN-H-14" was a leather helmet tested by the AAF in early 1944. It was not recommended for AAF use because it did not provide sufficient warmth for the ears and forehead.

On April 23, 1943, the Spec. AN-H-16 winter flying helmet was standardized for use by both the AAF and Navy. It was also constructed of one-fourth-inch pile shearling like the Type B-7 and proved quite satisfactory. The helmet was especially valuable on long bombardment missions where crewmen in exposed positions (e.g., B-17 and B-24 waist gunners) needed additional protection for their faces and necks. Acoustically insulated earphone receptacles were also used on this helmet. Forty thousand AN-H-16 helmets were procured, and it was still listed as standard issue for exposed gunners and airmen on special operations after the end of the war.[3] Specimens of this helmet are rarely found today.

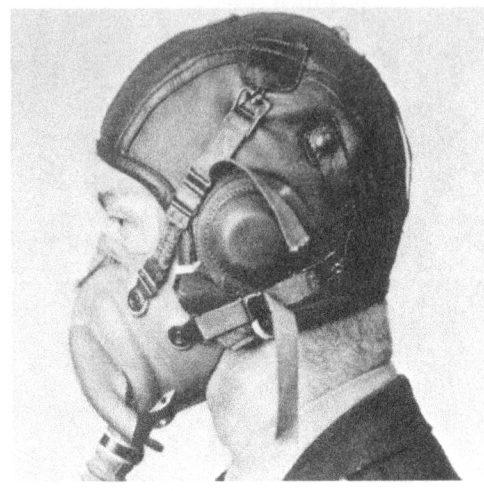

The Type B-6 winter flying helmet, with earphones, showing method of attaching the Type A-9 oxygen mask. (SI Photo 81-327)

Another little-known winter helmet was the Type B-8, which was similar to the B-6 except for changes in the B-8 to accommodate the Harvard-design 5-B earphone mounting cup. This helmet was adopted as standard about 1944 and probably was procured in very limited quantities.

The final type of winter helmet in the "B" series to be adopted for AAF use during World War II was the B-9, which was intended mainly for non-crew flying personnel, maintenance crews, and emergency ground use in cold weather. The B-9 extended far down over the neck and face for added protection against snow and extreme cold. It had

The AN-H-16 heavy winter flying helmet was standardized in 1943 for use by both the Army and Navy. Of shearling construction, it proved successful and was used in limited quantity through the end of World War II. It should be noted that the helmet in this 1944 photograph does not have oxygen mask attachments, which suggests that the photograph is of a prototype or early issue. (SI Photo A4855C)

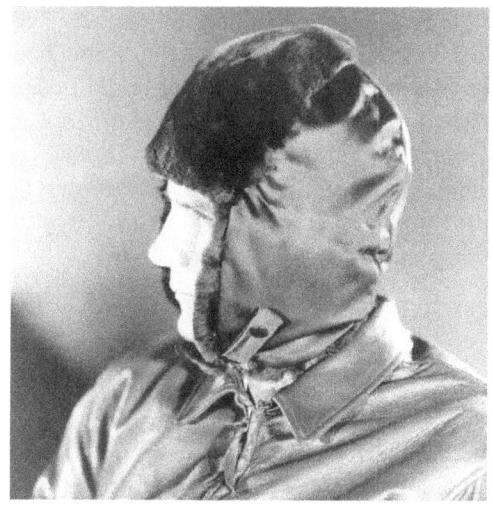

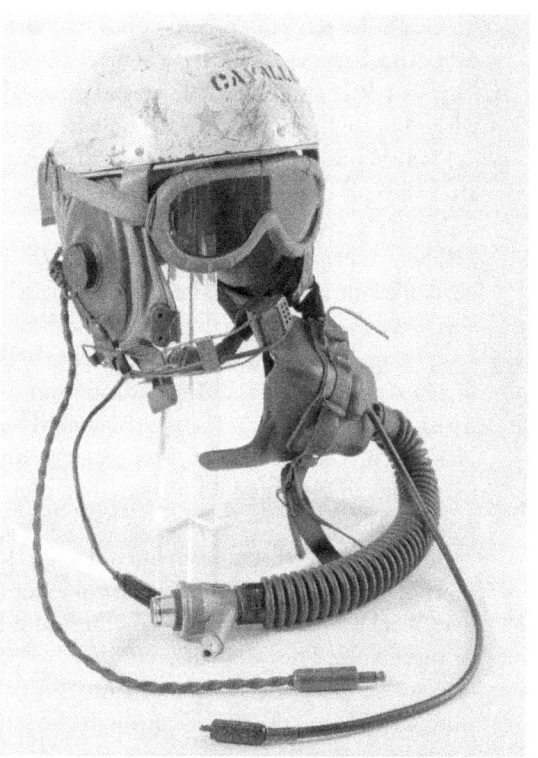

The Type B-9 combat and maintenance helmet of 1943 was mainly intended for use by non-crew flying personnel and maintenance crews. It was also designed for emergency ground use as protection against extreme cold and snow. The B-9 was made of two layers of pile fabric partially lined and trimmed with mouton fur. It could be worn over other types of headgear. (SI Photo A4855H)

Above, right: Experimental protective or "hard" helmet handmade by Stefan A. Cavallo, a test pilot for the National Advisory Committee for Aeronautics (NACA) in 1944. This was probably the first helmet to incorporate skull protection, optic shielding, communication facility, and an oxygen system, all capable of functioning independently of each other at all altitudes and conditions of flight. Although Cavallo was unsuccessful in his attempts to interest NACA in sponsoring a hard helmet development program in 1944, he flew hundreds of hours with this helmet during 1944–46, landing at many bases. He may have influenced AAF and Navy personnel in developing the protective helmets that were introduced after World War II. It was made from a fiberglass miner's hard hat attached to portions of an AN-H-15 summer flying helmet, with ANB-H-1 receivers. The accessories included the Army all-purpose goggle, carbon boom microphone, and Type A-13A oxygen mask with microphone. The helmet was painted white and sported five gold stars, one for each borough of New York, Cavallo's hometown. The stars often provided a surprise for ground crew personnel upon landing at military air bases. Although not an AAF item, this helmet is included because of its historical significance. A similar AAF experimental helmet is known to have been tested in June 1945. Specimens from NASM collection. (SI Photo 81–311) *Left:* The Type B-8 winter helmet of 1944 showing attachment of the Type A-14 oxygen mask by means of snaps or studs along the front edge. (SI Photo A4855E)

no earphone receptacles and could be worn over other headgear. The B-9 was made of two layers of piled fabric partially lined and trimmed with mouton fur. Standardized on September 7, 1943, it continued to be used for many years after the end of the war. This style continues today as a popular civilian winter hat.

There was one other winter flying helmet developed during the war, the Type N-1, which was listed as a "heavy" helmet. It was a shearling flying helmet similar in style to the AN-H-16 except that it was changed to accommodate the latest oxygen mask attachments. The N-1 was placed on limited procurement on November 9, 1944, and was declared obsolete on May 21, 1945.[4]

Several other nonstandard winter flying helmets of various types, all without type numbers, were procured over the years for limited or special use. They were listed in the various Air Corps Class 13 Stock Lists published from the 1920s through September 30, 1943. Most of the old items of nonstandard clothing and equipment were phased out of service by late World War II.

The June 1, 1938, issue of the stock list includes as nonstandard a "Hood, Flying, Winter, Fur Lined," but only in size 7. This item was still carried in the stock list dated September 30, 1942.

Gunner's Auxiliary Helmet

A special helmet for gunners, designated the "Type G-1, Gunner's Auxiliary," was standardized on August 26, 1940. It consisted of a hard, brown papier-mâché (fiber) shell into which cotton webbing was sewn. The helmet also included a sponge-rubber leather-covered strip that was cemented around the helmet to provide protection inside a turret against side impact. The G-1 resembled a tanker's helmet and had leather straps with snaps so it could be attached over any regular flying helmet. It was changed to limited standard on October 13, 1944, and was used in limited numbers during the war. This helmet might be considered in the category of a protective helmet.

Protective Flying Helmets

Experiments were conducted on a number of handmade protective, or hard, helmets at the Personal Equipment Laboratory beginning in 1943. William L. Moore, an engineer at the laboratory, personally tested most of the early designs by donning the sample helmet and hitting himself on the head with a mallet and banging his head on a post. Although no hard helmet was standardized during the war,

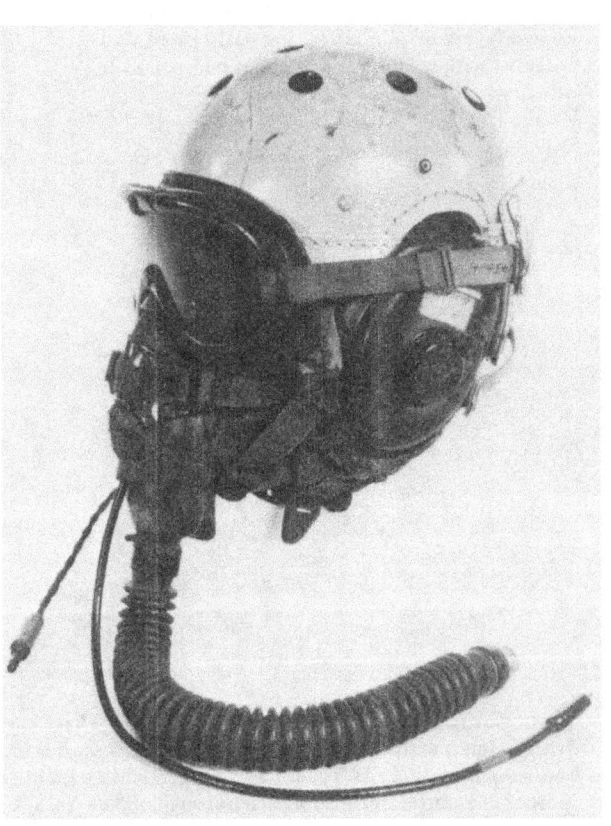

Improvised protective or hard helmet made for use of AAF jet pilots in 1945–46. This example was made for Capt. John Babel, test pilot of the YP-80A, by attaching an A-11 leather helmet inside a tank crewman's fiber hard helmet, which was painted yellow. Type B-8 goggles and A-13A oxygen mask were used with this helmet. Specimens from NASM collection. (SI Photo 81316)

Moore eventually designed the Type P-1 protective flying helmet, which was standardized in 1948 and proved quite successful in Air Force use.

Improvised protective helmets were made for use by AAF pilots of the new jet aircraft during 1945 and 1946. They were produced when it was determined that pilots of jet aircraft required hard helmets because of the buffeting they encountered while they were flying at high speeds through turbulent air. An example was the helmet made for Capt. John Babel and other test pilots of the YP-80A by the parachute rigger at Muroc Flight Test Base in California by attaching an A-11 leather helmet inside a tank crewman's fiber helmet. The Type A-13A oxygen mask, Type B-8 goggles, and Type T-30-Q throat microphone were used with this helmet. The AAF made 225 similar makeshift hard helmets for flying schools and organizations flying jet aircraft during that period. They were eventually replaced by the Type P-1 helmet.[5]

Attachable Sun Visor for Flying Helmets

On June 26, 1945, a sun visor for soft helmets was standardized as the "Type A-1 Visor, Flying, Attachable." It was an olive drab cloth visor that could be attached to flying helmets with snap (stud) fasteners added on each side to the earphone mounting sockets. This visor was believed to have originally been intended for the Type A-11 and AN-H-15 helmets; however, Technical Order no. 13-1-36, published on February 12, 1947, gave instructions for adding snap fasteners to the sides of the Types A-10, A-10A, A-11, AN-H-15, and AN-H-16 helmets.[6] The visor assembly was also listed in Technical Order no. 00-30-41, October 20, 1945 (reprinted here as Appendix C), which included all of the standard items of flying clothing, including helmets, at the end of the war.

Flying Caps

Many pilots and crewmen flying aboard aircraft with enclosed cockpits preferred to wear a cap or hat instead of a helmet. The famous "50-mission crush" cap of World War II fame was caused by the headbands of the earphones pressing down over the crown of the service cap that had had its grommet removed. To prevent the rigid brim and top of a service cap from interfering with the use of the radio headset, a tight-fitting baseball-type flying cap was developed. The Type B-1 summer flying cap was constructed of olive drab gabardine cloth with a leather sweat band and had a wide, stiff visor to shade the eyes from the sun. It was standardized on April 21, 1939, and changed to limited standard on June 3, 1942.

The Type B-2 winter flying cap was similar to the B-1, except that it was made of one-fourth-inch sheep shearling and had folding ear flaps and a stiff leather visor. The outside had, of course, a brown leather finish. It was also standardized on April 21, 1939, and changed to limited standard on June 2, 1942. This cap was quite popular with many crewmen during the war, despite later efforts to limit its use to ground crewmen.

The standard Army QMC olive drab wool knit M-1941 cap, called the "beanie," was also worn by crewmen, as was the garrison or "overseas" cap.

Beginning in 1942 the wearing of caps by military flyers was officially discouraged. Combat crewmen were urged to cover their faces and head completely with helmets, goggles, and oxygen masks, thereby avoiding exposure not only to severe cold but also to flash burns during a fire.

(Nurses and WASP flying caps are described in chapter 7 with other flying clothing for women.)

Face Masks

Some means of protecting the face was seriously needed during the period of the open-cockpit airplane. The face, or flying, mask appeared in World War I as the logical answer to this problem; however, difficulty was experienced in securing a fit sufficiently snug to exclude the strong blast of cold air and moisture to which flyers were subjected. Tests on face masks were made by the Equipment Section at McCook Field, and chamois was determined to be the most successful material.

The *Air Service Manual of Initial Equipment* for the AEF dated August 1918 listed a "Mask, Face, Soft Leather," as standard issue for each aviator and observer. This mask remained in use after the end of the war.

Tests of various face masks, including a combination mask and goggles, were continued at McCook and Wright fields during the 1920s. Lt. J.A. Macready wore a chamois-skin mask on some of his record altitude flights in 1925. He experienced a low temperature of -27° F at 20,000 feet while wearing this mask without any fogging of his goggles. Two hundred fifty face masks were procured in 1927, and 1,015 more were requested for use in 1928.[7] Some helmets came equipped with a face mask, and one type was still listed for issue in the Air Corps Class 13 Stock Catalog dated March 1929. The official listing was "Helmet—Flying, Winter, Fur Chin Pad."

The increased use of the enclosed cockpit in the 1930s and the development of the modern oxygen mask lessened the need to use the face mask as an article of flying clothing. However, World War II with its high-altitude, arctic, and cold-weather operations created new requirements for protective garments such as face masks.

Summer Masks

Masks in the "A" series were basically oxygen masks.[8] Some of the early oxygen face masks, however, not only included the oxygen function but also provided protection for the face against the cold weather conditions encountered when flying in open cockpit aircraft. The Type A-1 mask of the 1920s was made of rubber and had a metal nipple for the oxygen hose. The Type A-2 mask and helmet combination was tested during that period and then declared inactive.

The Type A-3 leather face mask was identical to the Type B-2 winter mask except that it was modified to allow the insertion of a rubber nipple for the oxygen tube. Service testing of the A-3 began on October 21, 1929, but the mask was placed in inactive status on January 13, 1931. The Type A-4 mask had a leather outer shell with chamois lining and was similar to the Type B-5 winter mask, which also had oxygen capability. An oxygen deflector connection was placed opposite the mouth cover and exhaling tubes extended from the sides of the nose and across the cheek part of the mask. Kapok was used to pad the lower sides of the eye openings to prevent fogging of the goggles. The A-4 was standardized on April 6, 1931, but was changed to limited standard on March 21, 1933. It was used until its stock was exhausted on March 12, 1942.

Horsehide was used for the outer shell of the Type A-5 oxygen face mask, and a chamois lining was cemented to it. The A-5 was a full-face mask that extended up over the eyes, down under the chin, and over the front of the neck. The eye openings were made large to permit the insertion of goggle cushions on the inside. The mask also had an improved oxygen distribution device and was designed to prevent the fogging of the goggles by exhalation. The A-5 was standardized on April 1, 1933, and was changed to limited standard on May 21, 1935. It was finally declared obsolete on August 11, 1943.

The Type A-6 oxygen face mask was service tested beginning on December 20, 1934, and standardized on May 21, 1935. It was changed to limited standard on July 15, 1939, and declared obsolete on August 11, 1943, along with the A-5 mask. The A-6 was a flexible leather mask that covered the lower part of the face. It consisted of the outer leather covering with a one-fourth-inch intermediate lining and a chamois inner lining. The nose and mouth portion had an opening for attaching a metal oxygen distributor that was also part of the mask. The distributor was connected with a single inlet to the oxygen vaporizer supply tube, which was inserted from the left side. The mask could also be worn without the oxygen distributor and tube for protection from the cold.

The Air Corps Stock List dated June 1,

1934, listed the Types A-5 and B-5 masks as standard issue, and the list dated September 30, 1943, listed the Types A-5 and A-6 masks. The 1943 catalog also listed two unnumbered masks—both leather, one cloth-lined and the other chamois-lined—as well as the Types B-2 and B-5 winter masks.[9]

Winter Masks

Heavy or winter face masks of the "B" series included the Type B-1 helmet and leather face mask combination, for high-altitude, as well as winter, flying. It was experimental and was tested in the mid 1920s. The B-2 was a leather mask that was standardized in the mid–1920s and used extensively. It was designated limited standard on April 6, 1931, and remained in use until it was declared obsolete on March 13, 1944. The Type B-3 was a chamois mask for Resistal goggles and received only service testing in 1925. The Type B-4 was an improved type that prevented the fogging of goggles but remained in an experimental status between 1926 and 1928.

The type B-5 was described as an oxygen face mask and was standardized on April 6, 1931. It had a special receptacle in the mouth area for the oxygen pipestem or tube. The B-5 probably could also be used without the oxygen tube. It was used in World War II until it was declared obsolete on March 13, 1944.

Other Masks

An extra heavy flying mask, the Type P-1, was standardized for limited procurement on December 7, 1944. It was made of cotton twill and was felt lined to protect the face, neck, and throat in low temperatures. It could be used with or without an oxygen mask and was intended for use by crewmen such as the gunners aboard high-altitude bombers with open firing positions, including the earlier B-17 and all B-24 models. Over the years, mechanics masks and locally improvised face masks were also used.

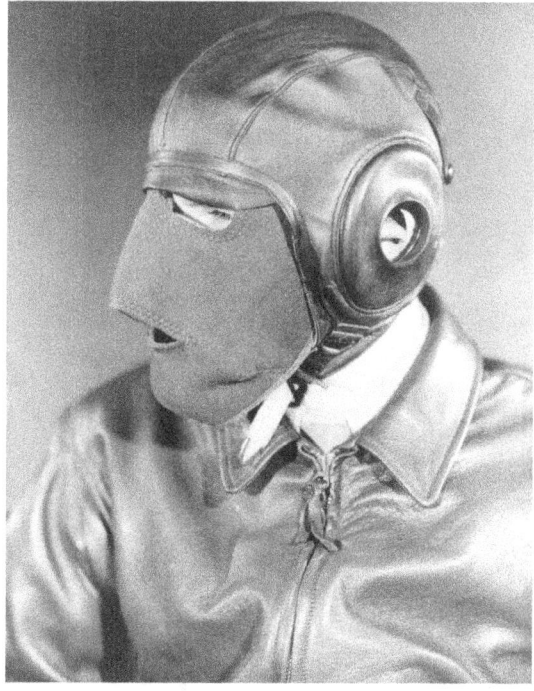

Type D-1 face mask being worn with the A-11 helmet and A-2 jacket. Of felt construction, the mask was standardized in March 1943. Although intended for mechanics and ground crew use, the D-1 was also worn occasionally by flying personnel and was included in arctic survival kits for use by downed aviators. (SI Photo A4855)

The Type B-2 winter face mask was typical of the flying masks developed for use during the 1920s. It was made of leather and was useful in providing protection to flyers in open cockpits or exposed crew positions. The B-2 remained in the inventory until 1944. (SI Photo A4856F)

Flying Goggles

The earliest aviators recognized that goggles were important for the safety and comfort of the eyes. There were many factors to be considered in the use of goggles and sunglasses by military aviators. In addition to their obvious uses (protection against wind, rain, dust, cold, and insects), tinted goggles were helpful in reducing glare and were important in decreasing the amount of ultraviolet and infrared radiation incident on the eye. Goggles were also useful to flyers in fires, since they completely shielded the wearers from flash fire and provided some protection against direct flame. They also offered modest protection against injury from low-velocity splinters, debris, and Plexiglas if an aircraft struck a bird or was hit by enemy ground or aircraft fire. All goggles were retained by an elastic headband.

During World II dark adaptation for flyers was accomplished by remaining in the dark for thirty minutes before a night mission or by wearing goggles with red lenses for the same length of time. The latter method was effective because the eyes' light-sensitive cells, which are used at night, are relatively insensitive to red light. The red goggles effectively shielded the night-vision cells from light, while they allowed the wearer to use his day-vision cells to read, to attend a briefing, or to study maps during the thirty-minute period.[10]

Resistal shatter-resistant goggles were widely used by both civilians and Army aviators during World War I and the 1920s, and some were still used as late as World War II. American airmen also wore many other types of U.S. and foreign goggles during the First World War, including the clear or tinted "Aviglas" goggles. Three types of flying goggles for pilots and observers were officially listed by the Army in the Aviator's Clothing List, Stencil no. 844, dated January 19, 1918: Type 1, featuring "no-vial" lenses; Type 2, with "super-tough" lenses; and Type 3, with "super-tough lenses and face mask."[11] Army Special Regulation no. 41, issued August 15, 1917, authorized the wear of improved type clear or amber-colored glass "Triplex" goggles by aviators and motorcycle messengers in the Aviation Section of the Signal Corps.[12] In addition, other types of goggles were procured, and many pilots preferred to purchase their own goggles. All of these were, of course, continued in use by the Army for several years after the end of hostilities.

Numerous types of goggles were service tested by the Army Air Service and later the Air Corps during the post–World War I years. These included the Type A-1 goggles

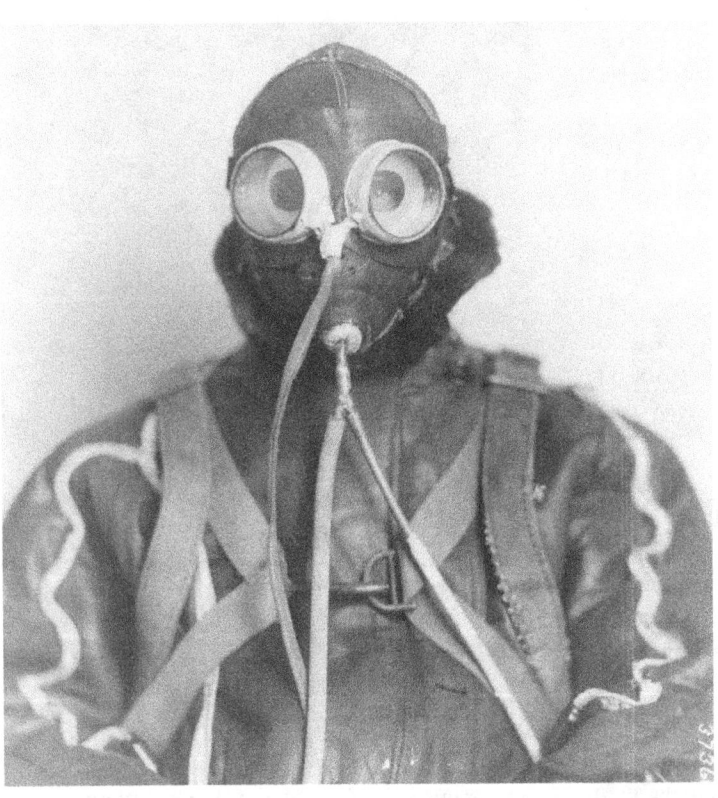

Experimental heated goggles worn with oxygen mask and fur-lined winter clothing for high-altitude flights in 1929. A heated version of the Type B-8 goggle was available for AAF use in 1944. (SI Photo A4856G)

Left: An example of the Type B-7 flying goggles, as manufactured at the beginning of World War II. A separate rubber cushion was attached to each half of the lens frame. The rubber on the B-7 in this recent NASM photograph deteriorated due to improper storage before it was donated to the museum. The small, tube-like ventilator on the top of each frame should be noted. Specimen from NASM collection. (SI Photo 81–310) *Right:* An early model of the AN-6530 flying goggles standardized in 1943 for use by both the Army and the Navy. The AN-6530 was almost identical to the Type B-7 goggles, including the separate cushions and the tube ventilators. Specimen from NASM collection. (SI Photo 81–309)

with flat, sealed "summer and winter" non-shatterable clear and amber lenses. The A-1, which resembled the Resistal type of goggles, was declared obsolete on September 17, 1930.

An electrically heated style of goggles, the Type C-1, was also service tested from 1931 to 1934. Some C-1 goggles may have been converted back to the standard Type B-6, on which they were based. However, the C-1 was carried as nonstandard issue in the Air Corps Class 13 Stock Lists until 1940.

Another type of goggles used in limited numbers during the 1930s was the "Goggle Assembly, Flying, Navy Mask Type." It was also carried in the stock lists as nonstandard issue until 1940.

Most flying goggles developed for the Air Corps were in the "B" series and had sealed, shatterable lenses. In the 1920s the Army standardized and procured the Type B-1—a Meyrowitz no. 6 with curved, shatterable lenses, metal frames, and rubber cushions. The B-1A, which was an improved B-1 with "de-center" lenses, was standardized on June 27, 1928, and continued to see service as limited standard from 1930 until it was declared obsolete on March 13, 1944. The B-1A was also available with corrective lenses.

The Types B-2, B-3, B-4, and B-5 were experimental goggles tested during the mid–1920s. The B-2 and B-3 had curved lenses, while the B-4 had electrically heated flat lenses. The B-5 also had flat lenses and was adjustable like the B-3.

The Type B-6 was an adjustable metal-frame goggle with curved, wide-vision lenses and removable cushions. It was standardized for use on December 19, 1928, and used as limited standard from May 3, 1933, until it was declared obsolete on March 13, 1944. Two variations were shown in the June 1, 1934, edition of the Air Corps Stock List; one style B-6 was made by E.B. Meyrowitz Company, and the other by the American Optical Company. Yet another variation, made by the Straus and Buegeleisen Company, was used as nonstandard in the 1939–40 period.

Probably the best-known goggles style of World War II was the Type B-7, which was standardized by the Air Corps on May 3, 1933, and used through the end of the war. The B-7 had nickel-plated steel lens frames and separate sponge-rubber eye cushions. A minor variation of it was standardized in 1943 for both Army and Navy use and was better known as the Spec. AN-6530 goggles. These goggles were marked "Type B-7," "AN-6530," or "A-N 6530" on the metal bridge between the lens frames. They were similar to the old B-6 except for a more rigid nose construction, simpler eyecup clamps, and fewer parts. The goggles were procured not as a unit but as separate

 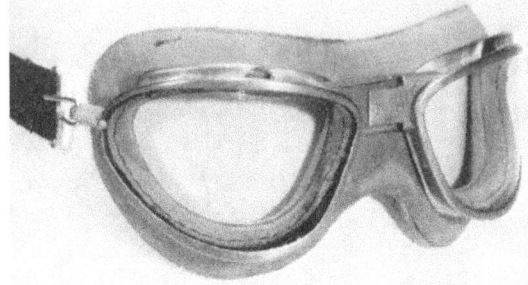

Left: AN-6530 flying goggles made in 1943 with old-style tube ventilators but incorporating the new one-piece rubber cushion, which was backed with chamois skin. Specimen from NASM collection. (SI Photo 81–308) *Right:* Improved model of the AN-6530 flying goggles, with not only the one-piece rubber cushion but also streamlined ventilators, to speed production, on top of each frame. Most of the AN-6530 goggles produced were of this type. Specimen from NASM collection. (SI Photo 81–307)

 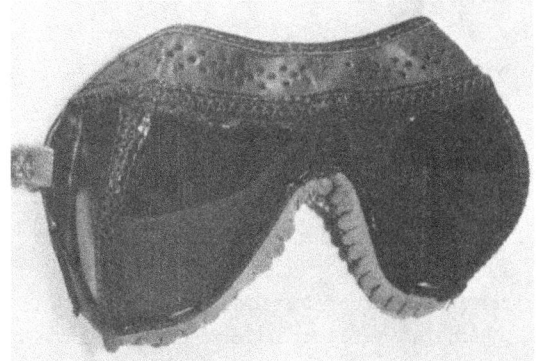

Left: The Type B-8 goggle of 1943 made by Polaroid featured a superior field of vision. The one-piece frame was constructed of dense black rubber and came in a kit with several interchangeable tinted and clear plastic lenses. The goggle flange could be trimmed so that a snug fit was obtained when wearing an oxygen mask. The B-8 remained in use with both the Air Force and Navy, under a different designation, through the Korean War period. Specimen from NASM collection. (SI Photo 81–306) *Right:* The "Goggle, Dark Adaptation, Type E-1," made by the American Optical Company. Standardized in 1943, it was worn by crewmen for thirty minutes before a night takeoff to allow their eyes to adapt to the darkness. The E-1 had red plastic lenses in a leather frame that could be folded to fit in the pocket. Specimen from NASM collection. (SI Photo 81–304)

parts: lens, Spec. 3047; vented frames, Spec. 3050; and cushion, Spec. 3051. Both clear and tinted tempered-glass lenses were available in green, grey, and yellow, and replacement was simple.

During early World War II certain objections were raised concerning these goggles, including excessive restriction of the visual field, fogging, and poor coordination with oxygen masks. The goggles were first made with separate rubber eye cushions, but this was changed to a more comfortable and protective one-piece cushion that was usually backed with chamois skin. Further small modifications were made during 1943 and 1944, including an improved type of ventilator on top of the metal frames, which facilitated mass production. This type of streamlined ventilator was also used on the "Willson" and "Skyway" commercial goggles sometimes used by Army aviators.

The final type of standard flying goggles to be developed during the war was the Type B-8, which was standardized for use on October 13, 1943. This goggle was distinctive because its frame was made of dense black rubber instead of metal and because it had a large, single-aperture lens. It was supplied in a kit with interchangeable plastic lenses: four green, two amber, and three clear. The lenses could be worn singly or in combination. The clear lenses were, of course, used at night. An electrically heated lens was also available; it eliminated fogging and frosting under all conditions and integrated with the Type F-3 heated suit by means of an electrical connection on the suit's chest.

The B-8 was more break resistant than the B-7 and was superior in its field of vision and its integration with oxygen equipment. If the goggle did not fit snugly over the oxygen mask, the rubber goggle flange could be trimmed. The B-8, sometimes referred to as the Polaroid because of the maker's name marked on most of them (Rochester Optical also made them), was used for many years after the end of World War II by the USAF, as well as by the U.S. Navy under a different designation. It was perhaps the last U.S. flying goggle ever to see service.

The Army also issued the M-1944 goggle for use by ground forces. The M-1944 was very similar to the B-8 but was slightly larger in overall dimensions. The lenses were not interchangeable with the B-8, and specimens examined did not have the chamois-skin backing attached to the black rubber frame. Some flyers probably acquired and used the M-1944, although the close resemblance between the M-1944 and the B-8 makes it difficult to confirm that supposition with wartime photos.

The Type E-1 pair of goggles was worn by pilots and crewmen to adapt their eyes to darkness. It was standardized on March 11, 1943, and used through the war with good results. The E-1 was a lightweight, leather frame, compactly folding style of goggles with red plastic lenses and could be carried conveniently in the pocket. For dark-adaptation, it was worn for thirty minutes before takeoff. It could be worn later during a flight if the lights were turned

The Army all-purpose goggle being worn with an AN-H-15 helmet and A-2 jacket by Capt. Carter C. Porter, North American A-36 dive-bomber pilot, on March 21, 1944. He is wearing a service uniform under his flight gear. (SI Photo 80–20363)

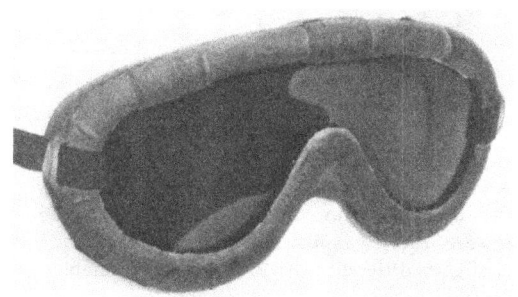

Left: Army all-purpose goggle, often called the "gunner's goggles." The frame was made of gray sponge rubber, and the goggle came with a kit that included clear, green, and red tinted plastic lenses. A red lens is shown in this NASM specimen photograph. With a red lens, it was possible for a gunner or pilot to see tracer bullets more clearly in daylight. Specimen from NASM collection. (SI Photo 81–305)

on in the plane for any reason. The E-1 was also used in blind flying training, behind a green-tinted windscreen, and, with some success, as an anti-glare goggle over enemy installations where powerful searchlights were encountered. (The blind flying goggles used by the U.S. Navy aviators had deep blue lenses, which, when worn behind an orange-tinted windscreen, produced identical results.)

The Type H-1 folding goggles, standardized on August 1, 1944, were made for emergency protection and were included as part of the B-4 and C-1 emergency kits. They were constructed of leather or water-repellent drilled back fabric, with sewed-in green-tinted, laminated plastic lenses. The H-1 had an adjustable plastic headband and came in a cotton carrying case.

The Army issued an all-purpose or general-purpose goggle made by the Polaroid Corporation. It was a non-polarizing type used not only by flyers but also by tank crewmen, paratroopers, dispatch riders, and similar personnel. Clear, light and dark green, amber and red tinted lenses could be used with this goggle. Flyers, who often called it the "gunner's goggles," usually received it with an amber or red plastic lens. With an amber lens, it was worn for sun protection; a red lens was used to adapt a flyer's eyes to darkness and, more important, to make it possible to see tracer bullets more clearly in daylight. This face-fitting goggle somewhat resembled the Type B-8 flying goggle but had a thinner frame made of molded gray or light green foam or sponge rubber. The manufacturer's type designation was "DA."[13] The number *1021* was marked on the flap of the leatherette or cloth case that also held the spare lenses. A version featuring a rubber nosepiece with a vent aiming downward was also produced and was marked "Polaroid Fog-Free No. 1040."

Sunglasses

Sunglasses have been important to aviators for many years and were particularly popular after aircraft with enclosed cockpits were introduced. During World War II sunglasses were worn by numerous pilots and crewmen, especially those flying aboard bomber and transport aircraft.

Some types of sunglasses were originally called goggles, which has led to occasional confusion in identification. The D-1 was a cushionless type of glasses with a metal frame and was used for glare protection. Although a pair of sunglasses, it was designated as the "Goggle Assembly, Flying, Type D-1"[14] when it was standardized on August 13, 1935, and when it was changed to limited standard on November 10, 1941. Perhaps funds were available in the 1930s for the procurement of goggles but not sunglasses. The Type D-2 was designed to accommodate the Type B-7 goggle lenses and was service tested from August 13, 1935, until it was declared obsolete on August 6, 1940. The Type D-3 was similar to the D-1 glasses, except for the frame construction and lens size. Procured under U.S. Navy Spec. M356B, it was service tested from September 21, 1940, until it was declared obsolete on

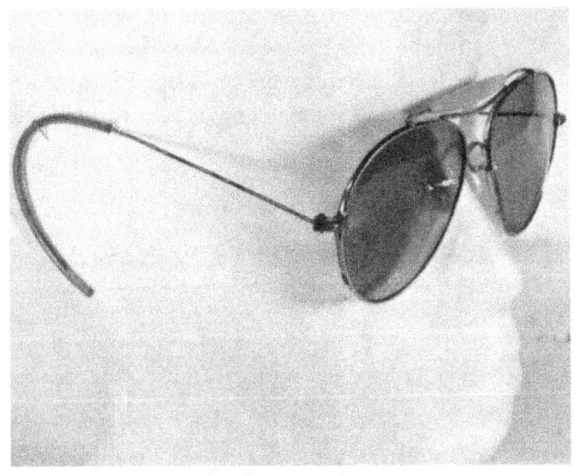

The "Glasses, Flying, Sun (Comfort Cable)," worn by AAF flying personnel during World War II. This example from the NASM collection has light green lenses and a gold-colored metal frame. It was issued to Lt. R.W. Morris, an AAF pilot, in 1944. These glasses were officially replaced by the "Glasses, Flying, Sun, Rose Smoke, Type 2," which were similar except for a slightly different sweat pad, adjustable temples, and an improved lens of greater density (SI Photo 81-11316)

September 26, 1941. The D-1 was officially replaced by the limited standard "Glasses, Flying, Sun (Comfort Cable.")" Experience showed, however, that they were not dense enough, since in particularly bright light the 50 percent decrease in brightness they provided was not even perceptible.

The comfort cable glasses were replaced late in the war by what became the basic sunglasses issued for the AAF—the "Glasses, Flying, Sun, Rose Smoke, Type 2." The comfort cable and rose-smoke glasses had the same face-form nickel-silver metal frames; but their sweat pads were slightly different, and the Type 2 had adjustable temples. The Type 2 was a sturdy style intended to reduce glare and was standard issue for all flying personnel. The replaceable lenses had an overall light transmission of 15 percent. Rose-smoke lenses were selected for the minimal color distortion and maximal apparent brightness they offered with lenses of such density. Their low transmission of blue helped to show contrast. Each pair was issued with an aluminum or leather carrying case. (Similar glasses are widely worn today.)

The glasses intended mainly for wear by ground personnel in the Arctic were the "Arctic Sun, with Rose Smoke Lenses, Type F-1." They were sometimes used by air-crewmen and were particularly useful where reflections from snow were a serious problem. They had the same lenses as the Type 2 and a plastic frame so that no metal could touch the skin at low temperatures. A leather carrying case was provided.

Another type of glasses that saw rather limited use by the AAF flying personnel was designated the "Goggle, Contrast, Type G-1," which was standardized on January 3, 1944. The G-1 had a nickel-silver frame and was similar to the comfort cable flying glasses, except that it was provided with an amber filter lens with approximately 40 percent light transmission. The amber lens had the effect of increasing contrast and making the spotting of small objects, such as a distant aircraft, much easier on dull, cloudy, or hazy days.

Communications Equipment
Headset and Throat Microphone

The standard HS-38 radio headset used by the AAF in World War II consisted of two adjustable brown leather-covered wire headbands supporting Type ANB-H-1 receivers. At least two variations of the black or brown

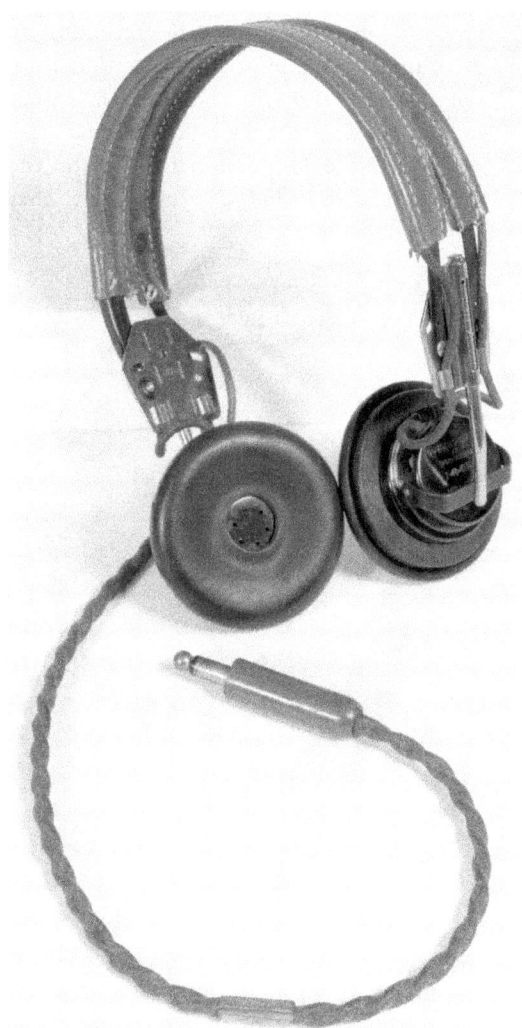

Standard HS-38 radio headset used by the AAF, featuring two adjustable leather-covered headbands that support Type ANB-H-1 receivers. The receivers were padded with black or brown sponge-rubber cushions, and the cord was equipped with a PL-354 jack. Specimen from NASM collection. (SI Photo 81315)

sponge-rubber cushions were used to pad the earphones and reduce outside noise interference. Similar earphones such as the Type HS-33 were also used. The standard ANB-H-1 earphones were also installed in the various types of flying helmets. The red plastic-covered plug or jack on the end of the connecting cord was marked "PL-354."

When oxygen masks containing microphones, such as the ANB-M-C1, were not employed, flyers used either a Type T-17 hand microphone or the Type T-30 throat mike. The T-30 was a vibration-sensitive carbon-type microphone designed for actuation by mechanical vibrations of speech that were present at the throat of the user. The throat microphones were made by several manufacturers, and the designation stamped on the rubber section included a suffix letter that probably originally indicated the manufacturer. For example, a Western Electric mike was marked "T-30-Q," while the same type of microphone made by the Shure Brothers Company was marked "T-30-V"; by the Kellogg Company, "T-30-R"; and the Universal Microphone Company, "T-30-S." A brown elastic band held the T-30 in place on the throat. Later production microphones featured a wire clip to hold the mike elements more firmly against the larynx to improve clarity of communication, but the clip was also more uncomfortable and was often removed and discarded by the pilot.

Communications equipment such as headsets and microphones was, of course, the responsibility of the Army Signal Corps.

The Gosport Communications System

During World War I researchers in England developed a means by which pilots and student pilots or crewmen could communicate with each other in an open-cockpit aircraft. Named the gosport system (after the Gosport Aerodrome), it was used mainly by flight instructors in later years. The system was utilized on the AAF's primary training aircraft during World War II. A flexible hollow tube or tubes connected the instructor to his student. The student could hear him through a special helmet or helmet attachment at the other end. The system was normally one way; that is, the pilot could speak to the student, but the student could not reply. (Two-way systems, however, were commercially available for many years from firms such as A.G. Spalding and Brothers.)

Metal gosport fittings were installed on both fabric and leather helmets. The fittings consisted of a downward curving tube about three inches long attached to a base that was mounted on the sides of the helmet in place of the earphones. The long, flexible tube between the cockpits would be plugged into these fittings.

Two types of helmets with built-in earpiece assemblies were procured by the AAF for use in primary flight instruction. Neither helmet

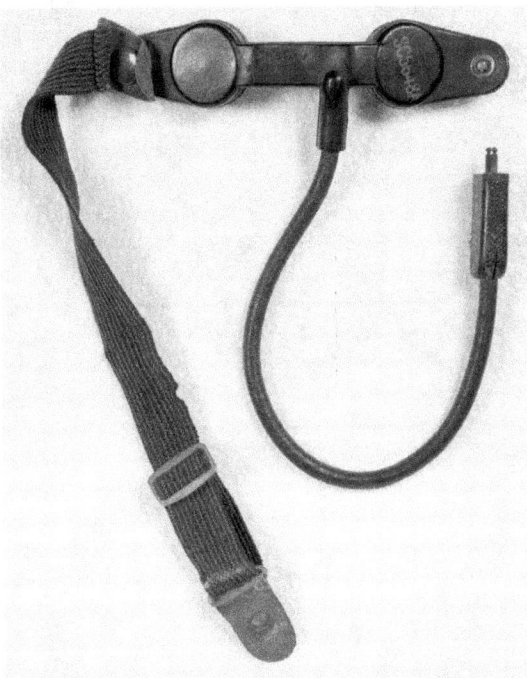

Standard throat microphone used by the AAF in World War II. This example was made by the Shure Brothers, Chicago, and was marked "T-30-V." The mike was retained by a brown elastic strap. This example from the NASM collection lacks the wire clip that was intended to hold elements more firmly against the "Adam's Apple" and was often discarded. (SI Photo 81–314)

was assigned a type designation. One was listed as the "Helmet and Speaking Tube Ear Piece Assembly—Summer Training" and consisted of an unlined olive drab gabardine helmet very similar to the Type A-9 summer helmet but with the curved tube sections built into the sides. The other was designated the "Helmet and Speaking Tube Ear Piece Assembly—Winter Training." It was a brown shearling design almost identical to the Type B-6 shearling winter helmet, except for the speaking tube earpiece assemblies.[15]

Sometimes an exasperated flight instructor would stick his gosport mouthpiece out of the open cockpit into the airstream. The resulting sudden, loud roar would not actually hurt the ears of the student pilot, but it would certainly gain his attention!

9

Handwear

Glove making is an ancient art dating back at least to the time of the pharaohs, so one might suppose that by World War II the optimum type of glove would have already been developed for every requirement. Such was not the case. Considerable research and testing was conducted during the war to solve the problem of providing adequate gloves for aviators.

The need for a solution to that problem was great since aviators at high altitudes regularly encountered temperatures below -50° F. The blast of air that came in through the waist gun windows of a B-17 or B-24 at that temperature could freeze a gunner's hands after only ninety seconds.

As late as September 1943, 32 percent of the 1,077 casualties in the Eighth Air Force in England were frostbite of the hands.[1] By the end of October 1943, however, the percentage had been decreased by approximately one-half because silk and electrical gloves had been improved and had increased in supply. Silk or rayon glove inserts were worn under the heated gloves, and a pair of Type A-9, and later Type A-9A, gauntlet-type shearling gloves were worn over both the silk and heated gloves. An electrically heated muff was also developed and issued for crewmen to use aboard bombers if their heated gloves ceased to function. Both heavy winter and light summer gloves also kept the wearer's hands clean and protected them from flashburn in the event of a fire.

Important Concerns

In their development of gloves, AAF researchers considered six closely related factors: heat insulation needs, the physiology of the hands, dexterity requirements, size and construction, the training of wearers in the use of gloves, and comfort provided by the gloves.

Protection against cold by insulation was determined by thickness of clothing. At 32° F protective covering for the hands needed to be approximately one-half-inch thick; at -22° F it had to be about one and one-fourth inches to afford an active individual some comfort. Such thickness was impracticable, however, if any degree of manual dexterity was required.

The thickness of the insulating material could be decreased if there was a source of auxiliary heat. Electrically heated gloves, when they were finally perfected, offered an excellent solution to the problem for crewmen who were not required to move very far from their positions in an aircraft.

AAF researchers determined a glove's effective insulating qualities (obtained in "clo" units[2]) by measuring the conduction of heat through the material, by finding the "tolerance time" for the glove, and by noting the rate at which the skin temperature of the hand changed, since human skin approaches a new level of temperature equilibrium after it is placed in a colder environment. The researchers recorded the skin temperatures at the fingertips and the back of the hands at specific intervals of time. They found that the tolerance time (the period it took for a subject's hands to become intolerably cold or numb in a low ambient temperature with a given air movement) usually was reached when the fingertips' temperature dropped to about 40.1° F. At that temperature manual dexterity abruptly decreased. The researchers also determined that tolerance time was greatly influenced by a wearer's activity, the protection given to the rest of his body, and the air movement around him, as well as by the ambient temperature and the extent of protection given his hands.

Physiological considerations were also very important to the AAF's glove designers. If an aviator's body heat was to be maintained at a suitable level, his hands had to be adequately protected. This was because a person's extremities, particularly the hands, play an important part in the physical regulation of body temperature. When the hands feel cold, one usually complains of being cold. However, if the extremities are warmed too much, the skin of the rest of the body is stimulated to lose heat more rapidly.

Another difficult problem for the researchers was finding a way to warm the palms of the hands and the ends of the fingers without causing a bulkiness that would interfere with dexterity. Among the changes in glove patterns introduced during the war to aid flexibility were the moccasin-type fingertip construction, flat seams, and the curved-finger pattern.[3] Mittens interfered with dexterity but were better than gloves for warming, since they allowed the fingers to touch each other.

A report from the office of the surgeon, Eighth Air Force, in 1943 stated that a shortage of winter flying gloves of the proper sizes made it necessary for some individuals to wear sizes that were too small. When any degree of manual dexterity was required, they had to remove their gloves, thereby causing frostbite of the fingers. This supply problem was corrected when proper sizing demand was established.

The size and construction of gloves had not only a direct effect on heat insulation, dexterity, and comfort but also an indirect effect on the heat regulation and cold sensation of the body. A glove that was too small was found to decrease more than just manual dexterity, which was so important to a flyer. In addition, it lessened the effectiveness of heat insulation. Gloves that were too large also reduced dexterity.

During the war the AAF began a program to train gunners to field strip and reassemble a mounted .50-caliber machine gun while they were wearing gloves. After the gunners had stripped and assembled the gun about twenty-five times, their speed was the same when they were wearing gloves as when they were barehanded. Only at very low temperatures were their rates with gloves slightly lower; the gun parts then were stiff and tight, and the shearling worn by the gunners had stiffened.

As it had always been, the comfort of gloves was purely personal and probably impossible to evaluate objectively. An individual's opinion of whether a pair of gloves was comfortable was, however, entirely influenced by the factors mentioned above—the gloves' heat insulation, dexterity, size, and fit and the wearer's confidence in his ability to do his job quickly with his gloves on when he was under stress and pressed for time. That confidence, a psychological factor, was a result of practicing whenever possible and as much as possible while wearing gloves.

A series of four conferences on handwear was held between October 1943 and February 1944. The third of these, held December 20, 1943, at the Aero Medical Laboratory at Wright Field, was concerned with such topics as dexterity tests for gloves, methods of analysis of tests for handwear, and glove design. Among the general results attained as a result of these meetings were (1) the formulation of a relatively standardized testing procedure for handwear, specifying the use of artificial (copper) models; (2) tolerance time and grading of sensation; (3) dexterity tests; and (4) a standard method for obtaining the average skin temperature of the hands.[4]

As the war progressed, a serious shortage of suitable leather for glove production developed, and representatives of the WPB, Wright

Field, and the men's glove manufacturers met in a conference held (appropriately) at Gloversville, New York, during the spring of 1944. They determined that the following quantities of leather would be needed to fill the requirements for the AAF gloves then on procurement: 3 million square feet of capeskin, and 2.3 million square feet of deerskin, and 1.05 million square feet of goatskin. Sufficient capeskin was available, but substitutions had to be made for some of the other leathers.[5] It was even suggested that the AAF herd the Arctic caribou so that an adequate supply of their skins could be available for use in mittens.

Unlike most other winter clothing standardized for use by the Army Air Corps, gloves intended for winter or high-altitude use were categorized as "A" types, while summer or warm-weather handwear was placed in a "B" series. This reversal of the norm probably occurred because the first glove to be standardized under the new system during the 1920s was a winter-summer combination glove and was given an "A" designation.

Winter Flying Gloves—Insulative Type

A variety of materials for both the outer shell and the lining of winter gloves were tried over the years, but no material was completely satisfactory. Horsehide, calfskin, and pigskin were among the materials used for the outer shell. Linings were constructed first of a variety of furs and then of lamb's wool, knitted camel hair, and wool fabrics.

During World War I many pilots wore one-finger coney-fur gauntlets with the cuff extended well up their arms to keep out drafts. Four-finger fur-covered types were also used. Both styles of gauntlets were usually constructed with a mitten-like cover or pocket over the ends of the fingers and a slit across the palm. The fingers could be extended through that slit to operate machine gun triggers or to make fine adjustments. This split-palm type of glove was not very popular with pilots during the 1920s, however, as aircraft became more complicated and had additional switches and controls in the cockpit onto which the bulky gauntlets and mittens could accidentally hook. Still, coney-fur and leather gauntlets, which lacked type numbers, were used as nonstandard items throughout the 1930s and well into World War II.

In addition to these items of handwear, the Types A-1 through A-8 gloves were officially called gauntlets by the Army. According to the Type Designation Sheets, the first gauntlet to be standardized by the Army for aviators was the winter-summer Type A-1. It was made of wool and leather and was declared obsolete on May 27, 1926. The Types A-2 through A-5, which were experimental designs of various materials, were made and service tested during the 1920s. The Type A-6 was standardized for the Air Corps on October 25, 1929, and was

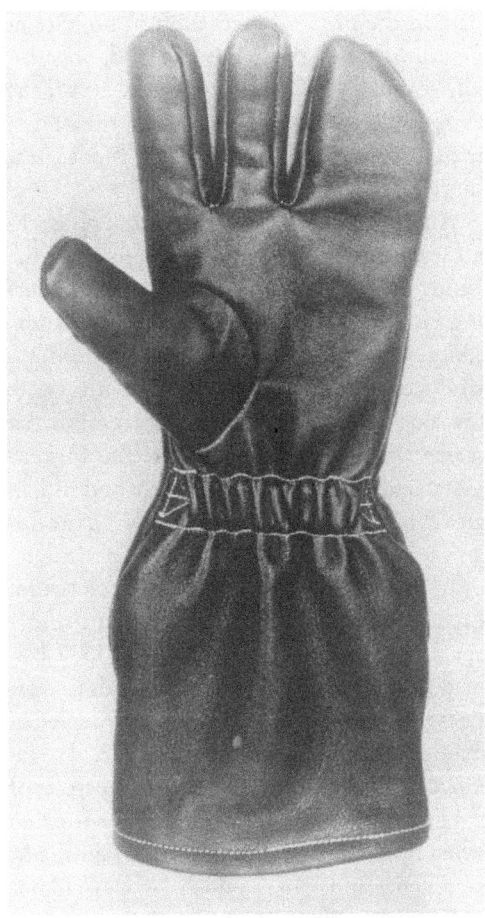

A two-finger winter flying glove with a leather outer shell used in 1925. (SI Photo A4857F)

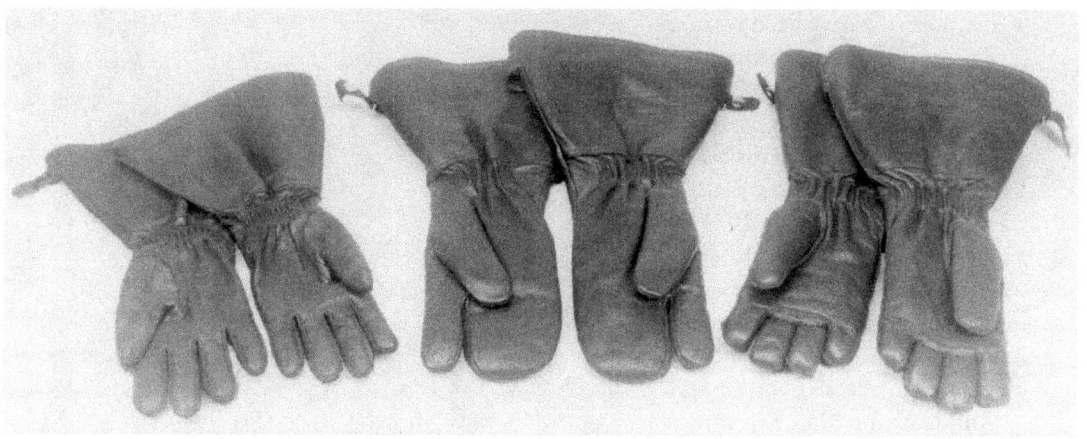

A 1934 photograph showing Air Corps flying gloves in standard use during the 1930s. All three types continued to be worn until 1944. Left to right: the Types A-8, A-6, and A-7. (SI Photo A4857H)

still used as limited standard during World War II. It was declared obsolete on March 27, 1944. The A-6 was a mitten-type leather gauntlet lined with lamb's wool and had one separate finger. Like the A-6, the Type A-7 gauntlet was standardized on October 25, 1929, and was used as limited standard until March 27, 1944. It was made of chrome-tanned calfskin, with baby lamb's wool lining, external seams, and four short fingers. The Type A-8, a medium-temperature gauntlet, was also made of chrome-tanned calfskin, but it had a camel's hair knitted-wool lining and four long fingers. The A-8 was standardized on October 20, 1930, and remained in use as limited standard until it was declared obsolete on March 31, 1944.

The Type A-9 gauntlet was an improved Type A-6 incorporating a seal-brown pigskin outer shell with lamb shearling lining and a short cuff. It was standardized on April 22, 1935, and in December 1941 had its nomenclature changed to "Type A-9, Glove, Flying, Winter." The A-9 remained in use until after the end of the war. An improved version, designated the A-9A, was standardized on April 11, 1944. It was a gauntlet type like the A-9, had a

thumb and one finger, and was made of either goatskin or pony hide with a lamb shearling lining. The A-9A was later procured with a brown deerskin shell. It could be worn over electrically heated gloves in emergencies, provided that the mitten was a size larger than

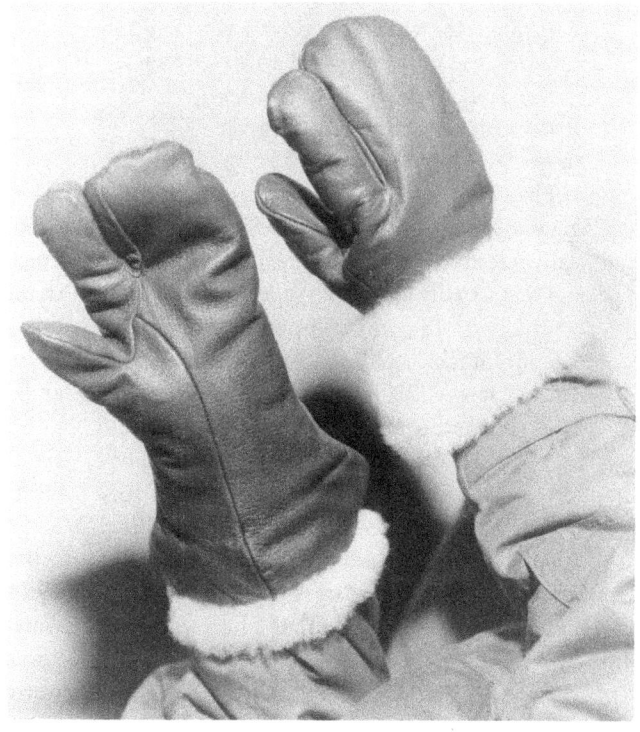

The popular Type A-9A heavy winter gloves with lamb shearling lining, 1944. (SI Photo A485QA)

would normally have been worn. A rayon insert could also be worn for added protection.

The Type A-10 was a five-finger goatskin leather glove with camel's hair lining and a knitted wristlet. It was standardized on July 20, 1938, and was used throughout the war. It was actually a "light" winter or "intermediate" glove and was noted for its very poor fit. In 1942 some A-10 gloves were made without lining.

On March 30, 1943, the Type A-11 winter flying glove, which was to see much service, was standardized. It had a brown cape leather shell and included removable knit woolen and rayon inserts. In 1944 a slight modification of the glove was adopted as standard and designated the Type A-11A. The A-11A's design was so improved that considerable manual dexterity was possible with the glove on. Although the intermediate range, for which this glove was intended, was only from 14° F to 50° F, the A-11A provided adequate protection at considerably lower ranges.[6]

The Type A-12 glove was also standardized on March 30, 1943. It was officially referred to as the "Glove, Flying, Arctic" and was actually a gauntlet-type mitten. It was covered with full-length, water-resistant cotton poplin fabric and was, at first, lined with fleece. Later A-12 gloves had wool-pile lining. The palm and thumb were faced with horsehide leather, and rayon glove inserts could be worn with it. The A-12 was recommended for wear in extreme cold where manual dexterity was not required. It could also be used as an "overglove" with the A-11A or, if there was a circuit or power failure, the F-2 heated glove.

The Type A-12 was a heavy gauntlet-type winter mitten with wool pile lining adopted in March 1943. The glove was made of water-resistant cotton poplin, and its palm and thumb were faced with horsehide leather. The co-pilot of this C-54 transport is also wearing a Type A-11 intermediate helmet. (SI Photo A4858D)

Glove Inserts

The rayon insert used with the A-9, A-11, and later insulative-type gloves was developed in 1942 to eliminate the danger of fingers freezing to metal when delicate manipulations precluded the use of heavy gloves during extreme cold. The insert was considered a significant development in military glove design. It was first intended for the use of mechanics and was later standardized for use by flying personnel.[7] In addition to their use with winter flying gloves, rayon inserts were used with electric gloves for the F-2 electric suit.

Tests were conducted at Ladd Field and other points in Alaska during the winter of 1942-43 to determine what types of gloves were best for very cold weather. Shearling gloves with wool-pile inserts proved to be warm enough for temperatures as low as -47° F, and gloves worn in two or more layers were reported as being the most satisfactory.[8]

Nylon had been tested as a substitute for

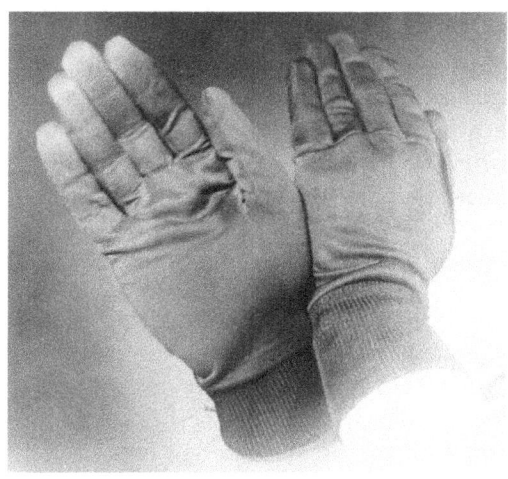

During World War II rayon inserts were worn with both regular and electrically heated gloves to provide additional warmth. They were a significant development in military glove design because they eliminated the danger of the skin of the fingers freezing to metal during extreme cold when the outer gloves had to be removed to allow delicate manipulations. (SI Photo A4857J)

rayon for inserts, and it was found superior in some ways. But the quantity of nylon available for gloves during the war was very limited.

Also during the war, the suggestion was made that the thumbs be centered in the sides of gloves, thus making them ambidextrous. This modification was later incorporated into the patterns for the wool and rayon inserts so that one could be saved if the match became useless. The change could only be made in very thin gloves, however, since the material was unavoidably bunched around the thumb.

Anti-Exposure Glove

The Type F-1 anti-exposure glove consisted of a yellow two-ply neoprene-coated nylon outer shell and an olive drab knitted-wool mitten-type insert. The insert had a dipped neoprene latex wristlet, which provided a seal at the wrist. The glove was intended to be worn as a part of the Type R-1 quick-donning anti-exposure flying suit. The F-1 glove was not standardized until January 26, 1945, and it therefore saw little service during the war. After the war, however, the AAF and USAF continued to use it for several years.

Emergency Rescue Gloves

Three types of heavy emergency-rescue gloves for the temperate zone were service tested beginning on June 4, 1945. They were the Type N-1, a four-piece mitten type; the N-2, a one-piece leather mitten; and the N-3, a one-piece knitted-wool mitten. They were not standardized for use before the end of the war. The N-1 was procured after the war

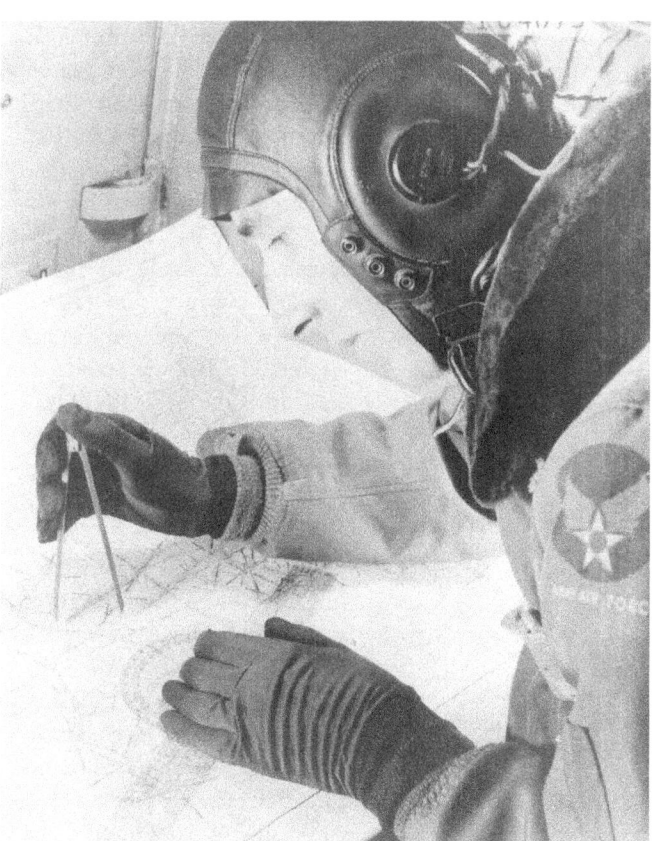

An AAF navigator wearing rayon glove inserts after removing his heavy gloves. His helmet is a Type A-11 with snaps for attaching the Type A-13 or A-14 oxygen masks. (SI Photo A4858)

and used by the USAF primarily as a component of emergency survival kits.

The Type D-3 glove was an AAF procurement of an Army quartermaster glove and was standardized on March 30, 1943. It was a mechanics, or utility, glove designed for extremely cold temperatures and would not be included here except that it was adopted for inclusion in the C-1 survival vest used by flyers. The D-3 consisted of a knitted-wool inner glove and a five-finger horsehide leather outer glove, with a strap on top for tightening. Either the wool insert or the leather outer shell could be worn alone. (This type of glove is still standard issue to enlisted men.)

Intermediate Flying Glove

The only intermediate glove to be standardized during the war was the Type M-1, which had a rayon cloth body and knitted-wool wristlets. Originally procured as a rayon glove insert, the M-1 was standardized on May 21, 1945.

Summer Flying Gloves

Officers frequently purchased their own light, brown leather gloves during and after World War I. A combination winter and summer gauntlet flying glove was procured and issued by the Army, and this type remained in service for several years after the war. One- and four-finger, unlined gauntlet-type gloves, without type numbers, were procured during the 1920s and 1930s and included in the Air Corps Class 13 Stock Lists.

The Type B-1 summer flying glove was a five-finger leather type with a chamois lining. It was service tested from March 1926 until October 20, 1930, before it was discontinued. The first summer glove to be standardized and procured for use was the Type B-2. It was a five-finger glove made of lightweight brown goatskin leather, which was considered fire resistant. The B-2 was standardized on August 17, 1942, was changed to limited standard on July 23, 1943, and was used through the end of World War II.

The Type B-3 was a five-finger, unlined brown leather glove standardized on July 23, 1943, as a replacement for the B-2. Deerskin and capeskin were both used in its construction, which featured perforated fourchettes and a take-up elastic inside wrist. In 1944 a

One of the most popular gloves developed during World War II, the Type B-3 summer flying glove was extremely comfortable, flexible, and lightweight, permitting a high degree of dexterity. The B-3A, a later modification, was often referred to as the ideal light flying glove and remained in use with the Air Force for many years. (SI Photo A4858C)

modification of the B-3 was standardized as the Type B-3A, and its changes were of major importance in the manufacture of flying gloves: The design was changed to a strip fourchette and half-pique construction, which greatly increased the fingertip sensitivity for the wearer. Elastic shirring was added to the B-3A's to help hold the glove on the hand. The flexibility and light weight of the B-3A permitted a high degree of dexterity, making it an ideal light flying glove. The long gauntlet guarded both hand and wrist against flash burns. The B-3A was also the first flying glove for which complete patterns and fabrication instructions were furnished to the manufacturer. It was made like a fine ladies' glove, usually with the finest quality soft capeskin but sometimes with seal-brown unlined goatskin and sheepskin. The B-3A was an excellent glove that was retained in use by the USAF until recent years.

The only very light flying glove designed during the war was the Type K-1, a mosquito-resistant pattern that was service tested beginning on June 4, 1945.

Electrically Heated Flying Gloves

Electrically heated glove inserts of the French pattern were procured for use by the U.S. Air Service during World War I. Like other articles of electric clothing, however, they were undependable, and few of them saw service with American aviators in the combat areas before the end of the war.

Experimental heated gloves and other articles of electric clothing were tested during the 1920s and 1930s. (Electrically heated suits and shoes are discussed in chapters 5 and 10, re-

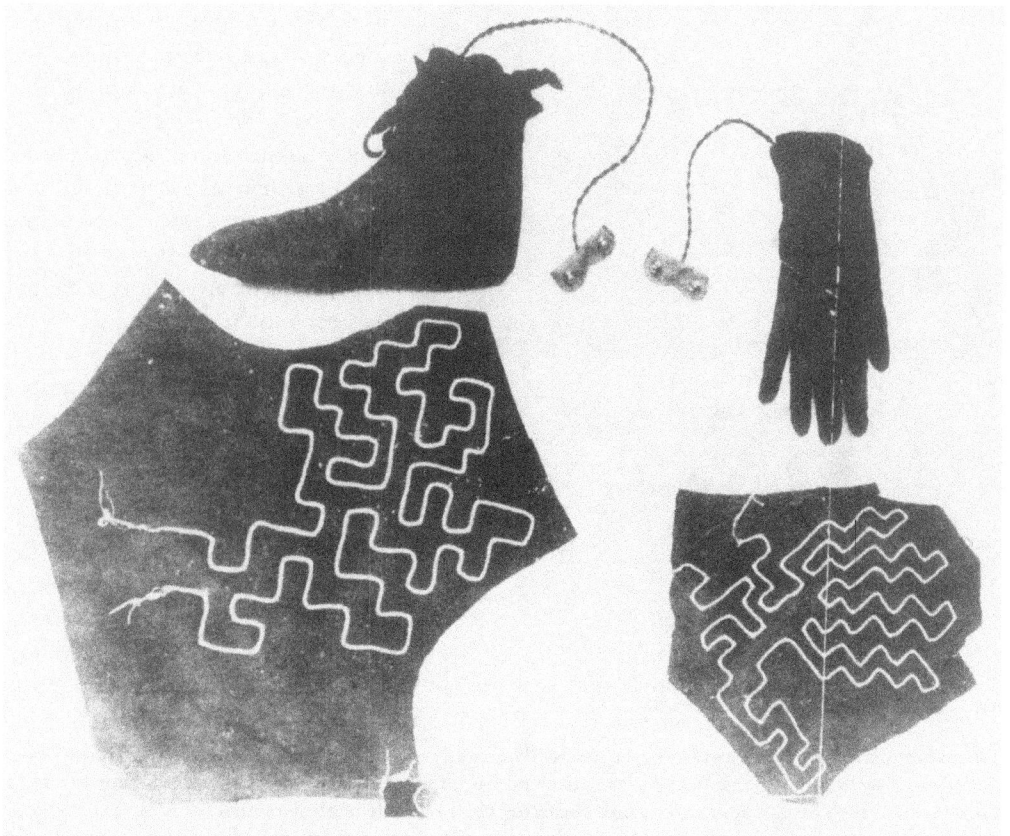

Electrically heated shoes and gloves, 1919. The usefulness of electric garments was limited by the lack of flexibility of the heating elements, which caused breakage and short circuits. (SI Photo 4858E)

spectively.) One type procured for limited use was the "Glove, Flying, Silk, Electrically Heated." This glove was an insert normally worn under other gloves or gauntlets. It was listed in the March 1929 edition of the Air Corps Class 13 Stock Lists but was replaced in the early 1930s by the Type C-4 electric glove.

The experimental heated gauntlet-type gloves included the Type C-1, a five-finger winter gauntlet made of wool with a leather shell and an asbestos-covered copper-wire insert. It was designed for twelve volts, as were all the "C" series electric gloves. The Types C-2 one-finger and C-3 gauntlets, converted from Type A-6 gloves, were also experimental and were service tested during the early 1930s. None of the three types proved to be sufficiently satisfactory for adoption, primarily because the heating elements were not flexible enough to prevent breakage during regular use. However, one size of each of the C-2 and C-3 gauntlets was retained in the Air Corps inventory and reintroduced into the Stock Lists published from 1938 through 1940 for issue as nonstandard items.

The Type C-4 was a one-finger, all-wool knitted gauntlet-type glove with rubber-covered heating elements placed over the thumb and first three fingers. It could be used alone or as an insert for the Type A-9 pigskin winter glove. Developed by General Electric, the C-4 was extensively service tested before it was standardized for use on April 22, 1935. The Air Corps procured and used the C-4 during the 1930s and the early part of World War II. Its status was changed to limited standard on April 4, 1941, and it was finally declared obsolete on April 4, 1944.

An electrically heated goatskin leather glove insert was listed in the Stock Lists in service-test status from 1939 through 1943. It was described as a five-finger, medium-size, twelve-volt, fifteen-amp glove,

The experimental Type C-3 twelve-volt electrically heated gloves made by General Electric, as they were undergoing testing in 1933. The C-3 was converted from the standard A-6 glove, which incorporated a thin lining in the glove proper and a lamb shearling cuff. Flexible heating connections were sewed into the lining. The project was discontinued mainly because the glove was not considered to be warm enough in case of power failure unless it was worn as an insert for a fur-lined gauntlet. As always, the heating elements were subject to breakage during ordinary use. The winter suit is the Type B-1 jacket with Type A-1 trousers. (SI Photo A4857)

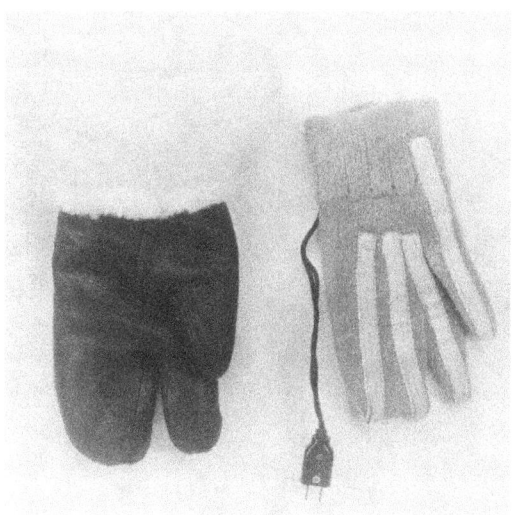 

Left: The Type C-4 twelve-volt electric glove (right) was often worn with the A-9 winter glove (left). Shown here in 1936, both saw service from 1935 until 1944. (SI Photo A4857A) *Right:* An experimental electric glove of 1938 showing pattern of wiring. (SI Photo A4857B)

made by the Colvinex Corporation. This insert probably was never type listed or standardized.

The Type C-5 electric glove was service tested for two years beginning January 4, 1938, but was declared obsolete on May 1, 1940. It consisted of a five-finger wool glove with a leather palm and had cotton-covered copper-wire heating elements located in the palm and over the ends of the fingers.

The last glove in the "C" series was the Type C-6, which was worn with the twelve-volt E-1 electric suit. It was a five-finger type fabricated with a goatskin or pony-hide leather outer shell and a knit wool lining between which were sewed the wire heating elements. It was designated as substitute standard on April 14, 1941, and was declared obsolete on February 24, 1944.[9]

The Type E-1 glove was similar to the Type C-6 except that it was designed for twenty-four volts for use with the F-1 electric suit. It was standardized on April 4, 1941, and was changed to limited standard on October 13, 1944. The E-1, however, was not very durable or dependable in use.

Another electric glove was developed for use with the twenty-four volt F-2 and F-3 electric suits. The heavy electric glove was a five-finger leather gauntlet type with a knit-wool lining. Its wires were placed over the back of the hand and fingers and were positioned be-

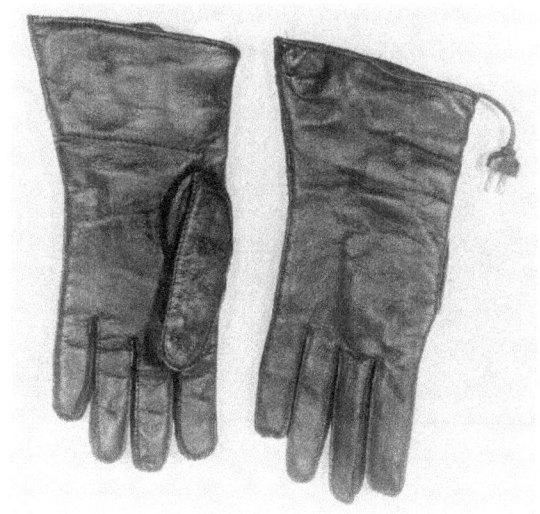

The Type E-1 twenty-four-volt electric glove was standardized in 1941 and was used with the F-1 electric suit. Like its predecessors, it did not prove to be very durable or dependable because of breakage of the heating elements during regular use. (SI Photo A4857C)

tween the two layers of the knit liner. More than 280,000 pairs of this glove were on procurement in November 1944. Several modifications were made to the glove during 1943–44, including the introduction of new, more flexible wire that almost doubled the flexing life. These thinner, more malleable wires and the development of an improved pattern for the leather shell both improved the glove's flexibility. The wires or heating elements were also relocated in relationship to the knuckles to avoid "hot spots."[10] The glove could protect the hands in temperatures as low as -60° F. It was considered essential, however, that this glove be worn with the rayon insert to provide protection in case the outer glove had to be removed at low temperatures.

The early electric gloves were connected to the arms of the suits by plugs, but during the war electric gloves and shoes for use with the Type F-2 and F-3 suits were connected to the arms by snap or stud fasteners. In October 1944 improved bayonet-type connectors were introduced for use, and the Type F-3 suit, so modified, was redesignated the Type F-3A.

With the marked improvement in the flexibility, and thus dependability, of the new more malleable heating elements used in electric clothing constructed after May 1944, heated gloves assumed a new importance in the field of flying clothing.

Heavy electrically heated glove used with Type F-2 and F-3 electric suits. Electric gloves, and other garments, were much more dependable after more flexible wire was developed in the spring of 1944, and they assumed a new importance in the field of flying clothing. This navigator is using the Astro Compass, AN-5738–1. (SI Photo A4857E)

10

Footwear

If one considers the number of different types of footwear that are available for specialized purposes, the list seems endless. Almost every type of trade, profession, craft, sport, and fashion seems to require a distinctive style of footwear, and many are quite necessary to adapt the human foot so that it can accomplish the particular task involved.

The Army Air Forces also used a variety of flying boots, called shoes in AAF terminology, as well as the basic Army shoes issued by the QMC during World War II. The standard QMC shoes most used by AAF personnel consisted of the low-quarter, tan or brown leather shoes and the high-top, brown leather service shoes, often referred to as "GI" shoes or "Boondockers." The high-top shoes were made with either the rough or smooth side of the leather on the outside. If the rough side was on the outside, a special preparation called "dubbing" was sometimes applied to make the shoes waterproof, although dubbing was discontinued in some commands because it prevented air circulation to the feet. In warm climates, especially tropical areas, a high shoe such as the GI was far better than a low-quarter since it gave protection from sand and insects and provided increased support for walking any distance over rough ground. Also, because the high-top shoe was less likely to come off during a bailout, flyers were urged during the war to wear shoes of this type and were discouraged from wearing low-quarter shoes.

Flying shoes or boots, along with good socks, proved to be a vital part of any outfit for any climate, and removable insoles were found to be most desirable for colder climates. In cold weather and at high altitudes, proper footgear was (and is) essential in preventing the feet from becoming frostbitten. The feet constitute about 10 percent of the total body surface. Under hot conditions, approximately 13 percent of the body's heat can be lost through the feet. However, under cold conditions, when the heat loss might be expected to increase, reductions in the blood's flow and temperature may cause the portion of body heat lost through the feet to fall as low as seven percent.

Insulative or Winter Footwear

The origins of many flying shoes and boots can be traced back to World War I. The Aviation Clothing Board, established in 1917, procured high-top leather boots and sheepskin lined "arctics" with clasps for winter wear by men in the Air Service during that war. High-top, brown leather, fleece- and fur-lined moccasin-type boots were also developed; they resembled the later Type A-6 boot but had a soft sole. A smooth-sole style of moccasin was often called the "barefoot" type since it had no separate sole and heel. Moccasin-type flying boots could be worn over standard Army service shoes or boots and proved to be both efficient and comfortable. They were further refined and developed at McCook Field

The prototype of the Type A-2 flying boot, officially called a shoe by the Army, was typical of the moccasin-type boots used since World War 1. This smooth-sole moccasin was called the "barefoot" type because it had no separate sole and heel. The A-2, produced with zipper closures, was standardized in 1928 and was made of leather with sheepskin lining. It was used as limited standard from 1937 until it was finally declared obsolete in 1944. (SI Photo A4859)

during the 1920s, and a low, brown leather, sheep-skin-lined type of aviator's moccasin, the Type A-1, Spec. 3000, was adopted as limited standard on February 19, 1924. The A-1 was not declared obsolete until March 13, 1944. It had a smooth sole and was secured by three straps with buckles. Originally called a moccasin, the A-1 was usually referred to in later years as a flying shoe.

Shoes were designated separate from moccasins. The A-1 designation for shoes was not used, perhaps to prevent confusion with the

Experimental insulated flying boot with heel and sole tested at Wright Field in 1931. (SI Photo A4859A)

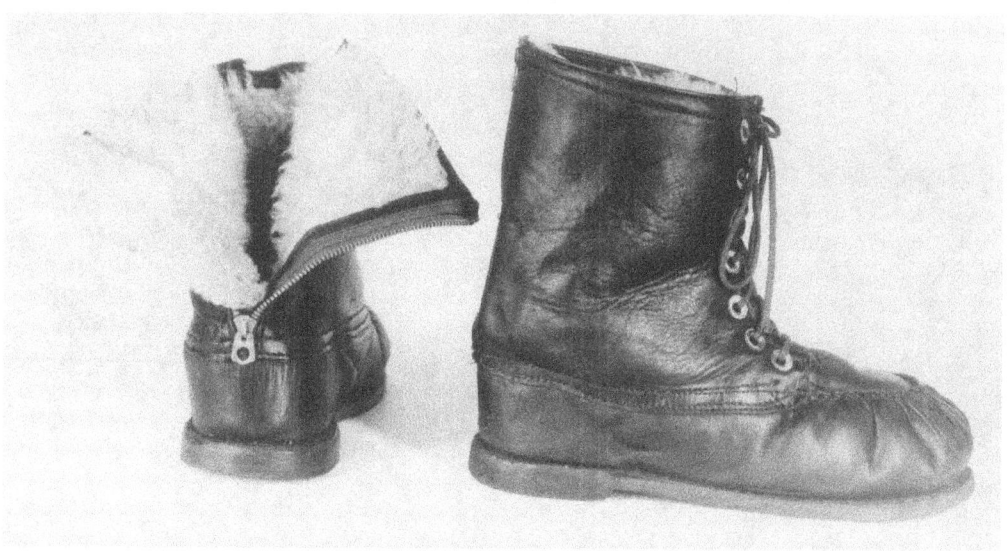

Type A-5 moccasin-type shoe with horsehide outer shell and sheep shearling lining. It had a hard leather sole and a low heel. The A-5 was adopted as limited standard in 1935 and was declared obsolete in 1944. (SI Photo A48598)

A-1 moccasin. The Type A-2 "Shoes, Aircraft, Pilot's," later called "Shoes, Flying, Winter," were standardized on August 29, 1928. The leather A-2 shoes were also of moccasin style, were sheepskin lined, and had zipper instead of buckle closures. Their status changed to limited standard on March 27, 1937, and a few were worn during World War II until they were declared obsolete on March 27, 1944.[1] The Type A-3 was an experimental leather high-top shoe similar to the A-2. It had a lace front, a zipper rear closure, and no heel. The A-4 was constructed of a leather outer shell and was lined with three-ply quilted-wool blanket material. It was laced up the front and had a hard leather sole and heel. The A-4 was service tested in 1930-31 and was maintained in small supply as nonstandard issue. The shoe was finally discontinued during World War II.

Most later types of shoes, beginning with

One of the best-known flying shoes ever developed was the Type A-6 shearling. This 1936 photograph shows the original model (right) during service testing, along with the shearling slipper insert provided for optional wear. The shoe was standardized as the Type A-6, and the slipper as the A-7, in 1937; both were used through the end of World War II. The A-6 shoe was originally made with an unfinished outer surface and was later weatherproofed, along with other shearling garments, by applying a brown polyacrylate dye and a lacquer top finish. (SI Photo A4859C)

the Type A-5, saw long service. The A-5 was a moccasin type with a horsehide outer shell and was lined with sheep shearling. It had a

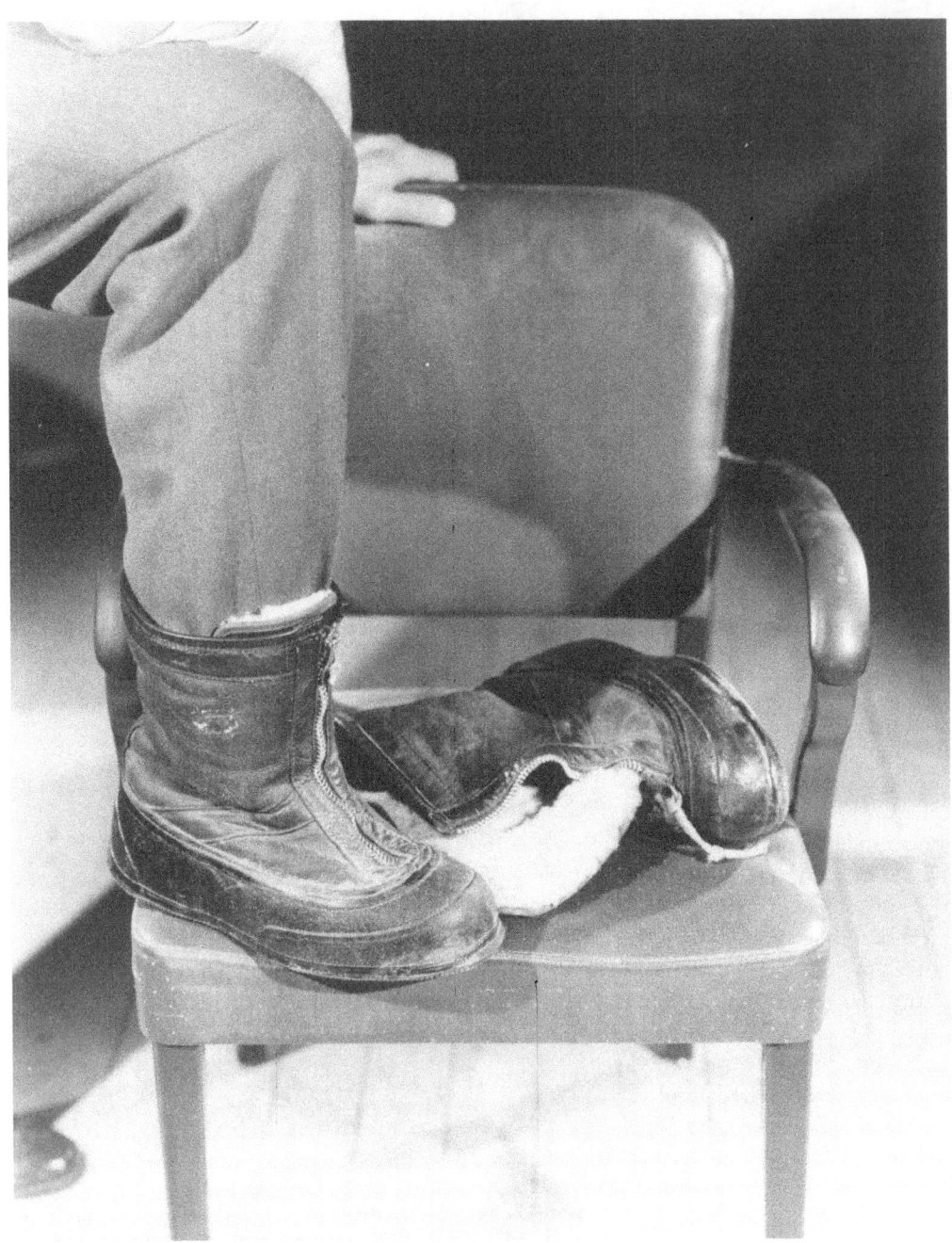

The Type A-6 shearling flying shoe as manufactured during World War II with the brown waterproof finish. The lower section of the shoe and the sole were made of rubber. (SI Photo A4859D)

hard leather sole and low heel, a lace opening front, and a zipper in back. The Type A-5 flying shoe was service tested beginning in 1934 and adopted as limited standard on May 22, 1935. It was declared obsolete on March 27, 1944, after almost ten years of limited use.

One of the best-known flying shoes ever used by the Army was the Type A-6. Its improved shearling design incorporated refinements learned during both extensive service testing of prototypes and service use of the A-5 shoe. The A-6 was a "heavy shoe" intended for use with shearling winter clothing, particularly the B-3 jacket, A-3 trousers combination. Service tests on the A-6 began on May 15, 1930, and the shoe was finally standardized on March 27, 1937. It was a shearling shoe made with three-fourths-inch fiber and had a zipper in front and a rubber sole. The outside of the ten-inch-high upper was waterproofed in later years with a brown polyacrylate dye and a lacquer finish. It provided suitable protection in the intermediate temperature range and was also satisfactory for wear over electric shoes and inserts. The A-6 proved, however, to be cumbersome and bulky for fighter pilots and ball turret gunners.[2]

The A-6 could be worn with or without a regulation shoe. Wartime experience, however, showed that a sturdy walking shoe was necessary since the

"Shoe, Flying, Winter, Type A-6A," showing the straps that were added to the A-6 in 1944 at the top and instep. (SI Photo 80-20365)

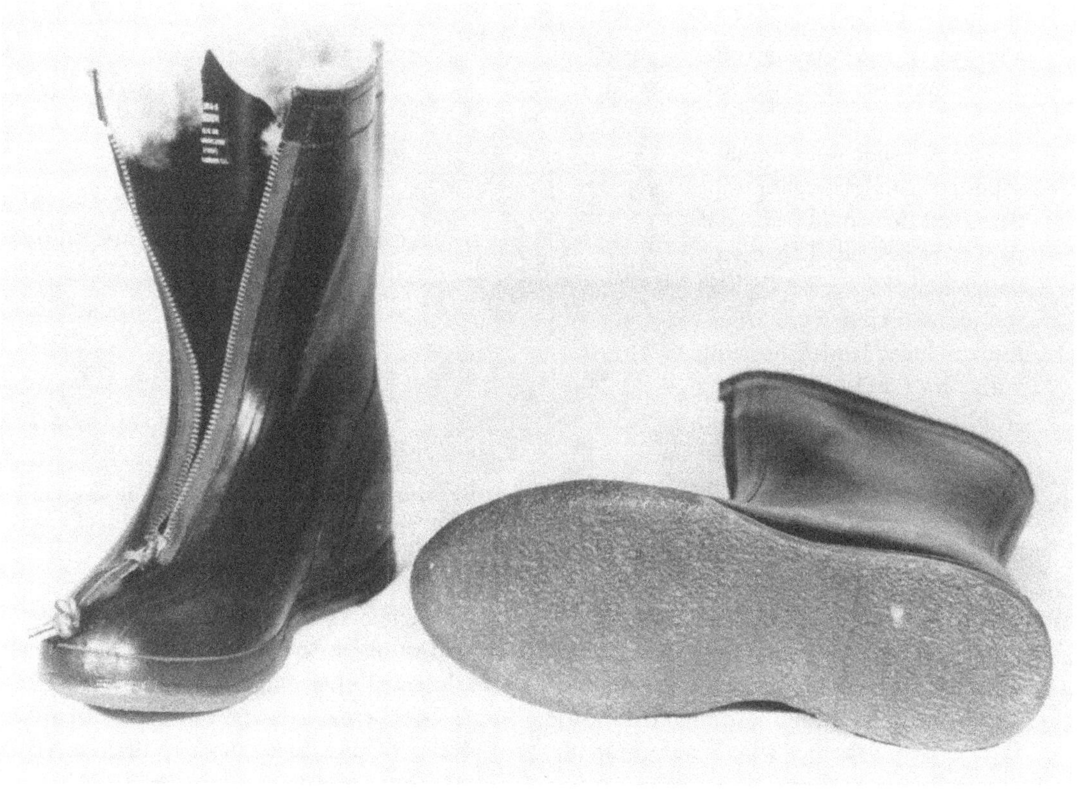

A rubber-coated fabric, fleece-lined shoe with crepe soles, the Type A-9 was introduced in 1941 and could be used with the C-1 and D-1 electrically heated shoes inserted. The rubber upper of the A-9 proved to be too hot in warm weather and too cold under winter conditions. (SI Photo A4859F)

A-6 made walking over rough terrain difficult. Another problem with the A-6 was that it could come off during a bailout, leaving a flyer with no shoes at all. On November 1, 1944, retaining straps were added around the shoe's top and over its instep in accordance with Spec. 94-3091-B. The straps were added to improve retention in mud and when parachuting. Moreover, the top strap was useful in securing the overshoe more closely to the leg, thus providing protection against cold drafts. The modified shoe, with straps, was officially standardized and designated the Type A-6A on August 7, 1945, and the plain A-6 was changed to limited standard. In addition, the A-6A was available in more sizes than the A-6 was.

The A-6 shoe was originally supplied with a shearling slipper insert that could be used if its wearer desired. This insert, designated the Type A-7 shoe, was constructed from three-fourths-inch lamb shearling with horsehide reinforcing strips and a pressed felt sole and heel. It was standardized on December 4, 1937, changed to limited standard on October 13, 1944, and used through the end of the war.

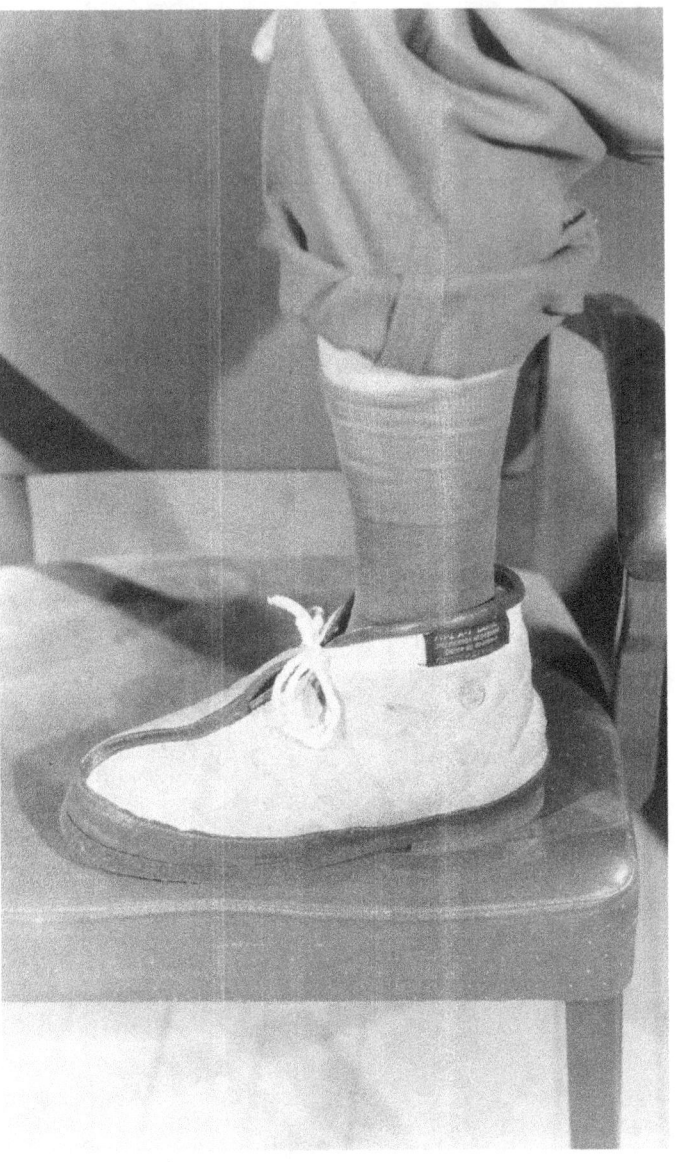

The Type A-7 shearling slipper or shoe in 1943 This shoe was standardized in 1937 and was originally intended for optional wear inside the A-6 shoe. (SI Photo A4859H)

The type A-8 was a fabric shoe with fleece lining and a flexible nonskid sole. An intermediate shoe, it was lighter in weight and less bulky than the A-6 and was intended for use in enclosed airplanes where extremely low temperatures were encountered. The A-8 was standardized on May 28, 1940, and declared obsolete on March 27, 1944.

The Type A-9 shoe was considered an improvement over the A-8 and had a rubber-coated wool fabric upper, a zipper closure, a wool-fleece lining, and a crepe sole. Snap fasteners were provided to permit Types C-1 and D-1 electrically heated shoes to be inserted. The A-9 was standardized on April 28, 1941, and changed to limited standard on June 2, 1942. It was a disappointment to AAF personnel because its upper was found to be too hot

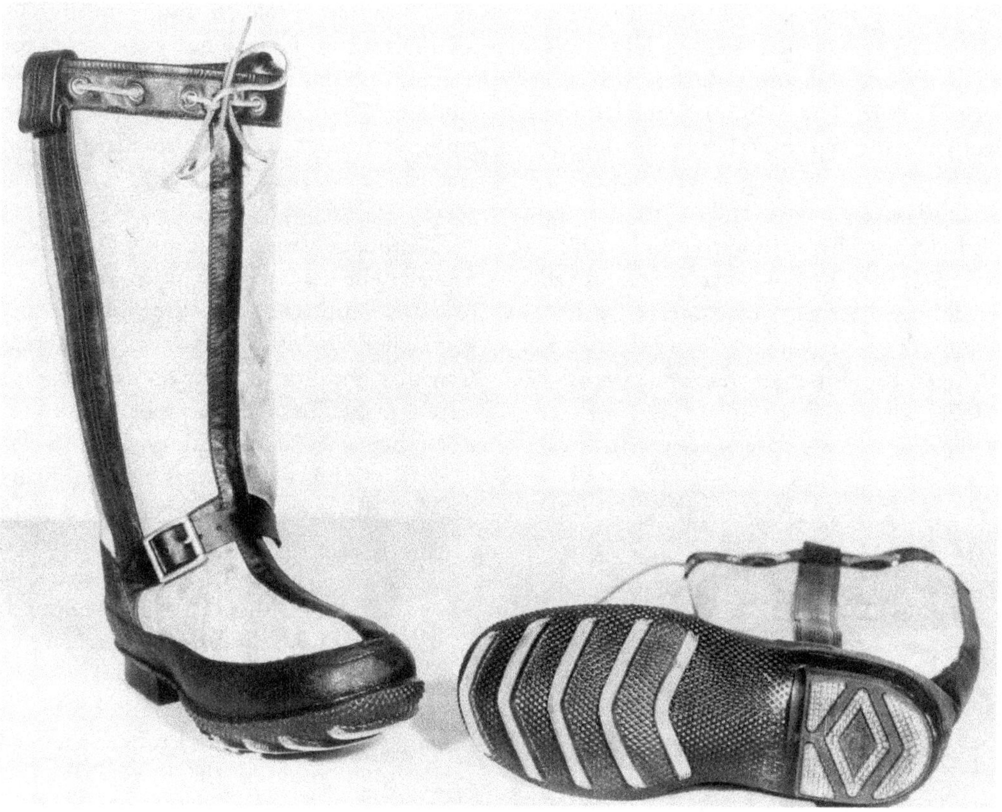

A version of the Type A-10 shearling winter shoe with the outside in the "raw." The A-10 was standardized for arctic wear in 1941, but turned out to be too impermeable to water vapor to be used successfully in the arctic regions. This experience led to the development of an arctic boot called a "mukluk." (SI Photo A4859G)

in temperate conditions and too cold in cold climates.

The next shoe, or boot, to be developed was the heavy winter Type A-10. It was knee-high and fabricated of three-fourths-inch-pile sheep shearling reinforced with horsehide. Its rubber sole had cord and rubber "Tire Cord" cleats to decrease skidding. The A-10 had no opening in front but did have a draw-

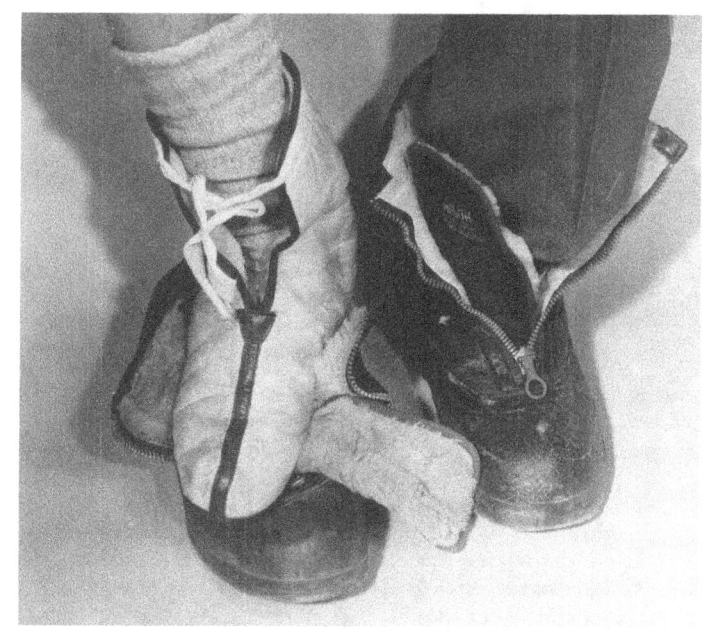

The Type A-11 shoe (left) was a slipper-style insert made of shearling. It was intended for wear with the A-10 shoe but could also be worn inside the A-6, as is shown in this 1944 photograph. (SI Photo A4859J)

string at the upper edge. Designed for Alaskan use, it was standardized on July 7, 1941, and was changed to substitute standard on August 17, 1942. The A-10 was intended to be worn with the Type A-11 shoe (a shearling slipper insert) over stockinged feet, and the B-7 and B-8 jackets and A-6 and A-7 trousers were also meant to be worn with it. The slipper-style A-11 shoe insert was made of one-fourth-inch sheep shearling with leather strips. It was standardized on January 29, 1942, but was changed to limited standard on August 17, 1942.

The Type A-12 shoe was made of heavy duck with leather soles. It was intended to be used instead of the very heavy A-6 shoes for walking and in case there was an emergency landing. Woolen socks and innersoles were worn with the A-12. It was standardized on August 19, 1942, and was declared obsolete on March 19, 1943.

Shearling footwear (such as the A-10 shoe) proved to be too impermeable to water vapor for successful use in arctic regions, leading many pilots and other crew members to wear Canadian and British flying boots when they were available. To solve this problem, the AAF developed special mukluk-type boots for Alaskan wear. Experiments were conducted during 1943 with a rubber-surfaced mukluk-type boot designated the Type A-13 shoe. Tests on it, however, were discontinued in favor of the Type A-14 mukluk.

The very successful A-14 was a canvas- and rubber-surfaced mukluk that was fashioned after the vapor-permeable footgear commonly worn in the Arctic. It was worn with an insert assembly of socks and insoles, with the complete combination including seven separate items that had to be worn in the following sequence: lightweight woolen sock, medium-weight woolen sock, heavyweight woolen sock, knit-worsted jumbo sock, felt duffel sock, felt insole, and the A-14 mukluk. The boot itself consisted of a fourteen-inch upper and a nonskid rubber sole. The upper, which was not completely waterproofed, was made of water-repellent, twelve-ounce olive drab canvas duck. It was closed by lacing at the instep and a tie at the top. Standardized on April 26, 1943, as the "Shoe, Flying, Arctic, Type

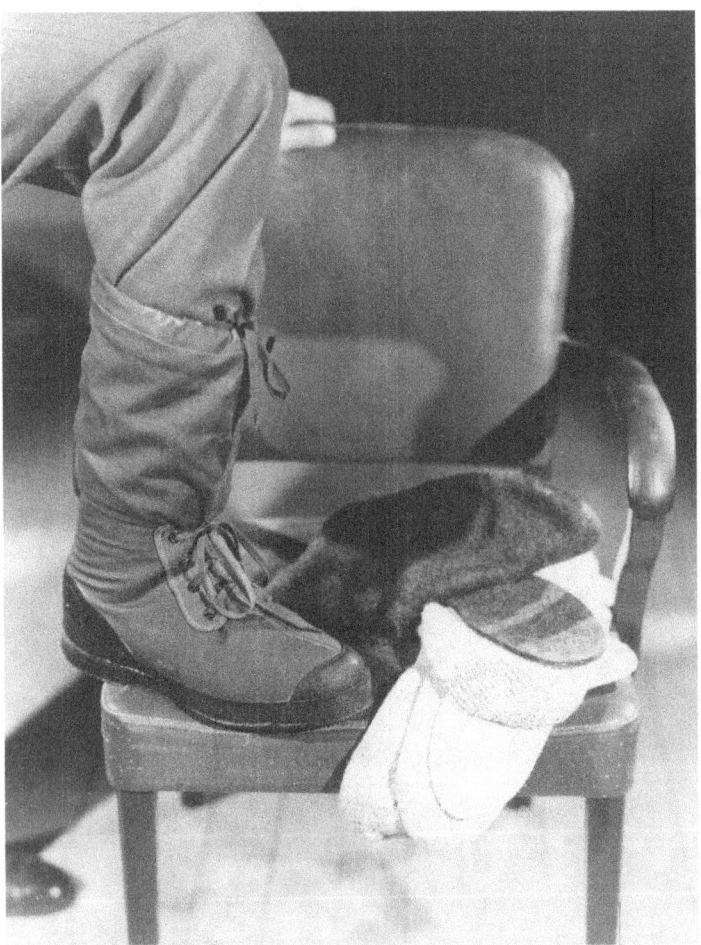

The very successful Type A-14 mukluk for arctic and extreme cold-weather wear. Made of canvas duck with a rubber sole, it is shown here with a felt insert, an inner sole, and four pairs of socks. The A-14 was standardized in April 1943 and remained in use long after the war. (SI Photo A4860)

A-14," it was retained in use, with modifications, for many years.

The type A-15 designation was assigned to an intermediate-weight leather "mosquito boot" that was never developed beyond a prototype. The Type A-16 intermediate shearling shoe was very similar to the A-6A but was smaller and without straps. It was intended for use by women pilots and nurses and was worn over regular shoes. It was standardized on May 2, 1944, and was used throughout the war.

The AAF developed one type of intermediate overshoe for flying personnel, the M-1. It was standardized on December 8, 1944, and was declared inactive on December 14, 1945. Made of rubber compounds and sheep shearling, the M-1 was intended for use over the combat or GI shoe at temperatures of 14° to 50° F.

Electrically Heated Footwear

Electrically heated innersoles for flight boots and shoes were part of the electric clothing equipment in production at the end of World War I. (See chapters 5 and 9.) Electric innersoles and shoes were also tested for use during the early 1920s, and those used with the Type C-1 experimental suit of 1924 were flameproofed and made of cork and canvas.[3] Electric "socks" were developed and were used in limited numbers during the 1920s; they were still listed in the Air Corps Class 13 Stock Catalog for March 1929.

Electrically heated footwear, like other electric clothing, was not very popular before World War II with either flying personnel or clothing engineers. In addition to the principal problem of inflexibility in the heating wires used in all electric clothing, the use of heated insoles made the standard footwear too tight for comfort; both electric shoes and electric insoles were reported to cause radio interference. In addition, heated innersoles worn in standard footwear did not furnish enough heat, and electric shoes proved to be inadequate during power failure or their forced use while away from a source of electricity. That final

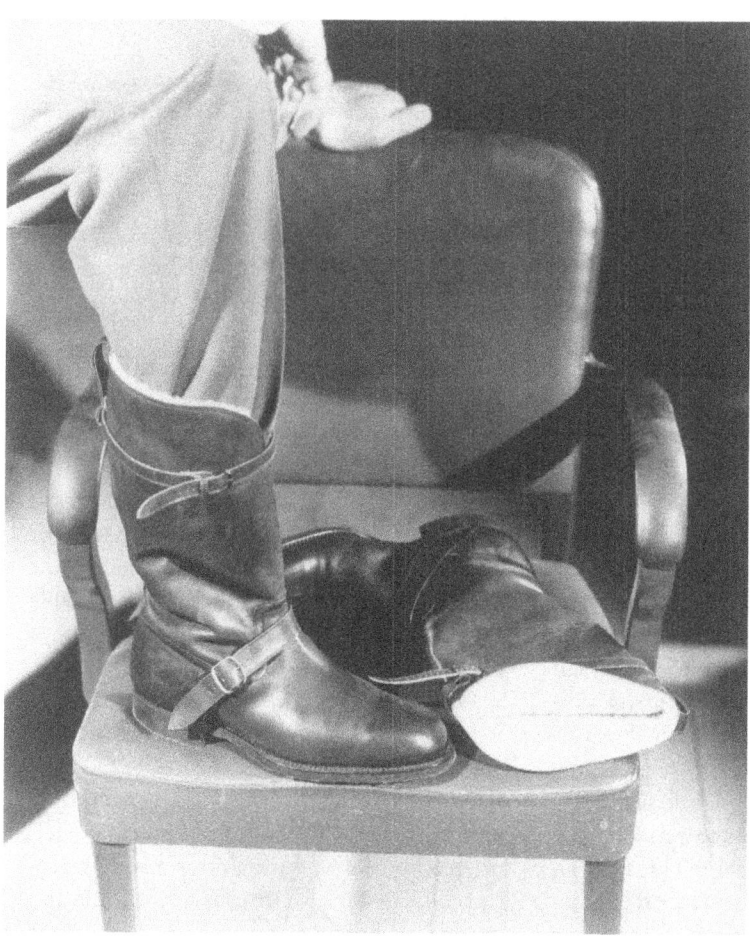

The Type A-15 "mosquito boot" was beautifully made of leather with fleece lining. It was never developed beyond the prototype stage. (SI Photo A48608)

A pair of Type D-1 electrically heated shoes made by the General Electric Company in 1941. Both the C-1 twelve-volt shoe for the E-1 electric suit, and the D-1 twenty-four-volt shoe, for the F-1 suit, were designed to be worn inside the A-9 winter shoe. They could not be used with the F-2 or F-3 suits. (SI Photo A4858F)

shortcoming was particularly important in case of a forced landing in winter.

By 1941 two new electrically heated shoes had been developed. They were less than ideal but were urgently needed by flying personnel in units equipped with new types of modern, high-flying aircraft such as single-seat fighters and bombers equipped with gun turrets. The shoes were designated as substitute standard and promptly procured for use. The twelve-volt Type C-1 was intended for use with the Type E-1 electric suit that had just been developed. It had an outer shell of olive drab overcoating and a moleskin lining, between which were sewed the wire heating elements. A rubber sole and heel were provided. The shoe furnished heat to all parts of the foot, including the sole. The C-1 was adopted as substitute standard on April 4, 1941, and was declared obsolete on February 24, 1944. The Type D-1 shoe was similar to the Type C-1 except that it was designed for twenty-four volts for use with the F-1 electric suit. Constructed of neoprene and wool and lined with moleskin, the D-1 was standardized on April 4, 1941, and was changed to limited standard on October 16, 1944. Both the C-1 and D-1 were actually inserts intended for use with the Type A-9 fleece-lined rubber overshoe.

After World War II began, sturdy walking shoes were particularly important in case a flyer had to escape from enemy-occupied territory after a bailout or forced landing. This problem was solved during the war, in part at least, by the development of heated inserts for wear with shoes that both furnished some warmth without the inserts and were suitable for land travel, including escape from behind enemy lines.

One such development was the electric and felt shoe combination produced for the F-2, and later the F-3, electric suits. The F-2 type shoe or insert was described in a wartime document as "a gray felt shoe to be worn in a felt or A-6 boot. The wiring on the sole is protected from abrasive wear by a felt insole and outsole. Webbing reinforces heel seam and toe to instep seam." Development on the F-2 shoe was started in November 1942, and the shoe, which could also be called a "slipper," was stan-

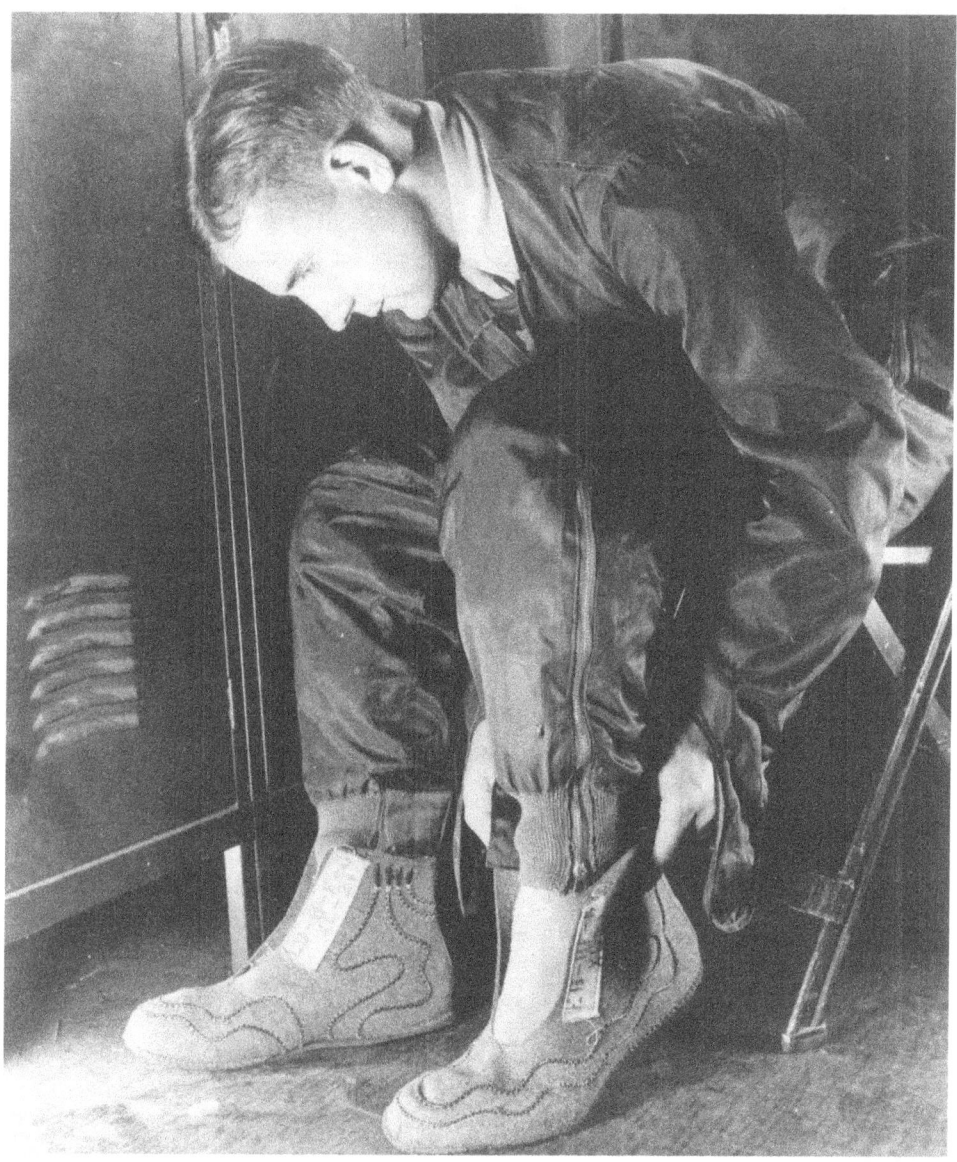

The electric shoe, actually a shoe insert, designed for use with the F-2 electrically heated suit. Standardized in 1943, this shoe was made of felt with heating wires sewn into the outer surface and was worn either inside an A-6 or A-9 winter shoe or inside a black felt overshoe of conventional style. Two separate circuits were connected in parallel. The insert was originally connected to the wiring in the trousers by attachment or connector studs on a flap. In late 1944, however, these were changed to bayonet-type connectors. In addition, the shoes were used with the F-3 and F-3A electric suits, as is shown in this photograph. (SI Photo A4858G)

dardized on August 13, 1943, along with the F-2 suit." An advantage of the felt insert and shoe combination was that it permitted the feet to "breathe" and thus kept the feet from getting moist, which was very undesirable at low temperatures. The shoe was originally attached with connector studs to the trousers of the F-2 electric suit. After October 1944, however, garments were made or modified to use the bayonet-type connectors.

As an insert in the Type A-6 or A-9 shoe, the felt electric shoe was worn over stockinged feet. It was also often worn with a conventional black felt high-top shoe, Spec. 3205, which laced up the front. An overshoe made of felt was not very sturdy, however, and the black felt shoe, with composition sole, proved to be rather unsatisfactory for extensive walking. Its use was later restricted mainly to ball turret gunners.

A later development during the war was the "Shoe—Insert, Flying, Electric, Type Q-1," which was standardized on October 31, 1944, for the Types A-6 and A-6A shoes. It consisted of an inner and outer layer of nylon cloth that enclosed a middle layer of cotton cloth; electric heating wire in two separate, parallel circuits was sewed to the cotton layer. The Q-1 also had a nylon outer sole and a cotton duck insole. It could be used with all variations of the F-2 and F-3 electric suits, but not with the F-1. Studs attached the shoe to the wiring in the trousers for the F-2, F-2A, and F-3 suits, while the F-3A suit used bayonet-type connectors. F-3 suits could be modified with the bayonet type connectors and then redesignated as F-3As. The Q-1's wire arrangement was improved over previous electric footwear to increase the heat supplied to the toe and heel areas. The insert also had the benefit of the new electric wires developed in 1944, which were much more flexible than earlier types had been. The opening of the Q-1 was at the back of the foot, and closure was made with a flap that was drawn around the ankle and fastened with laces.

The Q-1 insert was worn *over* regular QMC-issue Army leather shoes and socks in conjunction with complete electric clothing—a vitally important matter because of the dangers of aerial warfare and the need for good walking equipment after a bailout or forced landing. It was also important in case an aircrew member, after a bailout, was captured and interned in a prisoner of war camp for a long period of time. The sequence of wear was as follows: The flyer would first put on wool socks, over which he would wear regular QMC leather GI high-top shoes. The Q-1 electric shoe insert would follow, and finally a pair of A-6 or A-6A overshoes would be donned. This combination gave excellent results under most flying conditions and provided the crewman with serviceable shoes in case he was forced down.

The black felt shoe with composition sole being worn over the electrically heated shoe in conjunction with the F-2 electric suit. (SI Photo A4859E)

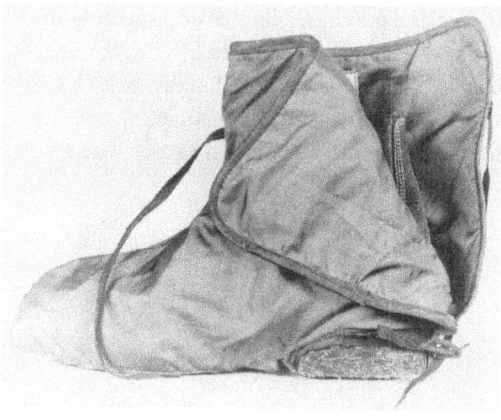

The Type Q-1 electric shoe insert being worn over a walking shoe, probably the black felt type. An overshoe, usually the A-6, also had to be worn over the insert. The Q-1, introduced in 1944, could be worn with both the F-2 and F-3 suits, but not with the F-1. (SI Photo A4858H)

Miscellaneous Footwear

The only light boot accepted during the war was designated the "Shoe, Flying, Light, Type L-1." It was an eight and one-half inch boot with full vamp leather outsole and a half rubber heel. The calf was foxed with kid top and lining. The L-1 was standardized for use on January 29, 1945.

Two final types of shoes were developed during World War II and were intended for use as "escape" shoes in case of a bailout or forced landing in enemy-occupied territory. The Type E-1 was designated the "Shoe, Flying, Light Combat," and was similar to the Marine Corps standard-issue shoe and the standard QMC-issue high-top GI shoe with rough leather outer shell. The E-1 laced up in front and had a composition sole and heel. The Type E-2 was the same design as the E-1 but had a leather sole and heel. Both were standardized on November 14, 1944, but were procured only in test quantities. Production problems at the time required concentration on the standard QMC service shoe and other military types, and the reconquest of France lessened the necessity of a special "escape" shoe for flying personnel.[5]

During the war the AAF experimented with many other types of boots and shoes. One attractive type was an experimental ten-inch-tall leather boot similar in design to the popular boot purchased by many flyers serving in Australia and Brazil. Reddish-brown leather boots obtained by crewmen passing through Brazil were called "gaucho" or "Natal" boots. They were similar to an American cowboy boot,

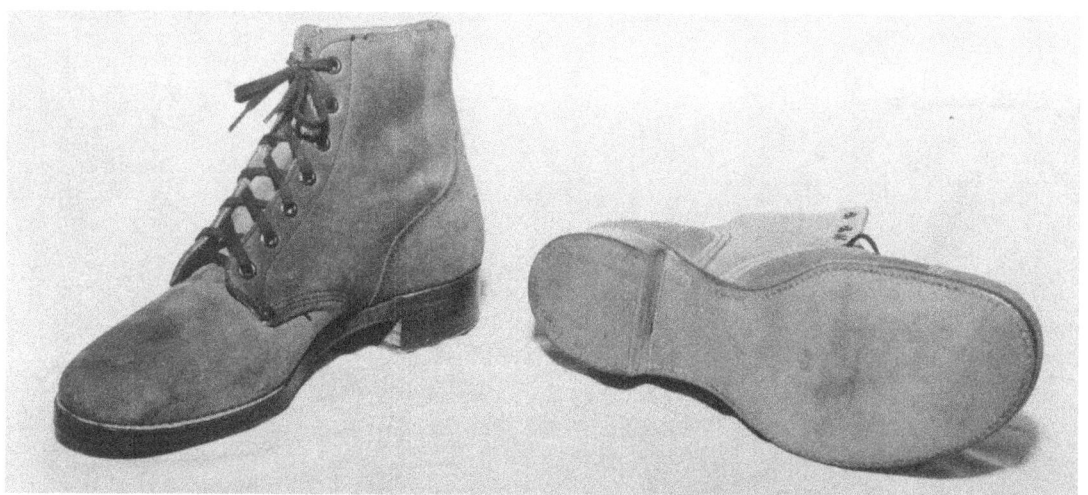

The Type E-2 escape- or combat-type shoe was standardized for AAF use in 1944 but was never procured. It was similar to the service shoes issued by the Marine Corps and Army QMC and was made with leather sole and heel and a rough outer surface. The Type E-1 shoe was the same but had a composition sole and heel. (SI Photo A4860C)

were quick donning, and served effectively against sand and mosquitoes.[6] AAF personnel in India could purchase custom-made "Karachi" boots from native shoemakers; these were made of dark brown leather, were loose fitting, had a smooth toe, and were rather short, reaching only to mid-calf. Many American aviators in England purchased fine, custom-made boots, usually of ankle height, from English commercial firms and shoemakers. Finally, British and Canadian winter-issue flying boots were excellent and were used by AAF crewmen whenever they could be obtained.

Appendices

Appendix A: "Program of the Personal Equipment Laboratory," *The Personal Equipment Officer* 2, no. 2 (c. 1946), p. 1.

PROGRAM OF THE PERSONAL EQUIPMENT LABORATORY

The Personal Equipment Laboratory is responsible for items of personal equipment related to the safety, efficiency, comfort and morale of all Air Force personnel under all operation conditions in conformance with the designs of operational aircraft as well as guided missiles. It is also charged with the development of equipment used in the dropping and supplying of airborne troops.

In keeping with its responsibilities, this laboratory has launched a comprehensive research and development program designed to meet the ever increasing changes in requirements attendant to the advancement in performance of aircraft. This program in general encompasses aircrewmen's clothing, certain other specialized clothing peculiar to Air Force needs, equipment and gear pertaining to rescue and survival, both land and sea, and parachutes and related equipment, both man carrying and cargo delivery.

It must be realized that the design and development of personal equipment encompasses practically all phases of engineering, in addition to the many physiological problems.

With respect to clothing, the highlights are those of partial pressure suits, electrically heated and air-conditioned clothing, including head, hand and foot gear, incidental to the operating conditions anticipated in high-speed and long-range aircraft.

Rescue and survival is most certainly undergoing radical changes influenced by present as well as projected ranges and speeds of aircraft and operation conditions evolving from their usage. The program covers those problems pertaining to the rescue of flight personnel from both land and sea, as well as their survival on both land and sea. Equipment includes life preservers, rafts, and attendant accessories such as signaling devices, sustenance kits, including solar stills, rigid and semirigid airborne lifeboats, crash rescue boats, and droppable emergency rescue and survival gear. We are now dealing not only with an individual or small number of individuals, but also with the problem of mass rescue and survival.

The parachute program is faced with particularly difficult problems. This can be appreciated upon realizing that canopy design for high-speed opening is an aerodynamic problem second to none. Further, the research and development of parachute canopies and attendant accessories and gear involve instrumentation development peculiar only to canopy designs. Problems are essentially associated with high speed and high altitude and include individual as well as capsule ejection, methods of reducing parachute opening shock upon the human, and automatic parachute opening devices; high altitude, precision delivery of cargo which entails suitable containers, parachute and equipment problems associated with ejection from aircraft, controlled descent, load arrestors upon impact, automatic canopy release devices upon impact, automatic container opening devices, and automatic container locating devices. Concurrently being studied with the canopy method of human and cargo delivery, is that of means other than canopy, such as rotary devices, etc.

The greater portion of the personal equipment program is a continuing research and development program, contributing factors being that human tolerances have not as yet been definitely established and the rapidly changing design of aircraft. Further, this whole program entails an intensive research in new materials, as well as the problem of integration; that is, the integration of flotation, restraint devices, items of apparel, to achieve simplicity and the elimination of as many separate items of personal equipment as possible.

MILLARD L. HASKIN, Colonel, Air Corps
Chief, Personal Equipment Laboratory
Engineering Division
Air Materiel Command

(The Personal Equipment Laboratory was located at Wright Field, Ohio.)

Appendix B: "Kit, Clothing, and Equipment, Flyer," Technical Order no. 00-30-41, Headquarters, Army Air Forces, Washington, D.C., Apr. 16, 1942.

RESTRICTED

WAR DEPARTMENT
HEADQUARTERS OF THE ARMY AIR FORCES
WASHINGTON

TECHNICAL ORDER
No. 00-30-41

April 16, 1942

KITS AND SETS OF EQUIPMENT
KIT, CLOTHING AND EQUIPMENT, FLYER

This Technical Order replaces Technical Order No. 00-30-41, dated September 12, 1941.

1. The Flying Clothing and Equipment Kit will be assembled to provide pilots and crewmen with supplementary outer clothing, oxygen masks and parachutes. These articles are for individual use and protection of personnel on flight operations in extreme climatic conditions or at high altitudes.

2. The Basis of Issue is set forth in the Table of Basic Allowances, Number 1, Section II, Air Corps Equipment, and authorizes the issue of six of these Kits to each Observation Squadron and Pursuit Squadron; four to each Air Base Squadron, Materiel Squadron and Depot Group Headquarters Squadron; three to each Pursuit Group Headquarters Squadron; and one to each Flyer, Bombardment Airplane, Reconnaissance Airplane and Photographic Airplane.

3. The Kit is issued to Flyers and Organizations in addition to regular clothing issues and consists of the following items:

Part No.   *Class 13*

Part No.				
40K3719	(a)	1 ea.	Bag assy., flyer's clothing, type B-4, Spec. 6-289.	
0158791		1 ea.	Bag, flyer's kit, type A-3.	
		1 ea.	Cap, flying, summer, type B-1, Spec. 3095.	
		1 ea.	Cap, flying, winter, type B-2, Spec. 3096.	
AN-6531		1 pr.	Glasses, sun, flying, Spec. AN-GG-G-401,	
			OR	
34B4023		1 pr.	Goggle assy., flying, type D-1, Spec. 94-3064.	
39D1569	(a)	1 pr.	Gloves, flying, winter, type A-10, Spec. 3093,	
			OR	
34D3414	(b)	1 pr.	Gloves, flying, winter, type A-9.	
33D4018		1 pr.	Goggle assy., flying, type B-7,	
			OR	
12843		1 pr.	Goggle assy., flying, type B-6 (American Optical).	
33G5979	(a),(c)	1 ea.	Helmet, flying, summer, type A-8,	
			OR	
42G6861	(a),(c)	1 ea.	Helmet, flying, summer, type A-9.	
32C-415	(a),(c)	1 ea.	Helmet, flying, winter, type B-5,	
			OR	
42G6431	(a),(c)	1 ea.	Helmet, flying, winter, type B-6.	
30-1415		1 ea.	Jacket, flying, type A-2.	
33H5595		1 ea.	Jacket, flying, winter, type B-3,	
			OR	
39H4825		1 ea.	Jacket, flying, winter, type B-6.	
42G4764		1 ea.	Mask, oxygen, type A-8B, Spec. 94-3107,	
			OR	
	(d)	1 ea.	Mask, oxygen, type A-9, Spec. 3125.	
		1 ea.	Parachute, complete.	

NOTICE: This document contains information affecting the National Defense of the United States within the meaning of the Espionage Act (U. S. C. 50:31:32). The transmission of this document or the revelation of its contents in any manner to an unauthorized person is prohibited.

RESTRICTED

RESTRICTED　　　　　　　　T.O. No. 00-30-41

Part No.　　　　　　　　　　Class 13 (Cont'd).

Part No.		
41B9606	1 ea.	Scarf, flying, silk.
	1 pr.	Shoes, flying, winter, type A-6, Spec. 3081.
30-732	1 ea.	Suit, flying, summer, type A-4 (olive drab).
33H5592	1 pr.	Trousers, flying, winter, type A-3,
		OR
39H 826	1 pr.	Trousers, flying, winter, type A-5.
	1 ea.	Vest, flying, winter, type C-2, Spec. 3055.
(e)	1 ea.	Vest, life preserver, type B-3, Spec. 94-3065.

NOTES: Size requirements should be carefully computed in order that total amounts authorized per squadron will permit satisfactory distribution.

(a) Substitute items will always be issued first.

(b) Gloves, flying, winter, type A-9 issued only in the Continental United States to personnel assigned to Aircraft having open cockpits and to personnel located outside the Continental United States, in extremely cold climates.

(c) Helmets issued only to personnel assigned to aircraft having open cockpits or other aircraft having sliding canopies and similar enclosures, the opening of which is necessary during flight, in the proper performance of all missions.

(d) Type A-9 Oxygen masks can be used only on aircraft equipped with A-12 demand type regulator.

(e) Life preserver vests issued only as required for overwater flights.

By Command of Lieutenant General ARNOLD:

H. J. F. MILLER
Major General, U.S.A.,
Commanding General, Air Service Command.

-2-

RESTRICTED

Appendix C: "Kit, Flyer's Clothing and Equipment," Technical Order no. 00-30-41, Headquarters, Army Air Forces, Washington, D.C., Oct. 20, 1945.

RESTRICTED
AAF DISTRIBUTION CODES: 00

HEADQUARTERS, ARMY AIR FORCES
WASHINGTON 25, D. C.

TECHNICAL ORDER
NO. 00-30-41

INDEXES AND PUBLICATIONS OF A GENERAL NATURE

20 October 1945

KITS AND SETS OF EQUIPMENT

KIT, FLYER'S CLOTHING AND EQUIPMENT

This Technical Order replaces T. O. No. 00-30-41, dated 15 February 1945. Approved changes accruing subsequent to the date of this Technical Order are published monthly in T. O. No. 00-30-1A, and reference will be made thereto in conjunction with this Technical Order.

TABLE OF CONTENTS

Section		Page
I	Basic Clothing and Equipment, AAF Personnel	2
II	Additional Clothing, Issued According to Type of Aircraft and Crew Positions	4
III	Additional Clothing for Air Transport Command and Troop Carrier Command Crew Members	6
IV	Additional Clothing for Special Operations as Required, AAF Personnel	7
V	Parachutes, AAF Personnel	8
VI	Basic Clothing and Equipment, AGF Liaison Pilot	8
VII	Additional Clothing, AGF Liaison Pilot	9

1. PURPOSE.

The kit will be assembled to provide pilots and crewmen with supplementary outer clothing and equipment for individual use and protection on flight operation, and is in addition to regular clothing issue.

2. SPECIAL INFORMATION.

<u>a</u>. Size requirements will be carefully determined and entered on the requisition in order that each individual will receive the correct size of each article.

<u>b</u>. THE ITEMS LISTED IN THIS TECHNICAL ORDER ARE THE LATEST STANDARD ITEMS OF AAF EQUIPMENT, HOWEVER, THE LIMITED STANDARD AND SUBSTITUTE STANDARD ITEMS OF AAF EQUIPMENT WILL BE ISSUED IN LIEU THEREOF UNTIL SUCH TIME AS AAF STOCKS HAVE BEEN SUFFICIENTLY DEPLETED TO PERMIT PROCUREMENT AND ISSUE OF THE STANDARD ITEMS LISTED HEREIN. REQUISITIONS FOR THIS EQUIPMENT WILL LIST THE STANDARD ITEM.

<u>c</u>. Flying clothing not suitable for climatic conditions of destination will be replaced accordingly at staging points.

<u>d</u>. The letters (NA) preceding an item denotes it is not presently available for issue and will not be requisitioned until the designation is removed either by a revision of this Technical Order or T. O. No. 00-30-1A.

<u>e</u>. This Technical Order consists of seven sections. Sections I through V list flying clothing for AAF personnel. Sections VI and VII list flying clothing for AGF liaison pilots.

(1) SECTION I - BASIC CLOTHING AND EQUIPMENT, AAF PERSONNEL.

(<u>a</u>) Items of individual clothing and equipment listed in this section will be issued to all qualified AAF flying personnel (commissioned or enlisted) who have attained a flying rating and who are on flying status. (Personnel on flying status are those who are entitled to and are receiving flying pay.)

(<u>b</u>) Additional clothing and equipment which may be required for special operations and/or conditions, locations, etc may be obtained according to the conditions set forth in the following sections.

(<u>c</u>) Oxygen equipment will not be issued to Glider Pilots, Helicopter Pilots or to personnel not on flying status who are issued flying clothing and equipment by T/E authorization.

(2) SECTION II - ADDITIONAL CLOTHING, ISSUED ACCORDING TO TYPE OF AIRCRAFT AND CREW POSITIONS.

(<u>a</u>) Items of individual clothing listed in this

NOTICE: This document contains information affecting the national defense of the United States within the meaning of the Espionage Act, 50 U. S. C., 31 and 32, as amended. Its transmission or the revelation of its contents in any manner to an unauthorized person is prohibited by law.

RESTRICTED
T. O. No. 00-30-41

section will be issued in addition to "Basic Clothing and Equipment" (Section I) according to type of aircraft and crew position.

(b) Clothing and equipment for pilots and crew members of tactical aircraft, other than types specifically mentioned in this section, will be covered under "Basic Clothing and Equipment" (Section I) and "Parachutes" (Section V).

(3) SECTION III - ADDITIONAL CLOTHING FOR AIR TRANSPORT COMMAND AND TROOP CARRIER COMMAND CREW MEMBERS.

(a) Items of individual clothing listed in this section will be issued to all crew members in addition to "Basic Clothing and Equipment" (Section I).

(4) SECTION IV - ADDITIONAL CLOTHING FOR SPECIAL OPERATIONS AS REQUIRED, AAF PERSONNEL.

(a) Items of individual clothing listed in this section may be issued in addition to "Basic Clothing and Equipment" (Section I) as special operations or conditions may require and when requested by the Air Force Commander.

(5) SECTION V - PARACHUTES, AAF PERSONNEL.

(a) Parachutes listed in this section, or any subsequent types developed, will be issued to all flying personnel on the basis of one each of the appropriate type.

(b) Parachutes will be issued on memorandum or hand receipt to personnel (commissioned or enlisted) who are on flying status at stations to which they are assigned. (Personnel on flying status are those who are entitled to and are receiving flying pay.) Upon change of station issue of parachutes will be governed by the following conditions:

1. If transfer is by tactical aircraft, the parachute will be retained by the individual.

2. If transfer is by other than tactical aircraft, the parachute will be turned in and another issued at the new station assignment.

3. If the individual is removed from flying status, the parachute will be turned in.

(6) SECTION VI - BASIC CLOTHING AND EQUIPMENT, AGF LIAISON PILOT.

(a) Items of individual clothing and equipment listed in this section will be issued to all qualified AGF Pilots.

(7) SECTION VII - ADDITIONAL CLOTHING, AGF LIAISON PILOT.

(a) Items of individual clothing listed in this section are for winter use of AGF Liaison Pilots and will be issued in addition to the items listed in Section VI, only when authorized by AGF, Division Commander.

f. Abbreviations used herein are in accordance with T. O. No. 00-35A-6.

3. CONTENTS.

The Kit consists of the following items:

SECTION I

BASIC CLOTHING AND EQUIPMENT, AAF PERSONNEL

(Refer to paragraph 2.e.(1) of "Introduction.")

	STOCK NO.	CLASS 13	UNIT	ISSUE
	8300-022100	Bag Assy - Flyer's clothing, type B-4, Specification No. 6-289	ea	1
	8300-022200	Bag - Aviator's kit, part No. AN6505-1	ea	1
(a)	8300-190500	Detector Assy - Demand oxygen mask leak	ea	1
	8300-290411	Glasses - Flying, sun, with rose smoke lens	pr	1
		Gloves - Flying, summer, type B-3, Specification No. 3176	pr	1
	8300-298310	Size 8		
	8300-298312	Size 9		
	8300-298314	Size 10		
	8300-298316	Size 11		
		Gloves - Flying, winter, type A-11, Specification No. 3143	pr	1
	8300-298880	Extra large		
	8300-298890	Large		
	8300-298900	Medium		
	8300-298910	Small		
	8300-331450	Goggle Assy - Dark adaptation, type E-1, Specification No. 3142	pr	1
	8300-336050	Goggle Assy - Flying, type B-8, Specification No. 3200	pr	1

RESTRICTED

Appendix C (continued)

RESTRICTED
T. O. No. 00-30-41

STOCK NO.	CLASS 13 (cont)	UNIT	ISSUE
	Helmet - Flying, intermediate, type A-11, Specification No. 3189	ea	1
8300-396000	Extra large		
8300-396010	Large		
8300-396015	Medium		
8300-396020	Small		
	Helmet - Flying, summer, type A-10A, Specification No. 3230	ea	1
8300-416580	Extra large		
8300-416590	Large		
8300-416600	Medium		
8300-416610	Small		
	Insert - Glove, rayon, for types A-11 and A-12 glove	pr	1
8300-456000	Extra large		
8300-456010	Large		
8300-456020	Medium		
8300-456030	Small		
	Jacket - Flying, intermediate, type B-15B, Specification No. 3220	ea	1
8300-470728	Size 34		
8300-470730	Size 36		
8300-470732	Size 38		
8300-470734	Size 40		
8300-470736	Size 42		
8300-470738	Size 44		
NA(b)	Mask - Oxygen, type A-13A	ea	1
8300-595885	Large		
8300-595888	Medium		
8300-595890	Small		
	Mask - Oxygen, type A-14A, Specification No. 3163	ea	1
8300-595891	Extra small		
8300-595892	Large		
8300-595893	Medium		
8300-595894	Small		
	Shoes - Flying, winter, type A-6, Specification No. 94-3081	pr	1
8300-720850	Extra large, modified		
8300-720950	Large, modified		
8300-721950	Medium, modified		
8300-722950	Small, modified		
8300-723200	XX Large, modified		
8300-723220	XXX Large, modified		
(c)	Suit - Flying, very light, type K-1, Specification No. 3232	ea	2
8300-809970	Large, long		
8300-809980	Large, regular		
8300-809990	Medium, long		
8300-810000	Medium, regular		
8300-810010	Medium, short		
8300-810030	Small, regular		
8300-810040	Small, short		
(d)	Suit - Flying, light, type L-1, Specification No. 3237	ea	2
8300-784850	Large, long		
8300-784860	Large, regular		
8300-784870	Medium, long		
8300-784880	Medium, regular		
8300-784890	Medium, short		
8300-784910	Small, regular		
8300-784920	Small, short		
	Trousers - Flying, intermediate, type A-11A, Specification No. 3219	pr	1
8300-878648	Size 28		
8300-878650	Size 30		
8300-878652	Size 32		
8300-878654	Size 34		
8300-878656	Size 36		
8300-878658	Size 38		
(e) 8300-667650	Preserver - Pneumatic, life vest, type B-5 (to be issued as required for over water flights only)		
NA 8300-981000	Visor Assy - Flying, attachable, type A-1	ea	1

RESTRICTED

RESTRICTED
T. O. No. 00-30-41

| STOCK NO. | CLASS 13 (cont) | UNIT | ISSUE |

NOTE (a) Issued to flyers equipped with demand type oxygen mask, for use in conjunction with Kit, Oxygen Testing, T. O. No. 00-30-156.

(b) Issued for use in photographic reconnaissance fighter and bombardment type aircraft capable of operating above 35,000 ft altitude when equipped with pressure demand regulators.

(c) Will be supplied for use in the Central Pacific, Southwest Pacific, South Pacific, Asiatic, and Caribbean Theaters of Operation. Will be issued at final staging areas in accordance with "Itemized Baggage Lists and Supplements (War Department Pamphlet No. 38-6, dated January 1945") and Movement Orders.

(d) Will be supplied for use in the European, Mediterranean and Alaskan Theaters of Operation. Will be issued at final staging areas in accordance with "Itemized Baggage Lists and Supplements (War Department Pamphlet No. 38-6, dated January 1945") and Movement Orders.

(e) To be issued as required for over water flights.

CLASS 16-A

	Stock No.	Description	Unit	Issue
	1600-207625000	Head Set - HS-38	ea	1
(f)	1600-208655800	Microphone - ANB-M-C1	ea	1

NOTE (f) Will not be issued to Glider Pilots or Helicopter Pilots. Will be installed in oxygen mask by competent personnel concurrently with the issuance thereof to using individual.

SECTION II

ADDITIONAL CLOTHING ISSUED ACCORDING TO TYPE OF
AIRCRAFT AND CREW POSITIONS

(Refer to paragraph 2.e.(2) of "Introduction.")

BOMBARDMENT (VH) - FOR ALL CREW MEMBERS

CLASS 13

Stock No.	Description	Unit	Issue
	Gloves - Electrically heated, insert and shell, for type F-2 and F-3 electrically heated flying suit	pr	1
8300-293485	Size 8		
8300-293490	Size 9		
8300-293495	Size 10		
8300-293500	Size 11		
	Gloves - Flying, winter, type A-9A, Specification No. 94-4070	pr	1
8300-298370	Extra large		
8300-298380	Large		
8300-298390	Medium		
8300-298410	Small		
	Jacket - Flying, winter, type B-11, Specification No. 3178	ea	1
8300-541700	Size 36		
8300-541705	Size 38		
8300-541710	Size 40		
8300-541715	Size 42		
8300-541720	Size 44		
8300-541725	Size 46		
	Shoe - Insert, flying, electric, type Q-1	pr	1
8300-701460	Small		
8300-701480	Medium		
8300-701500	Large		
8300-701520	X Large		
8300-701540	XX Large		

RESTRICTED

RESTRICTED
T. O. No. 00-30-41

STOCK NO.	CLASS 13 (cont)	UNIT	ISSUE
	Trousers - Flying, winter, type A-10, Specification No. 3179	pr	1
8300-933850	Size 36		
8300-933855	Size 38		
8300-933860	Size 40		
8300-933865	Size 42		
8300-933870	Size 44		
8300-933875	Size 46		
	Jacket - Flying, electrically heated, type F-3A, Specification No. 3213B	ea	1
8300-470670	Large, long		
8300-470673	Large, regular		
8300-470676	Medium, long		
8300-470679	Medium, regular		
8300-470682	Small, long		
8300-470685	Small, regular		
	Trousers - Flying, electrically heated, type F-3A, Specification No. 3212B	pr	1
8300-878525	Large, regular		
8300-878530	Medium, long		
8300-878535	Medium, regular		
8300-878540	Small, long		
8300-878545	Small, regular		

BOMBARDMENT (H) - FOR ALL CREW MEMBERS

STOCK NO.		UNIT	ISSUE
	Gloves - Flying, winter, type A-9A, Specification No. 94-4070	pr	1
8300-298370	Extra large		
8300-298380	Large		
8300-298390	Medium		
8300-298410	Small		
	Gloves - Electrically heated, insert and shell, for types F-2 and F-3 electrically heated flying suit	pr	1
8300-293485	Size 8		
8300-293490	Size 9		
8300-293495	Size 10		
8300-293500	Size 11		
	Shoe - Insert, flying, electric, type Q-1 (For all crew members except ball turret gunners)	pr	1
8300-701460	Small		
8300-701480	Medium		
8300-701500	Large		
8300-701520	X Large		
8300-701540	XX Large		
	Jacket - Flying, electrically heated, type F-3A, Specification No. 3213B	ea	1
8300-470670	Large, long		
8300-470673	Large, regular		
8300-470676	Medium, long		
8300-470679	Medium, regular		
8300-470682	Small, long		
8300-470685	Small, regular		
	Trousers - Flying, electrically heated, type F-3A, Specification No. 3212B	pr	1
8300-878520	Large, long		
8300-878525	Large, regular		
8300-878530	Medium, long		
8300-878535	Medium, regular		
8300-878540	Small, long		
8300-878545	Small, regular		

FOR BALL TURRET GUNNERS ONLY

STOCK NO.		UNIT	ISSUE
	Boots - Felt, outer shell, for type F-2 electrically heated insert	pr	1
8300-037730	Size 6		
8300-037740	Size 8		
8300-037750	Size 10		
8300-037760	Size 12		

RESTRICTED

RESTRICTED
T. O. No. 00-30-41

STOCK NO.	CLASS 13 (cont)	UNIT	ISSUE
	Insert - Electrically heated shoe, for type F-2 electrically heated flying suit, Specification No. 3159		1
8300-455300	Small		
8300-455310	Medium		
8300-455320	Large		
8300-455330	Extra large		

FOR EXPOSED GUNNERS ONLY

	Helmet - Flying, winter, Specification No. AN-H-16 (AN 6543)	ea	1
8300-429240	Extra large		
8300-429250	Large		
8300-429260	Medium		
8300-429270	Small		
	Jacket - Flying, winter, type B-11, Specification No. 3178	ea	1
8300-541695	Size 34		
8300-541700	Size 36		
8300-541705	Size 38		
8300-541710	Size 40		
8300-541715	Size 42		
8300-541720	Size 44		
8300-541725	Size 46		
	Trousers - Flying, winter, type A-10, Specification No. 3179	pr	1
8300-933845	Size 34		
8300-933850	Size 36		
8300-933855	Size 38		
8300-933860	Size 40		
8300-933865	Size 42		
8300-933870	Size 44		
8300-933875	Size 46		

FIGHTER PILOTS

(g)	Suit - Pilot, pneumatic, anti-"G," single pressure, type G-3A, Specification No. R-3231A	ea	1
8300-858460	Large, long		
8300-858465	Large, short		
8300-858470	Small, long		
8300-858475	Small, short		
8300-156100	Cushion - Parachute seat, 2-1/4 in. thick, Latex sponge rubber	ea	1

NOTE (g) One suit per Fighter Pilot, except P-59, P-61, and P-63 aircraft. Issue will be made at the AAF Combat Crew Processing and Distribution Center and record made on AAF Form 121. Upon completion of training these suits will be retained by the pilot. Upon departure for overseas pilots should have anti-"G" suits in their possession when they arrive at staging points and ports of embarkation. Replacement will be made only when suit is declared unserviceable.

SECTION III

AIR TRANSPORT COMMAND AND TROOP CARRIER COMMAND
FOR ALL CREW MEMBERS

(Refer to paragraph 2.e.(3) of "Introduction.")

	Jacket - Flying, winter, type B-11, Specification No. 3178	ea	1
8300-541695	Size 34		
8300-541700	Size 36		
8300-541705	Size 38		
8300-541710	Size 40		
8300-541715	Size 42		
8300-541720	Size 44		
8300-541725	Size 46		

RESTRICTED

RESTRICTED
T. O. No. 00-30-41

STOCK NO.	CLASS 13 (cont)	UNIT	ISSUE
	Trousers - Flying, winter, type A-10, Specification No. 3179	pr	1
8300-933845	Size 34		
8300-933850	Size 36		
8300-933855	Size 38		
8300-933860	Size 40		
8300-933865	Size 42		
8300-933870	Size 44		
8300-933875	Size 46		

SECTION IV

ADDITIONAL CLOTHING FOR SPECIAL OPERATIONS AS REQUIRED

(Refer to paragraph 2.e.(4) of "Introduction.")

	STOCK NO.		UNIT	ISSUE
		Boot - Felt, outer shell for types F-2 or F-3 electrically heated shoe insert	pr	1
	8300-037730	Size 6		
	8300-037740	Size 8		
	8300-037750	Size 10		
	8300-037760	Size 11		
		Gloves - Electrically heated insert and shell, for types F-2 and F-3 electrically heated flying suit, Specification No. 3184	pr	1
	8300-293485	Size 8		
	8300-293490	Size 9		
	8300-293495	Size 10		
	8300-293500	Size 11		
		Gloves - Flying, winter, type A-9A, Specification No. 94-4070	pr	1
	8300-298370	Extra large		
	8300-298380	Large		
	8300-298390	Medium		
	8300-298410	Small		
NA	8300-384550	Heater - Oxygen mask, electric, type E-2, for A-13A oxygen mask	ea	1
		Helmet - Flying, winter, Specification No. AN-H-16 (AN 6543)	ea	1
	8300-429240	Extra large		
	8300-429250	Large		
	8300-429260	Medium		
	8300-429270	Small		
		Insert Assy - For type A-14 shoe, Specification No. 3152	ea	1
	8300-455000	Large		
	8300-455010	Medium		
	8300-455020	Small		
		Jacket - Flying, winter, type B-11, Specification No. 3178	ea	1
	8300-541695	Size 34		
	8300-541700	Size 36		
	8300-541705	Size 38		
	8300-541710	Size 40		
	8300-541715	Size 42		
	8300-541720	Size 44		
	8300-541725	Size 46		
	8300-592250	Mask - Face, type D-1, cold weather, Specification No. 3146	ea	1
		Shoe - Insert, flying, electric, type Q-1	pr	1
	8300-701460	Small		
	8300-701480	Medium		
	8300-701500	Large		
	8300-701520	X Large		
	8300-701540	XX Large		
		Shoes - Flying, Arctic, type A-14, Mukluk, Specification No. 3151	pr	1
	8300-703290	Large		
	8300-703300	Medium		
	8300-703310	Small		

RESTRICTED

RESTRICTED
T. O. No. 00-30-41

STOCK NO.	CLASS 13 (cont)	UNIT	ISSUE
	Trousers - Flying, winter, type A-10, Specification No. 3179	pr	1
8300-933845	Size 34		
8300-933850	Size 36		
8300-933855	Size 38		
8300-933860	Size 40		
8300-933865	Size 42		
8300-933870	Size 44		
8300-933875	Size 46		
	Jacket - Flying, electrically heated, type F-3A, Specification No. 3213B	ea	1
8300-470670	Large, long		
8300-470673	Large, regular		
8300-470676	Medium, long		
8300-470679	Medium, regular		
8300-470682	Small, long		
8300-470685	Small, regular		
	Trousers - Flying, electrically heated, type F-3A, Specification No. 3212B	pr	1
8300-878520	Large, long		
8300-878525	Large, regular		
8300-878530	Medium, long		
8300-878535	Medium, regular		
8300-878540	Small, long		
8300-878545	Small, regular		

SECTION V

PARACHUTES

(Refer to paragraph 2.e.(5) of "Introduction.")

8300-635310	Parachute Assy - Complete, quick release harness, 24 ft back type B-10A	ea	1
	OR		
8300-635410	Parachute Assy - Complete, type A-5A, chest type, quick release	ea	1
	OR		
8300-637150	Parachute Assy - Complete, quick release harness, 24 ft seat type S-6A	ea	1

SECTION VI

BASIC CLOTHING AND EQUIPMENT, AGF
LIAISON PILOT

(Refer to paragraph 2.e.(6) of "Introduction.")

8300-022100	Bag Assy - Flyer's clothing, type B-4, Specification No. 6-289	ea	1
8300-022200	Bag - Aviator's kit, part No. AN6505-1	ea	1
8300-336050	Goggle Assy - Flying, type B-8, Specification No. 3200	ea	1
	Helmet - Flying, summer, type A-10A, Specification No. 3230	ea	1
8300-416580	Extra large		
8300-416590	Large		
8300-416600	Medium		
8300-416610	Small		
	Jacket - Flying, intermediate, type B-15B, Specification No. 3220	ea	1
8300-470728	Size 34		
8300-470730	Size 36		
8300-470732	Size 38		
8300-470734	Size 40		
8300-470736	Size 42		
8300-470738	Size 44		

RESTRICTED

Appendix C (continued) 145

RESTRICTED
T. O. No. 00-30-41

	STOCK NO.	CLASS 13 (cont)	UNIT	ISSUE
(h)		Suit - Flying, very light, type K-1, Specification No. 3232	ea	2
	8300-809970	Large, long		
	8300-809980	Large, regular		
	8300-809990	Medium, long		
	8300-810000	Medium, regular		
	8300-810010	Medium, short		
	8300-810030	Small, regular		
	8300-810040	Small, short		
		OR		
(i)		Suit - Flying, light, type L-1, Specification No. 3237	ea	2
	8300-784850	Large, long		
	8300-784860	Large, regular		
	8300-784870	Medium, long		
	8300-784880	Medium, regular		
	8300-784890	Medium, short		
	8300-784910	Small, regular		
	8300-784920	Small, short		
(j)	8300-667650	Preserver - Pneumatic, life vest, type B-5	ea	1
NA	8300-981000	Visor Assy - Flying, attachable, type A-1	ea	1

NOTE (h) Will be supplied for use in the Central Pacific, Southwest Pacific, South Pacific, Asiatic, and Caribbean Theaters of Operation. Will be issued at final staging areas in accordance with "Itemized Baggage Lists and Supplements (War Department Pamphlet No. 38-6, dated January 1945") and Movement Orders.

(i) Will be supplied for use in the European, Mediterranean and Alaskan Theaters of Operation. Will be issued at final staging areas in accordance with "Itemized Baggage Lists and Supplements (War Department Pamphlet No. 38-6, dated January 1945") and Movement Orders.

(j) To be issued as required for over water flights

SECTION VII

ADDITIONAL CLOTHING, AGF LIAISON PILOT

(Refer to paragraph 2.e.(7) of "Introduction.")

STOCK NO.		UNIT	ISSUE
	Gloves - Flying, winter, type A-11	pr	1
8300-298880	Extra large		
8300-298890	Large		
8300-298900	Medium		
8300-298910	Small		
	Helmet - Flying, intermediate, type A-11, Specification No. 3189	ea	1
8300-396000	Extra large		
8300-396010	Large		
8300-396015	Medium		
8300-396020	Small		
	Insert - Glove, rayon	pr	1
8300-456000	Extra large		
8300-456010	Large		
8300-456020	Medium		
8300-456030	Small		
	Shoes - Flying, winter, type A-6, Specification No. 94-3081	pr	1
8300-720850	Extra large, modified		
8300-720950	Large, modified		
8300-721950	Medium, modified		
8300-722950	Small, modified		
8300-723200	XX large, modified		
8300-723220	XXX large, modified		

RESTRICTED

RESTRICTED
T. O. No. 00-30-41

STOCK NO.	CLASS 13 (cont)	UNIT	ISSUE
	Trousers - Flying, intermediate, type A-11A, Specification No. 3219	pr	1
8300-878648	Size 28		
8300-878650	Size 30		
8300-878652	Size 32		
8300-878654	Size 34		
8300-878656	Size 36		
8300-878658	Size 38		

BY COMMAND OF GENERAL ARNOLD:

H. J. KNERR
Major General, U.S.A.
Commanding General
Air Technical Service Command

RESTRICTED

Appendix D: "Clothing—Refinishing Sheep Shearling Type Flying Clothing," Technical Order no. 13-1-10, Headquarters, Army Air Forces, Washington, D.C., Oct. 16, 1943.

RESTRICTED
DIST: 1
FILE: BEHS

WAR DEPARTMENT
HEADQUARTERS OF THE ARMY AIR FORCES
WASHINGTON

TECHNICAL ORDER
No. 13-1-10

October 16, 1943

CLOTHING, PARACHUTES, EQUIPMENT AND SUPPLIES

CLOTHING—REFINISHING SHEEP SHEARLING TYPE CLOTHING

NOTE *The work directed herein will be accomplished when necessary by service activities with the aid of the sub-depots, if necessary.*

1. GENERAL.

A wide spread condition of unserviceable and unsightly sheep shearling clothing has resulted due to extreme wear and the use of some poorly tanned leather in the manufacture of this clothing. After a period of service use these garments become faded, cracked, and peeled. To augment further serviceability and to enhance their appearance sheep shearling garments will be refinished in accordance with the procedure outlined herein.

2. PREPARATION OF SURFACE.

a. When necessary, shearling garments will be thoroughly cleaned and repaired before refinishing. Action to install dry cleaning units at all control depots has been initiated. However, until such a time as these facilities are available, shearling garments may be either forwarded to master local dry cleaning establishments using the Stoddard solvent method or to a fur cleaner using the sawdust method.

NOTICE: This document contains information affecting the national defense of the United States within the meaning of the Espionage Act, 50 U.S.C., 31 and 32, as amended. Its transmission or the revelation of its contents in any manner to an unauthorized person is prohibited by law.

RESTRICTED
T.O. No. 13-1-10

NOTE *THE USE OF CARBON TETRACHLORIDE AS A CLEANING AGENT IS PROHIBITED.*

b. Remaining old finish or paint insignias will be removed with a soft cloth saturated with acetone. An appearance of brown color on the cloth indicates old finish has been removed. The garment should then be dried for a period of 1 hour. THE ACETONE WILL BE APPLIED AND REMOVED AS QUICKLY AS POSSIBLE DUE TO THE FACT THAT IT IS EXTREMELY VOLATILE.

CAUTION *Acetone will be handled with extreme care, as it is highly inflammable; flash point being 3°F. The room in which the removal of the top finish is being accomplished will be well ventilated to prevent a high concentration of fumes. Due to the small amount needed to accomplish this work, only a small quantity will be stored in the department at any one time.*

3. APPLICATION OF LEATHER DYE (POLY-ACRYLATE).

a. Poly-acrylate will be applied with a paint brush or a piece of rug using the nap side. If these are not available a "wool" sponge may be used. A varnish brush will not be used for this work.

b. Before using, the poly-acrylate will be well mixed.

c. To four parts of the base color (poly-acrylate) add one part of water. This is the proper ratio for best results.

d. In applying the poly-acrylate dip brush into the solution, remove excessive acrylate by wiping brush against side of container.

e. The poly-acrylate should then be worked into the pores of the leather, care being taken not to leave any dry spots.

f. Hang garment to dry for 8 hours under ordinary room temperatures (70° to 75°F).

NOTE *The poly-acrylate will be kept in a warm room. If this solution freezes, it can no longer be used.*

4. APPLICATION OF THE TOP FINISH LACQUER.

a. Apply the top finish using a commercial-type paint-spray gun. Only a thin coat is necessary. Consult foreman of paint shop as to proper size of nozzle to be used and instructions as to the use of the spray gun. This procedure weatherproofs the garment, therefore extreme care should be taken not to leave dry spots.

b. The garment should then be dried for at least 2 hours at room temperature.

NOTE *To facilitate operation in spraying finish, the garment may be suspended from a clothes hanger.*

CAUTION *The spray gun will be washed out with acetone before being filled with the top finish. The spray booth in which the top finish is applied will be well ventilated and no smoking permitted.*

5. The following materials are required to accomplish this work:

QUANTITY	STOCK NO.	NOMENCLATURE	CLASS	SOURCE
As req	7300-003000	Acetone	07	AF Stock
As req	7300-382460	Poly-acrylate	07	AF Stock
As req	7300-538270	Lacquer - Top finish	07	AF Stock
1	7900-403920	Gun - Paint spray, DeVilbiss type P-MBC or equal	17-B	AF Stock

By Command of General ARNOLD:

WALTER H. FRANK,
Major General, U.S.A.,
Commanding General, Air Service Command.

RESTRICTED

Appendix E: "Preliminary Tests on Durability of Flying Clothing," Memorandum Report no. ENG-49-695-2S, Aero Medical Laboratory, Materiel Command, Wright Field, Ohio, Apr. 12, 1944.

AAFMC-266-WF-10-27-43-50M   P-1

D 23/51

ARMY AIR FORCES
MATERIEL COMMAND

MEMORANDUM REPORT ON

SUBJECT: Preliminary Tests on Durability of Flying Clothing.

CLT:jb:49
Date 12 April 1944

LABORATORY
SECTION ..... Aero Medical ....

Contract No. ....
Expenditure Order No. ..695-14..........

SERIAL No. ENG-49-695-2S ....

Purchase Order No. ....

A. Purpose:

To determine the effect of a moderate amount of wear on the thickness and thermal insulation of alpaca intermediate flying uniforms.

B. Factual Data:

1. Measurements of thickness and thermal insulation were made on two worn (60-90 hours under flight conditions), and two new alpaca intermediate flying uniforms. (Appendix 1.)

    a. Thermal insulation was determined in 4 tests on each uniform with the AML clometer. Values of clo were calculated from heat input, plate surface temperature, and clothing surface temperature.

    b. Thickness measurements were made at 16 points on each uniform. Data are in inches, measured under pressure of .1 lb. per square inch.

2. From the means and standard deviations of the new and worn series, the significance of difference in thickness and in insulation was assessed by conventional statistical methods. (Appendices 2 and 3)

C. Conclusions:

1. The differences in thickness and thermal insulation between the subject worn and new garments are insignificant.

Number of Pages - 5

AAFMC-266-WF-10-27-43-50M   Page 2

Engineering Division
Memorandum Report No. ENG-49-695-2S
12 April 1944

D. Recommendations:

    1. That this study be repeated when a larger number of uniforms is available that have been worn 300 hours or more.

Approved by *for E. A. Pinson, Capt., A.C.* A. P. GAGGE, Lt. Col., A.C.
Chief, Biophysics Branch

Prepared by *FOR Craig L. Taylor* T. JARDINEAUX, Pvt. WAC

Concurrence:

Prepared by ...CRAIG..L...TAYLOR,...1st..Lt.,..A.C.
              (Name)

Approved by W...RANDOLPH..LOVELACE,..II,..Lt.Col.
              Chief, Aero Medical Lab.   M.C.

Approved by F...O...CARROLL,..Brig..General, USA
              Chief, Engineering Division

Distribution:
  The Air Surgeon (12)

Engineering Division
Memorandum Report No. EMG-49-695-2S
12 April 1944

APPENDIX 1

Methods and Results.

1. Thermal insulation tests.
Each garment,* new and worn, was tested separately in the cold chamber at 32°F. The clometer** was placed as follows: in the jacket, the broad of the back was folded at the midline forming a single layer over each side of the clometer. The material was applied to the plate without compression. Temperatures of the clometer surface (T_s), the outer surface of the clothing (T_{ol}), and heat input were obtained every 15 minutes until equilibrium was maintained for 30 minutes. Since input was set at 100 cal/m^2/hr, temperature equilibrium was the criterion.

Two tests were made on each garment. Before the second of each, the clothing was loosened and reset on the clometer to simulate reapplication.

2. Thickness measurements.
Thickness under a pressure of .1 lb. per inch square was measured by a specially constructed metal disc and pointed steel pin.*** Six measurements were made on each garment at points within areas tested on the clometer.

3. Results.
Summaries of data in Appendices 2 and 3 show that the worn clothing has a slightly higher thermal insulation but a smaller thickness. This is contrary to established theory but is easily accounted for by the lack of significance between the means of new and used clothing for both thickness and thermal insulation. A larger number of measurements and clothing with longer wear would probably give a clearer indication of the true relationships, but the P values for the present series give no confidence that the differences are reliable either in sign or amount.

---

* The worn alpaca uniforms, supplied by the Flying Clothing Branch, were drawn from a supply which had been service tested by Capt. Monke and Lt. Wright at Biggs Field, Texas.

** The clometer is a three-layered plate, about 1/4 inch thick and 8 7/8 inches square with a total surface of .1 square meter. The inner copper layer carries constantan heating wires. The outer aluminum layers are grooved to hold a spirally wound copper wire element of a resistance thermometer. Heat input is controlled by a rheostat and read on a meter calibrated in Calories per square meter per hour. Plate surface temperature is read on a milliameter calibrated in °F.
This instrument was jointly conceived by Lt. Taylor and Dr. Guillemin and constructed, under the latter's direction by the Instrument Unit, Biophysics Branch.

*** The disc has a diameter of 3.5 inches and a thickness of .352 inch. With a face area of 9.62 square inches; Its weight of .96 lb. provides pressure of .1 lb. per square inch. It has an eighth inch hole in center.
The garment to be measured is laid flat on a steel base plate and the disc is laid over it without external pressure. The pointed steel pin is thrust through the center hole and through garment fabric to surface of under plate. The pin is then pulled out and measured.

Engineering Division
Memorandum Report No. ENG-49-695-2S
12 April 1944

APPENDIX 2

Experimental Data and Statistical Summary
of Thickness Measurements of New and
Worn Uniforms.

Measurements (64th of inch.)

	1	2	3	4	5	6
Worn jacket	11	8	10	9	8	10
Worn jacket	8	8	10	8	9	10
Worn trousers	18	10	9	9	8	9
Worn trousers	16	9	11	8	9	8
New jacket	12	11	12	11	11	11
New jacket	11	10	10	10	10	10
New trousers	9	9	9	15	10	10
New trousers	18	13	12	9	9	9

	Worn	New	Diff.	t	P
Mean	.152 in.	.170 in.	.018 in.	1.75	.09
Standard Deviation	.038 in.	.053 in.			

Appendix E (continued) 153

Engineering Division
Memorandum Report No. ENG-49-695-2S
12 April 1944

APPENDIX 3

Experimental Data and Statistical Summary
of Clo Determinations on New and Worn
Uniforms.

Garment	T_a^* (°C)	T_s (°F)	T_{cl} (°F)	$T_s - T_{cl}$ (°C)	Conductance (Cal/m²/hr/°C)	Clo $\left(\dfrac{1}{.18\ \text{Cal/m}^2/\text{hr/°C}}\right)$
Worn Jackets						
1 --	+1.0	82.7	39.7	23.9	4.184	1.32
--	-1.0	82.5	35.5	26.1	3.831	1.45
2 --	-1.5	83.4	34.0	27.4	3.649	1.52
--	-2.0	85.2	33.0	29.0	3.448	1.61
Worn Trousers						
1 --	+1.0	86.3	32.0	30.2	3.311	1.67
--	+2.8	82.9	36.0	26.0	3.846	1.44
2 --	-1.5	83.5	34.7	27.1	3.690	1.50
--	+1.3	83.0	41.0	23.3	4.291	1.30
New Jackets						
1 --	-0.7	80.1	33.0	26.1	3.831	1.45
--	0.0	81.3	33.0	26.8	3.731	1.49
2 --	-0.3	79.8	34.0	25.4	3.937	1.41
--	+3.5	81.5	37.0	24.7	4.048	1.37
New Trousers						
1 --	+1.0	85.5	41.2	24.6	4.065	1.36
--	+0.3	88.2	36.0	29.0	3.448	1.61
2 --	+1.6	85.4	38.0	26.3	3.802	1.46
--	0.0	84.5	35.0	27.5	3.636	1.52

	Worn	New	Diff.	t	P
Mean	1.48	1.46			
Standard Deviation	.118	.094	.02	.31	.76

* T_a = Ambient air temperature.

Appendix F: Type Designation Sheets (Wright Field, Ohio, 1920s through World War II)

Type Designation Sheets were forms prepared and maintained by the Equipment Branch and other sections at Wright Field from the mid-1920s through World War II. Items of flight materiel were recorded on these sheets as they were developed. The forms, a sample of which follows, constitute a valuable record of when different types of garments and other items of aeronautical equipment were tested, standardized for use, and finally declared obsolete. They also provide the specifications and drawing numbers and a brief description. Items with no dates indicating when they were declared obsolete were used on into the post—World War II period. A few items were standardized but never procured and issued. Many items of flying clothing had the same type number (e.g, the Type A-1 glove, Type A-1 helmet, Type A-1 jacket, etc.) Mechanics' clothing, oxygen equipment, anti-g garments and survival gear had similar type numbers as well. (They will be covered in a subsequent volume including their Type Designation Sheets.)

Most items of summer flying clothing were originally given type numbers in the "A" series, and most winter garments were assigned "B" series numbers. The Type A-2 summer flying jacket and the Type B-2 winter flying jacket were examples. There were exceptions: winter flying shoes, for instance, were given numbers in the "A" series, probably because there were no standard summer flying shoes when shoes were first assigned type numbers in the 1920s. In addition, the nomenclature for many items changed over the years.

The only extensive collection of copies of Type Designation Sheets known to exist today is in the possession of the National Air and Space Museum (NASM). This collection was found about 1974 among a group of old Wright Field files obtained from the U.S. Air Force. A few pages are missing, such as the sheet covering summer face masks ("A" designation). Still, the collection pertaining to flying clothing is believed to be essentially complete. Anyone who has any Type Designation Sheets is requested to send copies of them to the author at NASM for inclusion in the museum's archives.

Appendix F (continued) 155

Mat. Div. A. C. 71-Wright Field 2-3-39-2M

Type Designation Sheet

Classification Name .... Jacket ....

LETTER	BASIC CHARACTER
A	Pilot's (Summer)

Designation	Specification and Drawing Number	CHARACTERISTICS	Original Contract, Purchase Order or Expend. Order	STATUS						Obs.
				Exp.	Inact.	Service Test	Std.	Subst. Std.	Ltd. Std.	
A-1	074737	Cape with knitted wool wristlets and collar. O.D. Color.	E. O. 666-1	x		Dec. 12-26	Nov. 7-27		May 9-31	Sept. 29-44	Stock Exhausted.
A-2	31-1415 94-3040	Horse hide leather – spun silk lining; full leather collar and interlocking fasteners instead of buttons; knitted wool wristlets.				Sept. 20-30	May 9-31		April 27-43		Replaced by AN-J-3
A-3	AN-J-3 AN6552	Replaces Type A-2					April 27-43				
A-4	Norske	Commercial flight jacket constructed of whip cord with a wool fabric lining. Designed for use as a summer flying jacket for pilots.				May 1-40			Aug. 20-40		
A-4	Norske Style 1000M	Similar to the Type A-3 except that the jacket is unlined.				May 1-40			Aug. 20-40		Stock exhausted 2-12-42 Std. Cancelled
A-5	General Athletic Co. Type 31	Commercial light weight fabric jacket consisting of a "Tackletwill" outer shell somewhat similar in design to Type A-2 and a detachable knapped-wool backed twill lining.				May 19-41				July 1-43	Removed from Book
A-6		Commercial light-weight fabric consisting of a lastex whipcord outer shell, somewhat similar in design to the A-2 jacket.				Aug. 13-41				July 1-43	

Type— Jacket, Pilot's (Summer) Type A-1

Type Designation Sheet

Mat. Div. A. C. 71-Wright Field 2-3-39-2M

Classification Name ... Jacket ....

BASIC CHARACTER

Pilot's (Summer)

LETTER									
A									

| Designation | Specification and Drawing Number | CHARACTERISTICS | Original Contract, Purchase Order or Experml. Order | STATUS ||||||
				Exp.	Inact.	Service Test	Std.	Subst. Std.	Ltd. Std.	Obs.
A-7	U.S. Rubber Co. Style SA-2	Commercial light-weight fabric of a wool-backed twill material. Back lining panel of lastex material as are cuffs and waistband.				July 28-41				July 1-43 Removed from Book

Type— Jacket, Pilot's (Summer) Type A-7

Appendix F (continued)

Mat. Div. A. C. 71-Wright Field 2-3-59-2M

Type Designation Sheet

Classification Name .... Jacket

LETTER	BASIC CHARACTER
B	Pilot's (Winter)

Designation	Specification and Drawing Number	CHARACTERISTICS	Original Contract, Purchase Order or Expend. Order	STATUS							Obs.	
				Exp.	Inact.	Service Test	Std.	Subst. Std.	Ltd. Std.	Obs.	
B-1	94-3041 31-2410	Type B-10 two-piece suit separated to permit sizes to be interchangeable and closer fit when issued.					Dec. 15-31		May 8-34	Sept. 29-44	Stock Exhausted
B-2	94-3042 31-2412	Same change made on Type B-11 winter flying suit.					Dec. 15-31		May 8-34	Sept. 29-44	Stock Exhausted
B-3	94-3061 33H5595	Improved B-2 type; loose blouse effect with gusset under arm and bellows at shoulders; interlocking fasteners extend full length of front. (SHEARING) 1/2"				May 29-33	May 8-34		May 17-43		Replaced by AN-J-4
AN-J-4		Replaces Type B-3 (SHEARLING) 3/4"					May 17-43				
B-4	94-3072 35G1368	Designed in form of Alaskan parka with interlocking fasteners extending entire length of front. For pilots and mechanics in Artic temperatures.				Aug. 9-34	Nov. 7-35		April 29-41	Mar. 27-44	
B-5	3091 38H6529	Intermediate winter type for enclosed cabin. Wool fabric, warp knit, un-lined jacket with sheep shearling collar; interlocking features.				July 11-38			June 15-39	Mar. 27-44	
B-6	94-3097 39H4825	Similar to Type B-5 except fabricated from 1/4" lamb shearling.					June 12-39		May 17-43		
B-7	3120	Designed for use in Alaska; 8" longer than B-3 jacket; 1/4" shearling hood. Main body fabricated of 1" pile sheep shearling and sleeves of 5/8" sheep shearling. Front opening closed by loops and buttons.					June 12-41		Aug. 17-42		

Type— Jacket, Winter, Flying – Type B-1

Appendix F *(continued)*

Mat. Div. A. C. 71-Wright Field 2-3-39-2M

Type Designation Sheet

Classification Name ...... Jacket – Flight

LETTER	BASIC CHARACTER
B	Winter

Designation	Specification and Drawing Number	CHARACTERISTICS	Original Contract, Purchase Order or Expend. Order	Exp.	Inact.	Service Test	Std.	Subst. Std.	Ltd. Std.	Obs.
B-8	3129	Fabric knitted pile for use as Alaskian inner jacket.					Jan. 1943			
B-9	3156	Quilted casing filled with feathers. Used with Type A-8 trousers.					July 22-43	Apr. 7-44	Feb. 7-45	
B-10	3157	Intermediate Jacket. Outer shell of gabardine with alpaca pile fabric inner layer.					July 22-43			
B-11	3178	Winter Jacket. Cotton fibre windbreak outer shell with alpaca and wool pile fabric lining.			Nov. 22-43					
B-12	3203	Olive drab wool jacket used by officers as an alternate for regulation Officer's Blouse. Procured by AAF and resold to flying officers.					Oct. 30-43	Feb. 2-44		Sept. 29-44 Stock Exhausted
B-13	3214	For Flying Officer personnel.					Mar. 14-44		Jan. 8-45	
B-14	3216	For flying enlisted personnel.					Mar. 14-44		Jan. 8-45	
B-15	3220	Intermediate Pilot's flying jacket; improved design over the B-10.					Apr. 7-44		Nov. 4-44	

Type— Jacket, Pilot's, Winter, Type B-8

Appendix F (continued) 159

Mat. Div. A. C. 71-Wright Field 2-3-89-2M

Type Designation Sheet

Classification Name .... Jacket

BASIC CHARACTER
Flying (Intermediate)

LETTER
B

Designation	Specification and Drawing Number	CHARACTERISTICS	Original Contract, Purchase Order or Experml. Order	STATUS						
				Exp.	Inact.	Service Test	Std.	Subst. Std.	Ltd. Std.	Obs.
B-15A	3220	Similar to B-15 except for incorporation of oxygen hose clip and communication wire lead tabs and other minor refinements.					Nov. 4-44	May 21-45		
B-15B	3220	Basically similar to B-15A except for incorporation of rayon lining over alpaca interlining together with other minor requirement as result of service use of latter type.					May 21-45			
B-16	3224	WASP					May 4-44		Mar. 1-45	
B-17	3225	Nurse's					May 4-44			

Type—
JACKET – Flying, Intermediate, Type B-15A

Appendix G: The Preservation of Vintage Flying Clothing and Accessories

Conservation is a very complicated field of endeavor that involves dealing with a great variety of materials and conditions and an infinite number of problems. Sometimes the remedy for one problem will create another. For instance, applying a good leather dressing may help preserve a leather garment but can corrode its metal fittings. A suitable course of treatment for one object may be unsatisfactory for a similar item. In many cases, slowing further deterioration by placing an object in a safe environment is the best course of action that can be taken.

The following comments and recommendations concerning the basic care and preservation of vintage flying clothing and accessories are offered as general guidelines only. They are furnished with the concurrence of the Conservation Analytical Laboratory, Smithsonian Institution. It is strongly recommended, however, that the advice of a professional conservator be sought before any untrained person tries to treat valuable specimens. The Smithsonian Institution accepts no responsibility for any possible ill-effects that may result from applying the following suggestions to any object.

Old garments tend to become rather fragile with age, and items of old flying clothing are no exception. From its beginning, flying clothing usually was constructed quite sturdily and was normally stronger and more durable than ordinary clothing. It was intended to withstand exposure to the elements and hard usage. Still, wear-and-tear and the inevitable aging process weaken even the strongest garments, and care must be taken to preserve old flying gear if it is to survive.

The wearing of vintage flying clothing is not recommended. Because many items are now quite scarce and valuable, owners of antique aircraft and others wishing to wear period flying clothing should consider retaining original garments in a collection or exhibit and purchasing reproductions that are now available from several commercial firms. Many replica helmets, jackets, and other items are quite realistic in appearance, and some even include authentic-looking labels.

General Protection

Clothing, like most objects in a collection, requires protection from the various adverse elements of the environment. These include dust, air pollution, humidity, temperature, light, vibration, insects, rodents, molds and microorganisms, and even man himself.

The most important characteristics of the atmosphere that influence the preservation of clothing are dust, air pollution, and humidity. There is no such thing as total protection, but certain measures can be taken to help retard the deterioration process.

Enclosing objects in display or storage cases smoothes out the day-to-night variation in relative humidity caused by temperature changes and also minimizes exposure to dust and polluted air. A polyethylene dust cover is also helpful, so long as it is not sealed along the bottom.

To care for and treat any object, a collector basically should take the following steps:

1. Examine the specimen, and record its history and data while the information is readily available. Detailed photographs or drawings help.
2. Remove dirt or harmful foreign matter, or fumigate as required using methods that do no harm to the object itself.
3. Determine the specific causes of any deterioration that is found, and take action to remove or counteract them.
4. Reattach broken parts, and strengthen weak points where possible.
5. Place the specimen in a safe environment by exhibiting or storing it under as close to ideal conditions as possible.
6. Inspect the specimen periodically for signs of deterioration, mold, insect infestation, etc. Photographs or drawings are useful at this stage to help slight changes be noticed.
7. Provide the specimen additional preservation treatment as necessary. This can involve better support, fumigation, application of leather preservative at intervals, and other actions.

Before cleaning or treating any specimen, a careful check should be made to be sure that no damage will be done and that the action to be taken will cause no injurious "side effects." When any doubt exists, a professional conservator should be consulted. If this is not possible, the planned procedure should be tested either on an inconspicuous part of the object or on a similar object of no value; at least one week should be allowed for gross ill effects to become visible.

Dust

Dust is composed largely of minute mineral particles and of fibers of such items as paper and clothing. It is also often an abrasive and may collect air pollutants. When water condenses around dust particles, some of them become aggressive chemical agents that may attack a collected specimen directly. Dust disfigures items by soiling their surfaces, and its removal involves at least wiping or shaking, and perhaps even washing, which accelerate wear-and-tear and increase the risk of physical damage. Protecting clothing and other items from dust is therefore of great importance.

Air Pollution

Air is contaminated by a number of chemical compounds, especially in urban areas. Industrial fumes, motor vehicle exhaust, and emissions from heating equipment contribute chemicals that alone or in combination produce sulfuric acid and other very corrosive or oxidizing agents. Some pollutants attract water, which facilitates harmful chemical reactions.

Another source of damage from pollution is often overlooked: The air inside closed exhibit cases may become polluted by organic acids from inadequately seasoned wood or by sulfur-containing gases released from certain paints (even some latex paints), textiles, or foam rubber. Cases and exhibit materials should be carefully examined, and the use of materials that release harmful vapors should be avoided. A good dictum to remember is "If it has an odor, it can't be good." In the construction of exhibit cases or storage equipment, oak should be avoided unless it is seasoned and sealed thoroughly with paint; also to be shunned are other inadequately seasoned woods, acidic papers, paints containing lithopone, unpainted hardboard, and any materials (like plywood) made with synthetic resins that may release formaldehyde or formic acid. Display cases should be fitted with ventilation holes loosely plugged with cotton to serve as a dust filter.

Collections should be inspected frequently for indications that pollutants are causing damage. Pollutants can cause silver or gold braid to tarnish heavily and bright copper to discolor. The sulfur in some latex paints can also tarnish silver badges in a few days. Lead, such as that used in some bullets, can change into a white powdery incrustation. On other metals, crystals may form, and objects may change color because of polluted air. Iron items may rust, and brass, copper, and various alloys may corrode. Leather may become very brittle or red with rot, and heavy pollution may cause textiles to rot. Even continuous or heavy smoking in closed areas may eventually coat objects with nicotine and tar deposits and may discolor textiles, books, and paper materials. Ozone from electrostatic air filters causes rubber to crack.

Efficient air conditioning helps greatly to minimize damage from air pollution.

Humidity

Water vapor in the air and the condensation that can result from it form a potential hazard to objects in a collection. When the relative humidity rises, all organic materials absorb water. This may cause chemical reactions as in the corrosion of metals. A damp environment encourages the growth of mold, which may damage an object and leave unsightly stains. If the relative humidity falls in an exhibit or storage area, water is extracted from some materials. If too much moisture leaves, damage results: paper and leather become brittle, glue dries out and loses adhesive strength, wood warps, etc. The attic and basement are not good locations to store specimens because they frequently are either excessively damp or dry, depending on the season.

Cyclic changes in relative humidity can cause materials to swell and contract. Constant movement against the constraints of mountings causes damage. Wood may warp and chip, oil paintings may crack and flake, and other damage can occur.

The ideal humidity level varies with the type of specimen, but generally it is best to maintain a relative humidity of between 45 and 55 percent or as close to that as possible. If the relative humidity should fall below 45 percent in an area with sensitive materials such as paintings or furniture, an attempt should be made to raise it by lowering the temperature. A 10° F (6° C) fall in air temperature can cause a 20 percent rise in relative humidity. If a collection has settled into a stable condition during years of "wrong" conditions, however, it is best to leave well enough alone.

Dial-type hygrometers for determining relative humidity can be purchased at a moderate price. Often, they also indicate the temperature. Hygrometers of this type do not provide a record, so they must be checked at regular intervals and the readings recorded. If air-conditioning is not available or does not do an efficient job, the purchase of humidifying and dehumidifying appliances should be seriously considered. In selecting a humidifier, one that supplies water vapor by evaporation should be chosen. During the winter a humidifier can be used to overcome the drying effect of central heating. A dehumidifier can help significantly during the summer when the weather is often humid. If necessary, silica gel may also be used as a desiccant to extract water in storage cases; it can even be used as a ballast to stabilize cyclic changes. Again, it is always wise to consult an expert.

Temperature

The heating of objects, especially variable heating, hastens their deterioration. For example, the rubber padding on goggles and the rubber parts of flying boots are particularly vulnerable to deterioration if they are kept at high temperatures. Once rubber has become sticky or has hardened because of chemical changes, the damage is irreversible.

Lamps and ballast units should be located outside exhibit cases. If spot lamps are used they should be of the "Coolbeam" pattern that projects forward only one-third of the usual total output of radiant heat. Specimens should, of course, be kept out of the sun and other bright light.

Specimens should always be stored in a cool location. Attics should be avoided if at all possible. A temperature of between 40° and 60° F (5° and 15° C) is best, and 70° F (21° C) should be a maximum, if at all possible. Temperatures above 70° F speed the growth of molds if the relative humidity is also high, and may accelerate the life cycles of harmful insects. Low temperatures do not usually harm specimens, but fluctuating temperatures can be doubly destructive, since matter tends to expand and contract as the temperature rises and falls. If a specimen is made of two or more substances that respond to temperature changes at different rates, dangerous strains can develop. In addition, another, more serious effect of temperature variation may occur: When the air temperature drops in a closed space, relative humidity rises, and vice versa. The presence of objects may alter the effect, but any change is bad. The temperature usually must be controlled to hold relative humidity within safe limits.

Light

Excessive illumination, especially ultraviolet light, may cause chemical changes that severely damage an object. Organic materials are especially vulnerable, but even materials such as glass may be affected. One of the most common results is the fading of dyes or the changing of colors. Other types of damage include the weakening of fabrics and the deterioration of paper and leather goods. Not only the intensity of the light, but also the duration of exposure should be controlled. Sunlight should be avoided in exhibit and storage areas. If possible, the exhibit and storage areas should be kept dark when not in use.

Both natural and artificial light, especially fluorescent illumination, should be screened to protect against ultraviolet light. To accomplish this, "Plexiglas UF3" or "Lucite AR-UF3" can be used on windows, and UF4 can be used for display cases. Rolls of self-sticking plastic material called P-19, made by the 3M Company, are also available for use on windows, but they may eventually shrink and expose bare glass at the edges. Plastic tubes that slide over lamps may also be obtained from many suppliers of plastic products. Ordinary incandescent lamps, however, do not normally require UV filters because the glass bulbs filter out weak near-ultraviolet light.

Vibration

Vibration tends to increase the wear on fabric or leather items that have become fragile with age. Its effect can be minimized if textile or leather garments are free of abrasive dust and are fully supported while on exhibit—that is, lie in contact with a mannequin or with unbleached cotton padding. If tape or glue is used to hold padding, it must not come in direct contact with a specimen of clothing.

Insects

Insects can cause severe damage to organic materials, so clothing should be closely inspected for infestation upon receipt and at regular intervals thereafter. Insects can work rapidly, and the damage is often permanent. A collector should always check when a light is turned on, a book or object is opened, or a specimen is lifted. The most common insects encountered are clothes moths, silverfish, beetles of various types, and cockroaches.

Garments that are dirty or soiled with food particles or perspiration or are suspected of insect infestation should be carefully hand or custom cleaned or washed, as applicable. This should be done before the garments come in contact with other items in a collection. If the items are clean, then consideration should be given to fumigation instead of washing. Objects should be brushed inside and out before they are placed in storage. Special attention should be given to seams to make sure that insects or larvae are not present. Insects are usually attracted not so much to a fabric itself as to stains—food, beverages, perspiration—that may be on it.

Insects can also wreak havoc with other specimens in a collection. They eat the sizing in paper, the glue in book bindings, and even paper itself. They attack wood and can bore tunnels that may not be obvious except by careful examination of inside surfaces.

Moth crystals or balls consisting of paradichlorobenzene are usually effective as both an insecticide and a fungicide; they are available from most drug stores. They should, however, neither come into direct contact with a garment nor be used with objects made of patent leather. They soften not only such leather but also pyroxylin book bindings and can cause some pigments, particularly red-brown, to fade. In addition, their vapors may damage modern paints and some plastics. To be effective, insecticide concentrations such as these should be enclosed in a tightly sealed container for at least forty-eight hours. Prolonged breathing of the fumes should be avoided, since heavy doses are harmful. When any doubt exists about insect infestation, a professional exterminator should be consulted.

Rodents

Mice and rats work rapidly and can cause a lot of damage in a single night. They may eat some kinds of organic materials and use others for nest building. A close watch should be kept for droppings and for signs of gnawing on specimens or storage containers. Good storage cabinets can protect a collection against both rodents and insects. Infestations in buildings can be eliminated with traps or an Environmental Protection Agency-registered poison with prescribed safeguards, and it should be remembered before items are placed in a barn that squirrels can also cause a lot of mischief if allowed to enter storage areas.

Molds and Micro-organisms

Molds and micro-organisms will not be a problem if ambient relative humidity is maintained at all times at a level of between 45 and

50 percent. Mold (also called mildew) can be expected if a collection of specimens containing organic material is kept at or above a temperature of 70° F (21° C) and the relative humidity is allowed to exceed 65 percent. Once it starts, mold growth proceeds fastest in warmth, so a cool environment is desirable. Temperatures of between 40° and 60° F (5° and 15° C) are recommended, but higher temperatures are acceptable if the relative humidity is within the safe range.

Mildew is usually observed on specimens as a superficial, often whitish growth, produced by fungi. Clothing should be cleaned as soon as possible to prevent further discoloration and damage, and, of course, it should be moved to a more favorable environment.

If relative humidity cannot be kept low, then good circulation of air should at least be ensured. Pockets of stagnant air favor mold growth.

Damage from Careless Handling

Man is one of the greatest single sources of damage to objects. Careless handling can damage, soil, or corrode specimens, and parts can be misplaced or lost. For example, over an extended period of time the oil and moist salts on a person's hands may cause metals to rust and may stain or damage delicate fabrics. Ideally, plastic or clean cotton gloves should be worn whenever objects in a collection are handled. Spilled drinks, careless opening or dropping of objects, picking them up improperly, and "trying on" clothing may cause permanent damage. Trying on an old cap, helmet, or garment, for instance, may seem innocent enough, but hair oil and perspiration may stain the lining, attracting insects, and weak seams or zippers may split or become damaged. Careless smoking may cause small burns on fabric objects and darkening by tars. In addition, smoking certainly can present a real fire hazard if it is allowed in work or storage rooms.

Leather and Sheep Shearling Clothing

The various existing tanning, dressing, and finishing processes are intended to produce leathers that will last for long periods of time and perform certain functions. The processes yield leathers with qualities designed to suit numerous needs: leathers that are waterproof, windproof, especially flexible, or particularly suited for dyes, paints, adhesives, etc.

Leather garments of different origins do not always react to their environment in the same way and do not always benefit from the same treatments. For example, cleaning or lubricating products darken many light finishes. Some products may even cause further damage to cracking and powdery leather. Some substances may further damage leather suffering from irreversible "red rot" due to acidity caused by pollution. As previously stated, deterioration may also be caused by conditions that are excessively damp, causing mold, or too hot or dry.

Deterioration is often caused by materials other than leather that are part of the object—e.g., rusting iron snaps, hooks, or buckles will darken and embrittle adjacent leather, requiring special treatment. Leather dressings and residues of saddle soaps may cause the corrosion of adjacent brass or copper fittings such as snaps, rivets, buttons, buckles, and zippers, usually resulting in the formation of a waxy green deposit. This corrosion should be removed by carefully using a wood pick, brush, or chemical applied to a swab. Trichloroethane is excellent for this purpose; it has no solvent effect on some paints but might on others. "Shell Solv 71" gives excellent results but has an objectionable odor. Naphtha is good but somewhat slower acting. Such substances should always be used in well-ventilated areas and away from open flames or any persons who are smoking. A metal polish with "longterm" properties may help delay the formation of the green corrosion on brass and copper parts. Of course, any substance or treatment should always be tested on an inconspicuous part of an item before it is used on the main portion of the object. Substances such as polish or leather dressing should be kept off adjacent materials.

Before boots and shoes are stored in boxes or fabric shoe bags, they should have dirt and salt removed from them and should either be polished with a shoe cream or have a leather dressing applied to them. They should not be stored in plastic bags because they could mildew. Items of footwear should be stuffed with crumpled paper or have shoe trees inserted to help them retain their shape.

Zippers should be lubricated after cleaning, but care must be taken to use a lubricant sparingly to prevent flaking and smearing on adjacent areas. Plain beeswax is probably a safe lubricant to use on most zippers, but it is better to use micro-crystalline wax because beeswax may corrode copper. Some zippers made during World War II and used on flying clothing were manufactured from substitute alloys that corroded very easily. Nothing much can be done for a badly corroded zipper except to replace it with a modern zipper of the same size and style.

There is no perfect leather dressing for use on all occasions. Excellent results have been obtained with British Museum Leather Dressing, a flammable mixture of lanolin, beeswax, cedarwood oil, and hexanes. It may become somewhat sticky in warm weather, however, so it should be applied thinly. In warm climates Cerlsin wax should be used. Another leather product, Lexol, has also given good results for most uses and is readily available from most leather and craft shops. The dressing should be applied to a cheesecloth pad and rubbed gently into the leather's surface. A second application may be necessary in a day or two if the leather is very dry. The beeswax in the British Museum Leather Dressing will act on the surface of the leather as a polish. After the item has been left for two days to allow the dressing to be absorbed into the leather, it may be polished by rubbing with a soft, clean cloth. The dressing should not be rubbed into leather that is flaking or cracking. Instead, it should be lightly patted onto the surface of the leather to prevent further damage. The leather dressing should be kept off metal fittings because the wax may contain or develop acids that can eventually cause corrosion.

The preservation of shearling garments, made with the flesh side of a sheep's pelt worn on the outside, was a problem even during World War II, as flaking was common. (A polyacrylate brown dye and a lacquer top finish usually had been used on the flesh side.) Technical Order no. 13-1-10 was published to instruct AAF personnel how to refinish sheep shearling (see Appendix D), and those guidelines are still valid today. Two other points not included in that order should also be remembered: the fleece in shearling clothing is an especially attractive nesting place for insects, and shearling clothing should never be hung up since its weight might cause the hanger to tear through the shoulders.

Fabric Clothing

It is especially important that fabric garments be protected from excessive illumination, especially sunlight, to retard fading and deterioration. They should be kept clean and free of dust, oil, grease, and perspiration. Any traces of food particles may attract insects, and garments should be regularly inspected for signs of insect infestation. Proper storage is essential: fabric items should not be hung up but should be laid flat in sturdy, dust-free boxes. These boxes should then be placed in a cool location with a constant day and night relative humidity level of between 40 and 60 percent. Creasing can be prevented by stuffing with cotton or cotton muslin.

Repairs can be made by using matching colors, weights, and types of threads. When an old garment is being sewed, the type of stitch originally used in the garment should be copied, if possible. The threads holding the buttons and seams often weaken with age and may require reinforcement. If a small piece of the same type of material is needed for a repair, it may be possible to snip a piece from a seam or other area inside the garment where it will not show.

As was mentioned above, the wearing of old garments is not recommended, but if it is necessary, the wearer should make sure that the clothing is large enough so that excessive strain is not placed on the seams, buttons, and zippers. Other clean garments should always be worn under vintage clothing to protect it from perspiration. Needless to say, food particles should not be allowed to touch the clothing or collect in its pockets.

Rubber

Oxidative attack by the atmosphere—accelerated by the presence of ozone, ultraviolet radiation, and strong light—causes rubbers to harden and crack. Steps can be taken to control oxidation, however: Ozone can be excluded by avoiding electrical discharge in the vicinity (such as that caused by electrical flytraps and malfunctioning electrostatic air filters), and specimens should be protected from ultraviolet light. Unfiltered daylight, xenon-arc and mercury-arc lamps, and unfiltered fluorescent lamps should be avoided in both exhibit and storage areas. Storing specimens in a suitable box that excludes light is particularly important not only for rubber, but for other types of specimens as well. Specimens, especially rubber items, should never be stored in an attic, where high or fluctuating temperatures are encountered.

Protective dressings that incorporate ultraviolet absorbers and antioxidants are available for rubber. "Armor All Protectant," for example, claims to shield most rubbers and several other types of material against ozone, ultraviolet rays, and oxygen. Armor All is compounded of highly resistant polymers and is intended to provide a protective barrier at and beneath the surface of treated material. It is available from local auto supply and drug stores.

Unfortunately, once rubber is damaged by hardening or cracking, little can be done. The same is true of sponge rubber, such as that used as padding on goggles, once exposure to high temperatures has caused it to become sticky. As a result, prevention is of the utmost importance in preserving goods made totally or partly from rubber.

Cleaning

Frequent dry cleaning or washing fades and weakens clothing, so garments should not be cleaned on a routine or frequent basis. Fumigation should be considered if a clean garment is suspected of having insect infestation. Soiled clothing should be gently hand washed with a neutral detergent; it should never be washed with soap. Dry cleaning is also not recommended for old garments. If clothing is to be dry cleaned, however, collectors should locate cleaners who do their own work on their premises without tumbling the garments and who test the colors and fabrics before commencing work. A little more may have to be paid for such care, but it will be well worth the added expense. Cleaning will also prevent food or perspiration spots, which oxidize or "set up" with age, from turning into permanent, unsightly stains.

Garments should never be ironed or pressed to set a sharp crease, because it would cause the fibers eventually to weaken along the crease lines. Caution must also be exercised when brushing old clothing, and stiff brushes, in particular, should be used with extreme care. If a vacuum cleaner must be used (e.g., on the fleece lining of a shearling flying suit), the end of the tube should be covered with cheesecloth or other porous material to reduce the suction on the object and damage from the edges of the tube. This will lessen the possibility of damage to the garment and decrease the chance of losing buttons and badges during vacuuming. Another method of reducing suction and avoiding damage is to vacuum the specimen through a frame covered with plastic window screen. For best results, the object should be laid on a similar frame covered with plastic screening material.

Touching a metal object with bare hands should be avoided. Instead, cotton gloves should be worn, and the object should be wiped clean after it is handled. Some types of wax can provide metals with a safe protective barrier to water vapor and oxygen and can help retard rust and corrosion. In addition, a Kerodex hand cream has been designed for electronic equipment workers to use when touching metal components.

Storage

Placing an object in a safe, stabilized environment is the most important action that can be taken to preserve a specimen. Maintaining an object under favorable conditions not only is important in retarding deterioration but also is a lot safer than most types of treatment that a layman can provide. Basements, like attics, are not recommended for storing specimens.

As has already been explained, garments should be stored by laying them flat in a dark, dust- and insect-free container in an area with a relative humidity of between 45 and 55 percent and a temperature of between 40° and 60° F (5° and 15° C). A collector may not be able precisely to meet these conditions in a private home but should try to come as close to them as possible. It is important that containers allow enough ventilation to avoid condensation and buildup of acid vapors. Acid-free cardboard boxes are preferred for storing clothing; sizes up to 60 inches long by 28 inches wide by 6 inches deep are recommended. Clothing that is laid flat should not be tightly packed, folded, or creased. Any necessary folds should be filled with tissue paper or stuffed with unbleached cotton padding, since folds readily become set and may eventually be impossible to eradicate. Acid-free long-fiber paper and "alkali-reserve" paper are available from some paper-product companies and should be used for lining boxes or storage containers. Newspapers and ordinary cardboard should never be used because of their high sulfur and lignin content. In addition, the ink on newspapers can rub off and soil fabrics. Anyone who has a problem finding acid-free paper should check with a local museum or library for a nearby source.

It is emphasized again that clothing should not be stored on hangers since the weight of a garment might weaken its fabric and cause a jacket or suit to become "round-shouldered." Hangers may eventually tear through the shoulders of heavy garments; this is an especially common problem with shearling and leather flying suits. Hangers used temporarily should be well padded. Caps and hats should be stuffed with acid-free paper to maintain their shape while they are on exhibit or in storage.

Insects and mice can severely damage specimens, and clothing should be closely inspected for them upon receipt and regularly thereafter. Garments that are dirty, soiled with perspiration, or suspected of insect infestation should be carefully hand or custom cleaned or fumigated, as appropriate, before they come in contact with other items in a collection. For health reasons, it is currently considered bad practice to maintain insecticide concentrations in storage containers unless insects are suspected to be present.

Nothing should ever be stored directly on a floor because of the possibility of water damage. Instead, all items should be raised at least six inches to allow flood water to pass by. It is a good idea to cover cartons and other objects in storage with sheeting in case a leak develops in the roof or a water pipe.

Common sense should always be used in dealing with any collector's item. It cannot be stressed too much that anyone who is not sure what to do in treating a specimen should do nothing until professional advice is obtained.

The following books are recommended for further study:

Guldbeck, Per E. *The Care of Historical Collections: A Conservation Handbook for the Nonspecialist.* Nashville, Tenn.: American Association for State and Local History, 1972.

Leene, Jontina E., ed. *Textile Conservation.* Washington, D.C.: Smithsonian Institution, 1972.

Lewis, Ralph H. *Manual for Museums.* Washington, D.C.: National Park Service, U.S. Dept. of the Interior, 1976.

Abbreviations

Most of the following abbreviations are used in the text, appendixes or reference sections of this book. Other abbreviations listed below are frequently encountered by collectors of flying clothing and are included for their assistance.

AAF	Army Air Forces		Capt.	Captain
AC	Air Corps		CBI	China-Burma-India Theater of Operations
Actg.	Acting			
Adm.	Admiral		CF	Central Files
AEF	American Expeditionary Forces (World War I)		CG	Commanding General
			Cir.	Circular
Aero Med.	Aeronautical Medical		Civ.	Civilian
AFB	Air Force Base		CO	Commanding Officer
AG	Adjutant General		Co.	Company
AMC	Air Materiel Command		Col.	Colonel
AML	Aero Medical Laboratory		Cont.	Contracting
AN, A-N	Army-Navy		Dept.	Department
ANC	Army Nurse Corps		Dir.	Director
AR	Army Regulations		Div.	Division
ARC	American Red Cross		Elect.	Electric
AS	Air Service, U.S. Army		EM	Enlisted Man
Asst.	Assistant		Eng.	Engineering
Assy.	Assembly		Equip.	Equipment
ATC	Air Transport Command		ETO	European Theater of Operations
ATSC	Air Technical Service Command		Exec.	Executive
AUS	Army of the United States		Exp.	Experimental
AVG	American Volunteer Group (Flying Tigers)		F	Fahrenheit
			FAA	Federal Aviation Administration
Avn.	Aviation		Fld.	Field
Bd.	Board		FM	Field Manual
Br.	Branch		Ftr.	Fighter
Brig. Gen.	Brigadier General		FY	Fiscal Year
BuAer	Bureau of Aeronautics, U.S. Navy		G.E.	General Electric Company
C	Celsius (or Centigrade)		Gen.	General
c.	Circa		GHQ	General Headquarters, U.S. Army

GI, G.I.	Government Issue	Prod.	Production
GO	General Order	Pur.	Purchasing
Gp.	Group	PX	Post Exchange
GPO	Government Printing Office	QMC	Quartermaster Corps
Hist.	History, Historical	RA	Regular Army
HQ, Hq.	Headquarters	RAF	Royal Air Force, Great Britain
L	Large or Light	RCAF	Royal Canadian Air Force
Lab.	Laboratory	Rear Adm.	Rear Admiral
Lib.	Library	Res.	Reserve
Lt.	Lieutenant	Ret.	Retired
Lt. Col.	Lieutenant Colonel	Rpt.	Report
Lt. Gen.	Lieutenant General	S	Small
Ltr.	Letter	S., St.	Staff
M	Master or Medium	Sect.	Section
Maint.	Maintenance	Serv.	Service
Maj.	Major	Sgt.	Sergeant
Maj. Gen.	Major General	SigC.	Signal Corps
Mat.	Materiel	SO	Special Order
MC	Materiel Command or Medical Corps	SOS	Services of Supply
		Spec.	Specification
MD	Materiel Division	Sq., Sqdr.	Squadron
M.D.	Doctor of Medicine	SR	Special Regulations
Mech.	Mechanic	S/Sgt.	Staff Sergeant
Memo.	Memorandum	Sup.	Supply
Mil.	Military	Sv.	Service
Misc.	Miscellaneous	T., Tech.	Technical
M/Sgt.	Master Sergeant	Tel.	Telegram
MTO	Mediterranean Theater of Operations	TM	Technical Manual
		Tng.	Training
NACA	National Advisory Committee for Aeronautics	TO, T.O.	Technical Order
		TR	Training Regulations
NAF	Naval Aircraft Factory, Philadelphia	T/Sgt.	Technical Sergeant
		UK, U.K.	United Kingdom
NASM	National Air and Space Museum	USAAF	United States Army Air Forces
NCO	Noncommissioned Officer	USAF	United States Air Force
OCQM	Office of the Chief Quartermaster	USN	United States Navy
O.D.	Olive Drab	WAC	Woman's Army Corps
Off.	Officer or Official	Wash.	Washington, D.C.
O.G.	Olive Green	WASP	Woman's Airforce Service Pilot
OQMG	Office of the Quartermaster General	WD	War Department
		WF	Wright Field, Ohio
Orgn.	Organization	Wg.	Wing
Per.	Personnel	WPB	War Production Board
POW	Prisoner of War	X	Extra
Pr.	Pair	ZI	Zone of Interior

Notes

Introduction

1. The collection in the NASM archives includes catalogs for the E.J. Willis Company, New York, 1913; the Roold Company, France, 1913; and the General Aviation Contractors Ltd., England, 1913.

2. Benedict Crowell, *America's Munitions, 1917–1918,* Publication of the Office of the Assistant Secretary for War, Director of Munitions (Washington, D.C., 1919), pp. 317–19.

1. Problems in the Development of Flying Clothing

1. Maj. W.G. Kilner, Office of the Assistant Secretary of War, to Brig. Gen. H.C. Pratt, Mar. 19, 1932, Wright Field Central File; quoted in Edward O. Purtee, "Development of AAF Clothing and Other Personal Equipment Peculiar to Air Operations" (Three-volume unpublished study prepared for the acting director of the Air Technical Service Command, Wright Field, Ohio, May 22, 1945), vol. 1, p. 1 (hereafter cited as ATSC Study).

2. Brig. Gen. H.C. Pratt to Maj. W.G. Kilner, Apr. 7, 1932, Wright Field Central File; quoted in ibid., p. 1.

3. Memorandum Report no. EXP-M-54-653-96B, prepared by Capt. A.P. Gagge, Medical Corps, Apr. 7, 1942, Wright Field Central File; quoted in ATSC Study, vol. 1, p. 2.

4. ATSC Study, vol. 1, pp. 4–5.

5. Thomas M. Pitkin, *Quartermaster Equipment for Special Forces,* Quartermaster Corps Historical Studies no. 5 (Washington, D.C., February 1944), pp. 134–42, discusses this matter of inadequate cooperation between the AAF and the QMC. It is interesting to note, however, that the official U.S. Army history of the QMC in World War II (Erna Risch, *The Quartermaster Corps, vols.* 1 and 2, Washington, D.C., 1953–55) does not disclose any jurisdictional disputes with the AAF concerning the development of flying clothing and equipment or any other wartime difficulties that may have developed between the QMC and the AAF.

6. ATSC Study, vol. 1, p. 6.

7. Donald Huxley, Johnstown, N.Y., letter to the author, Nov. 11, 1980 writes:

It is my opinion that the most important and significant step in the development of military personal equipment was the formation of the Personal Equipment Laboratory. The Laboratory was the direct result of General [Henry H.] "Hap" Arnold's oft stated dissatisfaction with the existing flight clothing and related gear.

Fortunately, those who were responsible for the organization of the Laboratory were able to benefit from the mistakes of the many Armed Services agencies previously responsible for the development of personal equipment. First, they manned the staffs of the various branches with personnel drawn from the parent industries. For example, the Clothing Branch was staffed with textile engineers, anthropologists, clothing designers, pattern designers and graders, specification writers, sample makers, test engineers and had the services of thousands of field testers who thought that each item was long overdue. Each member of the Laboratory was made aware of the importance of his or her efforts to the successful completion of the mission of the AAF. We were told, quite forcefully, that the final responsibility was ours alone. We could request assistance from the various segments of the industry but that we were to personally prepare all specifications and related documents. This then was the end of total dependence on any part of the industry for the preparation of procurement data. We made mistakes but they were consistent mistakes and as such were easily correctible. Perhaps our greatest accomplishment was the standardization of patterns. For example if the AAF procured size Medium Regular flight suits from twelve sources, all garments had the same finished dimensions.

However, it is my firm belief that the most important contribution to the eventual development of all Armed Services personal equipment was the separation of the developmental agencies of the Army and the Army Air Forces. The resulting competition, although never acknowledged by either service, certainly expedited development and vastly improved the quality of all military clothing and personal equipment.

It is my fondest hope that those who are now interested in the history of World War II personal equipment will recognize the fact that the very few years of the Personal Equipment Laboratory resulted in the guidelines and parameters of personal gear design that has protected the airmen of our country through three wars and many unsettled years.

8. "Program of the Personal Equipment Laboratory," *The Personal Equipment Officer* 2, no. 2 (c. 1946), p. 1 (reprinted here as Appendix A).

9. Lt. Col. (later Col.) A.P. Gagge, Special Report on "New AAF Clothing in the U.K.," Jan. 31, 1944, Aero Medical Laboratory Files; quoted in ATSC Study, vol. 1, p. 10. Structural improvement to aircraft made during 1943–44, especially the closing of open radio hatches and waist gun positions with Plexiglas windows, also contributed to the decrease in frostbite cases.

2. The Manufacture and Supply of Flying Clothing

1. ATSC Study, vol. 1, p. 16.
2. Ibid., p. 13.
3. Ibid., p. 14.
4. Ibid., p. 10. To fill the AAF's most pressing needs, some winter clothing was received from the RAF and other U.S. Army units and was worn by American airmen in the United Kingdom during this period.
5. Royal D. Frey, Wright-Patterson AFB, Ohio, letter to the author, June 17, 1980. Former lieutenant Frey was shot down during a mission over Germany in 1944 and survived the war in a prisoner-of-war camp. He later was curator of the Air Force Museum at Wright-Patterson AFB for many years.

Other former pilots and gunners recalled, in interviews with the author, their experiences with AAF clothing between 1943 and 1945. Former sergeant Murray M. Rawlins, who was a radio operator and gunner on a B-17 flying out of England just before D-Day in 1944, was issued the old shearling flying clothing but no electrically heated clothing. He was also provided with the M1 steel infantry helmet, which he wore on combat missions until his plane was damaged by anti-aircraft fire over Germany and crash-landed behind enemy lines. After escaping, he was hospitalized but eventually returned to flying status in the spring of 1945. He was issued new AAF flying clothing (for which he retained the receipt). The issue included the Type B-15 jacket, A-11 trousers, A-6 boots, B-3 gloves, A-11 flying helmet, AN-H-15 summer helmet, and B-4 life vest. (Interview with the author, Washington, D.C., June 27, 1980.)

Richard Morris, a lieutenant and B-17 pilot with the 92d Bomb Group of the Eighth Air Force stationed in England, began flying combat missions in January 1945. He usually wore electrically heated clothing, which he remembers as being very serviceable, but carried shearling clothing close at hand in case there was a failure in the electric suit at high altitude. He also was issued one of the new steel helmets especially designed for aviators, which resembled the M1 infantry helmet but had large steel ear flaps that fitted over the earphones in the leather A-11 helmet. (The specific steel helmet assigned to Morris was probably an M3.) (Interview with the author, Washington, D.C., June 27, 1980.)

In China very little flying clothing was received during 1944, according to Lt. Col. David Toplon, USAF (Ret.), then a lieutenant serving as a bombardier-navigator in a B-25 bomber squadron. Personnel needing clothing or high-top shoes either borrowed items to wear on a mission or received garments that had belonged to personnel killed or wounded in action. Other items of clothing were available from personnel returning to the United States. The M1 steel infantry helmet, "stretched" to accommodate the earphone headset, was worn as protection while flying over enemy territory. (It should be noted that priority on the delivery of clothing and equipment was given to units in the European theater of operations until late 1944.) (Interview with the author, South Hadley, Mass., June 6, 1980.)

6. ATSC Study, vol. 1, p. 17.
7. Mae Mills Link and Hubert A. Coleman, *Medical Support of the Army Air Forces in World War II*, Report of the Office of the Surgeon General, USAF (Washington, D.C., 1955), p. 275.
8. Two books edited by Maurer Maurer of the U.S. Air Force Historical Division, Air University, provide further information about, and illustrations of, AAF unit insignia during World War II: *Air Force Combat Units of World War II* (Washington, D.C., 1961), and *Combat Squadrons of the Air Force in World War II* (Washington, D.C., 1969).
9. J. Duncan Campbell, *Aviation Badges and Insignia of the United States Army, 1913–1946* (Harrisburg, Pa., 1977).

3. Research and Testing of Flying Clothing

1. ATSC Study, vol. 1, p. 18.
2. Foreign Equipment Catalog, Section IX, *Cloth-*

ing and Aerial Delivery Equipment, Air Materiel Command, Wright Field, Mar. 10, 1946.

3. ATSC Study, vol. 1, p. 20.

4. Ibid., p. 21.

5. The amount of insulation provided by an item of clothing was measured in "clo" units. One clo is the insulation necessary to maintain comfort under the following conditions: an ambient temperature of 70° F; relative humidity of less than 30 percent; air movement at a rate of 20 feet per minute; and a metabolic rate of 50 calories per square meter of surface. In addition to the thermal man, a "clometer" was developed for the Aero Medical Laboratory to use in testing clothing. (An example of a typical clothing test report, with a description of the clometer, is reproduced in Appendix E.)

6. ATSC Study, vol. 1, p. 24. It was generally estimated that about 40 percent of the total body heat that escaped left through the head, 40 percent through the trunk, and 20 percent through the legs.

7. This information was first published in Hickman Powell, "The Typical American Flyer," *Popular Science,* Mar. 1943.

8. "High Altitude Flight Testing of Flyers' Personal Equipment in Specially Engineered B-17E No. 41-2407," Memorandum Report no. ENG-49-697-1H, prepared by Lt. Col. W. Randolph Lovelace II, Engineering Division, Air Materiel Command, Wright Field, Mar. 20, 1944.

9. Donald Huxley, Johnstown, N.Y., telephone interview with the author, June 5, 1981; and "Final Test of Summer Flying Suits Treated for Flame Retardency," Air Proving Ground Report no. 7-43-27, prepared by 2d Lt. George A. Edwards, Eglin Field, Florida, Nov. 23, 1944. In the postwar years some flying clothing was treated with a flame-retardant compound, but it was not until the mid–1960s, during the Vietnam War, that effective flame-retardant clothing made of "Nomex" fabric was developed for service use.

10. See "Kit, Flyer's Clothing and Equipment," Technical Order no. 00-30-41, Headquarters, Army Air Forces, Washington, D.C., Oct. 20, 1945 (reprinted here as Appendix C.)

4. Heavy Winter Shearling Flying Suits

1. ATSC Study, vol. 1, p. 29.

2. Col. (later Maj. Gen.) Malcolm C. Grow was honored for his work in developing aviator's body armor in England during World War II. Among his many other accomplishments was the establishment of the Aero Medical Laboratory at Wright Field.

3. Maj. (later Lt. Col.) E.L. Hoffman won the Collier Trophy in 1926 for his work in parachute development. He was the chief of the Equipment Branch at Wright Field for many years and was involved in the development of all types of equipment. See also "Fawn Reindeer Pelts and Lamb Shearlings for Winter Flying Suits in the Air Corps," Memorandum Report no. M-56-2653, prepared by C.J. Cleary, Materiel Division, Wright Field, Apr. 17, 1934.

4. ATSC Study, vol. 1, p. 31. Two-piece winter suits appeared after the summer jacket (Type A designation), and hence their components were identified as Type B jackets and Type A trousers. Although the jackets and trousers were designed and purchased as "suits," stock-listing methods required their separation. As a result, winter clothing could not be satisfactorily listed until the new Class 13 catalog system was implemented after World War II.

5. Ibid., p. 32.

6. Ibid., p. 33.

7. For more details, see "Clothing—Refinishing Sheep Shearling Type Clothing," Technical Order no. 13-1-10, Headquarters, Army Air Forces, Washington, D.C., Oct. 16, 1943 (reprinted here as Appendix D).

8. ATSC Study, vol. 1, p. 36.

9. Lt. Gen. Henry H. Arnold and Rear Adm. J.H. Towers, "Report on Requirements of Shearling, etc.," Apr. 18, 1942; cited in ATSC Study, vol. 1, p. 37.

10. Interview with the author, New Haven, Conn., June 5, 1980.

11. ATSC Study, vol. 1, p. 39.

12. AAF Illustrated Catalog, *Class 13 Clothing, Parachutes, Equipment and Supplies,* Headquarters, Air Service Command, Patterson Field, Ohio, Sept. 30, 1943, p. 54.

13. ATSC Study, vol. 1, p. 40. By 1942 the OQMG had decided to shift away from using furs and animal skins in cold-climate clothing for the Army ground forces. In their place, multi-layer pile fabrics were increasingly utilized. Wool continued to be used extensively by the QMC for such items as sweaters, underwear, mufflers, and mittens.

14. Ibid.

15. Type Designation Sheets, Equipment Branch, Wright Field (reprinted here as Appendix F). Shearling garments survive today as expensive civilian winter coats and as reproductions of AAF shearling clothing produced for sale to owners of vintage aircraft and other aviation buffs.

5. Electrically Heated Flying Suits

1. Crowell, *America's Munitions,* p. 318.

2. ATSC Study, vol. 1, p. 44.

3. Type Designation Sheets.

4. "Use, Test, and Repair of Electrically Heated Clothing," Technical Order no. 13-1-8, Headquarters, Army Air Forces, Washington, D.C., Nov. 27, 1942. The order emphasized that the electrically heated suit furnished little protection against cold if the electrical circuit of either the airplane or the suit became inoperative: "Electrically-heated clothing is designed to be worn as a unit.... [A]n undersuit ... and any type of

flying suit may be worn over the electrically-heated suit depending on the outdoor temperature."
5. ATSC Study, vol. 1, p. 48.
6. Type Designation Sheets.
7. ATSC Study, vol. 1, p. 49.
8. Type Designation Sheets.
9. Lt. Col. A.P. Gagge, "F-2A Electrically Heated Suit," Memorandum Report no. ENG-49-695-2P, Materiel Center, Wright Field, Apr. 14, 1944.
10. ATSC Study, vol. 1, p. 51.
11. Type Designation Sheets.
12. Lt. Col. A.P. Gagge, "Flight Demonstration of AAF Flying Clothing Requirements," Memorandum Report no. ENG-49-695-2M, Materiel Command, Wright Field, Mar. 1, 1944. See also *Handbook of Instructions with Parts Catalog-Type F-3 Electrically Heated Flying Suits,* no. AN 13-1-16, Joint Publication of the Army Air Forces, the Bureau of Aeronautics of the U.S. Navy, and the Air Council of the United Kingdom, June 25, 1944.
13. Type Designation Sheets.
14. "F-2 and F-3 Electrically Heated Flying Suits," *Air Surgeon's Bulletin,* May 1944, p. 17.

6. Other Types of Flying Suits

1. ATSC Study, vol. 1, p. 56.
2. Type Designation Sheets.
3. Ibid.
4. "Army Develops Two-piece Flying Suit of Horsehide and Wool to Combat Cold," *New York Times,* April 24, 1932.
5. Interview with the author, Washington, D.C., May 21, 1980.
6. ATSC Study, vol. 1, p. 35.
7. "Comparative Tests with Shearling and Pile Garments," Memorandum Report no. ENG-M-49-695-3B, Engineering Division, Air Materiel Command, Wright Field, Dec. 17, 1942. The OQMG had accepted the layering principle even before the war and had used it in the development of arctic clothing and, later, in the standard winter combat uniforms for American ground troops.
8. ATSC Study, vol. 1, p. 59.
9. Type Designation Sheets. During 1942 alpaca- and mohair-pile winter field clothing was introduced by the Army QMC for wear by ground forces in the Arctic. (See Pitkin, *Quartermaster Equipment for Special Forces,* p. 27.)
10. ATSC Study, vol. 1, p. 60.
11. Type Designation Sheets.
12. Ibid.
13. Ibid.
14. Maj. Samuel R.M. Reynolds, "Human Engineering in the Army Air Forces," *The Personal Equipment Officer* 2, no. 1 (c. 1946): 2–10.
15. ATSC Study, vol. 1, p. 61.
16. Ibid., p. 62.

17. *Spalding Aviator's Equipment,* Catalog of A.G. Spalding and Brothers (New York, c.1928), p. 27.
18. Type Designation Sheets. The Soviet Air Force also used quilted eider-down flying clothing for its winter wear during World War II.
19. ATSC Study, vol. 1, p. 63.
20. Type Designation Sheets.
21. ATSC Study, vol. 1, p. 65.
22. Type Designation Sheets; and ATSC Study, vol. 1, pp. 64–66.

7. Other Items of Body Clothing

1. "Aviator's Clothing," Stencil no. 844 (AHP), Office of the Chief Signal Officer, War Department, Washington, D.C., Jan. 19, 1918.
2. Type Designation Sheets.
3. Roger A. Freeman, *The Mighty Eighth* (Garden City, N.Y., 1970), pp. 101–2.
4. Col. Hubert A. Zemke, USAF (Ret.), Oroville, Calif., telephone interview with the author, June 27, 1980. Colonel Zemke was commander of the 56th Fighter Group in World War II.
5. Type Designation Sheets.
6. "Kit, Flyer's Clothing and Equipment," Oct. 20, 1945. Many earlier types of garments remained in use as substitute or limited standard after new standard items were introduced. Some flyers preferred to continue wearing their old garments, such as the popular A-2 jacket.
7. Type Designation Sheets.
8. "Dreadnaught Safety Suit for Fliers," *Air Service Journal,* Mar. 29, 1919.
9. "Non-Sinkable Suits," *Aircraft Journal,* June 28, 1919.
10. Actual flotation coats (with sleeves) had been made in the 1920s and could be ordered from the 1928 catalog, *Spalding Aviator's Equipment.*
11. Maj. M.P. Kelsey, MC, "Acute Exposure of Flyers to Arctic Waters," *Air Surgeon's Bulletin,* Feb. 1944, p. 7.
12. ATSC Study, vol. 1, p. 72.
13. Type Designation Sheets.
14. Capt. J. Herbert Nagler, MC, Eleventh Air Force, "Electrically Heated Rescue Suit," *Air Surgeon's Bulletin,* Oct. 1945, p. 338.
15. Huxley, telephone interview.
16. This type of sweater vest was issued to Lt. (later Lt. Col.) Donald S. Lopez upon graduation from flying school and was worn by him frequently between 1943 and 1945 while he was serving in China. Interview with the author, Washington, D.C., June 25, 1980.
17. ATSC Study, vol. 1, p. 67.
18. Ibid., p. 69.
19. "Wearing of Service Uniform," Army Regulation no. 600-40, War Department, Washington, D.C., Aug. 28, 1941, as amended and March 31, 1944, as

amended. See also "Prescribed Service Uniform," Army Regulation no. 600-35, War Department, Washington, D.C., Nov. 10, 1941, as amended, and Mar. 31, 1944, as amended.

20. ATSC Study, vol. 1, p. 68. See also "Women's Flying Clothing," Memorandum Report no. ENG-695-32-N, Aero Medical Laboratory, Materiel Center, Wright Field, Mar. 4, 1944.

8. Headgear

1. Type Designation Sheets.
2. ATSC Study, vol. 2, p. 4.
3. "Kit, Flyer's Clothing and Equipment." AAF crewmen generally preferred to wear the Type A-11 intermediate helmet even during winter and on high-altitude missions.
4. Type Designation Sheets.
5. Steel or armored flyers' "flak" helmets are not included in this volume, but will be discussed with body armor in volume 2 of this study.
6. "Clothing—Modification of Flying Helmets Type A-10, A-10A, AN-H-15, A-11, and AN-H-16," Technical Order no. 13-1-36, Headquarters, Army Air Forces, Washington, D.C., Feb. 12, 1947.
7. ATSC Study, vol. 2, p. 8.
8. These masks will be described in detail with other items of oxygen equipment in volume 2 of this study.
9. AAF Illustrated Catalog, *Class 13*, Sept. 30, 1943.
10. *Reference Manual for Personal Equipment Officers*, AAF Manual no. 55-0-1, Headquarters, Army Air Forces, Washington, D.C., June 1, 1945, pp. 7-A-1–7-B-2.
11. "Aviator's Clothing."

12. "Regulations for the Uniform of the United States Army," Special Regulation no. 41, War Department, Washington, D.C., Aug. 15, 1917.
13. *Index of Army and Navy Aeronautical Equipment*, vol. 3, *Oxygen Equipment*, Air Materiel Command, Wright Field, n.d. (c. 1943), p. 152.
14. AAF Illustrated Catalog, *Class 13*, Sept. 30, 1943, p. 37.
15. Ibid., p. 45.

9. Handwear

1. Lt. Phillips M. Brooks, "Gloves for Flyers," *Air Surgeon's Bulletin*, Apr. 1944, p. 21.
2. See chap. 3, n. 5.
3. ATSC Study, vol. 2, p. 11.
4. Link and Coleman, p. 277.
5. ATSC Study, vol. 2, p. 15.
6. *Reference Manual for Personal Equipment Officers*, p. 5-D-1.
7. ATSC Study, vol. 2, p. 14.
8. Ibid., p. 13.
9. Type Designation Sheets.

10. Footwear

1. Type Designation Sheets.
2. ATSC Study, vol. 2, p. 19.
3. Ibid. p. 16.
4. Ibid. p. 17.
5. *Class 13, Special Clothing and Personal Equipment-Clothing, Flyers*, Supply Catalog of the U.S. Air Force, Air Materiel Command, Wright-Patterson AFB, Ohio, 1948, p. 20
6. ATSC Study, vol. 2, pp. 20–21.

Bibliography

Books and Book-Length Reports

Campbell, J. Duncan. *Aviation Badges and Insignia of the United States Army, 1913–1946.* Harrisburg, Pa., 1977.

Crowell, Benedict. *America's Munitions, 1917–1918,* Report of the Assistant Secretary of War, Director of Munitions. Washington, D.C., 1919.

Freeman, Roger A. *The Mighty Eighth.* Garden City, N.Y., 1970.

Greer, Louise, and Harold, Anthony. *Flying Clothing, The Story of Its Development.* Shrewsbury, England, 1979. This book deals with flying clothing in general from before World War I to the present, with emphasis on the RAF.

Link, Mae Mills, and Coleman, Hubert A. *Medical Support of the Army Air Forces in World War II.* Report of the Office of the Surgeon General, USAF. Washington, D.C., 1955.

Lovelace, W.R.; Gagge, A.P.; and Bray, C.W. *Aviation Medicine and Psychology.* Publication of Air Materiel Command, AAF. Wright Field, Ohio, 1946.

Maurer, Maurer, ed. *Air Force Combat Units of World War II.* Publication of the USAF Historical Division, Air University. Washington, D.C., 1961.

_____. *Combat Squadrons of the Air Force in World War II.* Publication of the USAF Historical Division, Air University. Washington, D.C., 1969.

Newburgh, L.H., ed. *Physiology of Heat Regulation and Science of Clothing.* Philadelphia and London, 1949.

Pitkin, Thomas. *Quartermaster Equipment for Special Forces.* Quartermaster Corps Historical Studies no. 5. Washington, D.C., Feb. 1944.

Purtee, Edwin O. "Development of AAF Clothing and Other Personal Equipment Peculiar to Air Operations." 3 vols. Unpublished study prepared for the acting director of the Air Technical Service Command, Wright Field, Ohio, May 22, 1945. This manuscript provided much valuable information for the preparation of this study.

Risch, Erna. *The Quartermaster Corps,* 4 vols. Publication of the Office of the Chief of Military History, Department of the Army. Washington, D.C., 1953–55.

_____, and Pitkin, Thomas. *Clothing the Soldier of World War II.* Quartermaster Corps Historical Studies no. 16. Washington, D.C., 1946.

Catalogs, Stock Lists, and Manuals

"Aviator's Clothing." Stencil no. 844 (AHP). Office of the Chief Signal Officer, War Department, Washington, D.C., Jan. 19, 1918.

Class 13, Clothing, Parachutes, Equipment and Supplies. Illustrated Catalog, Headquarters, Air Service Command, AAF. Patterson Field, Ohio, Sept. 30, 1943.

Class 13, Clothing, Parachutes, Equipment and Supplies. Stock List, Materiel Division, Air Corps; and later Air Service Command, AAF. Fairfield, Ohio, various dates, 1920s through mid-1940s.

Class 13, Special Clothing and Personal Equipment—Clothing, Flyers.' U.S. Air Force Supply Catalog, Headquarters, Air Materiel Command. Wright-Patterson AFB, Ohio, 1948 and 1953 editions.

Clothing and Aerial Delivery Equipment. Foreign Equipment Catalog, Section IX. Headquarters, Air Materiel Command, AAF. Wright Field, Ohio, Mar. 10, 1946.

Enlisted Men's Clothing and Equipment. Quartermaster Supply Catalog no. QM 3-1. Headquarters, Army Service Forces. Washington, D.C., Aug. 1, 1943.

Handbook of Instructions with Parts Catalog—Type F-3 Electrically Heated Flying Suits. No. AN-13-16. Joint publication of the Army Air Forces; the Bureau of Aeronautics, U.S. Navy; and the Air Council of the United Kingdom. June 25, 1944.

Index of Army and Navy Aeronautical Equipment. Vol. 3, *Oxygen Equipment.* Headquarters, Air Materiel

Command, AAF. Wright Field, Ohio, n.d. (c. 1943).

Reference Manual for Personal Equipment Officers. AAF Manual no. 55-0-1. Headquarters, Army Air Forces, Washington, D.C., June 1, 1945. This manual contains interesting details of flying clothing and equipment used late in World War II.

Type Designation Sheets. Equipment Branch, Wright Field, Ohio. This extremely valuable source of information on flying clothing and equipment was maintained at Wright Field from the mid–1920s through World War II. (See Appendix F.)

Also valuable in the preparation of this study were the catalogs of flying clothing and equipment published by various commercial companies between 1913 and 1941 and found in the NASM archives.

Journals

Air Service Journal. Publication of the Gardner-Moffat Company, New York, 1917–19.

Air Surgeon's Bulletin. Publication of the Office of the Surgeon General, AAF. Washington, D.C., 1944–45.

The Personal Equipment Officer. Publication of the Personal Equipment Laboratory, AAF. Wright Field, Ohio, 1945–46.

Memorandum Reports

"Comparative Tests with Shearling and Pile Garments." Memorandum Report no. ENG-M-49-695-3B. Engineering Division, Materiel Command, AAF. Wright Field, Ohio, Dec. 17, 1942.

"F-2A Electrically Heated Suit." Memorandum Report no. ENG-49-695-2P. Headquarters, Materiel Center, AAF. Wright Field, Ohio, Apr. 14, 1944.

"Fawn Reindeer Pelts and Lamb Shearlings for Winter Flying Suits in the Air Corps." Materiel Division, Air Corps. Wright Field, Ohio, Apr. 17, 1934.

"Flight Demonstration of AAF Flying Clothing Requirements." Memorandum Report no. ENG-49-695-2M. by A.P. Gagge, Headquarters, Materiel Command, AAF. Wright Field, Ohio, Mar. 1, 1944.

"High Altitude Flight Testing of Flyers' Personal Equipment in Specially Engineered B-17E No. 41-2407." Memorandum Report no. ENG-49-697-1H, Headquarter's, Materiel Command, AAF. Wright Field, Ohio, Mar. 20, 1944.

"Preliminary Tests on Durability of Flying Clothing." Memorandum Report no. ENG-49-695-2S. Aero Medical Laboratory, Materiel Command, AAF. Wright Field, Ohio, Apr. 12, 1944. (Reprinted here as Appendix E.)

Regulations

"Prescribed Service Uniform." Army Regulation no. 600-35. War Department, Washington, D.C., Nov. 10, 1941, as amended, and Mar. 31, 1944, as amended.

"Wearing of Service Uniform." Army Regulation no. 600-40. War Department, Washington, D.C., Aug. 28, 1941, as amended, and Mar. 31, 1944, as amended.

Technical Orders

"Clothing—Refinishing Sheep Shearling Type Clothing." Technical Order no. 13-1-10. Headquarters, Army Air Forces. Washington, D.C., Oct. 16, 1943. (Reprinted here as Appendix D.)

"Kit, Clothing and Equipment, Flyer." Technical Order no. 00-30-41. Headquarters, Army Air Forces, Washington, D.C., Apr. 16, 1942. This T.O. included a complete inventory of the standard types of clothing and equipment issued to flyers just after the entry of the United States into World War II. (Reprinted here as Appendix B.) This T.O. should be compared to the one that follows.

"Kit, Flyer's Clothing and Equipment." Technical Order no. 00-30-41. Headquarters, Army Air Forces, Washington, D.C., Oct. 20, 1945. This T.O. provides a complete inventory of standard types of clothing and equipment for flyers available at the end of World War II. It also states that older substitute standard and limited standard items could be issued in lieu of the standard items if necessary. (Reprinted here as Appendix C.)

"Use, Test and Repair of Electrically Heated Clothing." Technical Order no. 13-1-8. Headquarters, Army Air Forces, Washington, D.C., Nov. 27, 1942.

Index

AAF School of Applied Tactics, Orlando, FL 60
AAF units, numbered:
  Eighth Air Force 14, 22, 68, 69, 70, 77, 108, 109
  Ninth Air Force 56
  XI Fighter Command, Eleventh Air Force 76
  Fourteenth Air Force 70, 71, 72
  Fifteenth Air Force 14
  23d Fighter Group, Fourteenth Air Force 79
  55th Fighter Squadron 13
  56th Fighter Group, Eighth Air Force 70
  75th Fighter Squadron 79
  92d Bomb Group, Eighth Air Force 70
  303d Bomb Group, Eighth Air Force 8
  322d Bomb Group, Ninth Air Force 56
  351st Bomb Group, Eighth Air Force 64
  390th Bomb Group, Eighth Air Force 68–69
  479th Fighter Group, 70
Abbreviations 168–169
Aces, AAF 70, 79, 82
Aero Medical Laboratory (AML), Wright Field, OH 8, 27, 28, 29, 55, 109
  human centrifuge 29
  low-pressure cold chamber 29
  thermal man 27–28
Air Mail 34
Air Technical Service Command (ATSC) 8, Appendices B and C
Air Transport Command (ATC) 55
Alaska 7, 8, 9, 55, 76, 118
"Alaskan suit" *see* Jackets, flying, winter, Type B-7; Trousers, flying, winter, Type B-6
Alaskan Test Expedition 8, 55, 9;
see also Cold Weather Test Detachment; Ladd Field
Alpaca pile *see* Clothing, Alpaca pile
American Optical Company 101, 102
A-N Standardization System 11, 12, 18
Anthropologists 28
Antiaircraft fire (Flak) 21, 100
Anti-G garments 23
Aregard, M/Sgt. Howard 72
Army-Navy Munitions Board 11
Arnold, Gen. Henry H. ("Hap") 8, 38, 40, 69
Asiatic-Pacific Theater of Operations 11
Astro compass, Spec. AN-5738–1 118
Attachés, American 24
Aviation Clothing Board *see* Clothing Board, Aviation

Babel, Capt. John 96, 97
"Bare Foot" moccasins *see* Moccasins, aviators, Type A-1
Battle dress or battle jacket *see* Jackets, flight, Type B-13 and B-14
BB bronze *see* wires, electrical
Bedford cloth and Bedford cord 33, 34; *see also* Suits, flying, winter, Bedford cloth
Benson, Col. Otis O., Jr. 28
Beraloy *see* Wires, electrical
Blanket lining 34, 50, 54; *see also* Suits, flying, winter, Type B-2 and B-7
"Blood chits" 20, 70, 71, 72
"Blue Bunny" suit *see* Suits, flying, electrically heated, Type F-1
Boeing Aircraft Co. 30
Boeing B-17 "Flying Fortress" 8, 21, 22, 30, 36, 39, 41, 45, 47, 60, 69, 70

Boeing B-29 "Super Fortress" 82, 99, 108
Boots:
  felt, outer shell for Type F-2 electrically heated suit 130–131
  flying *see also* Footwear; Shoes, flying
    RAF 12, 63
    RCAF 126
  "Gaucho" 131
  "Karachi" 131–132
  "Mosquito" *see* Shoes, flying intermediate, Type A-15
  "Natal" 131
Borsodi, Maj. Frederick 63
Buoyancy suits: *see* Jackets, flying, winter, Type B-9; Suits, exposure; Suits, flotation; Trousers, flying, winter, Type A-8; Vests, life preserver
Byrd cloth 65, 66

Calfskin 34, 110
Camel hair 10
Capeskin 110, 114
Caps:
  "50-mission crush" 68, 70, 81, 82, 97
  flying 97
  flying, nurses,' Type C-1 83; Type K-1 86; Type L-1 85–86
  garrison (overseas cap) 82, 83, 97
  knit, M-1941 "beanie" or "Jeep cap" 97
  pilots, Type B-1 22, 37, 56, 89, 97; Type B-2 40, 89–97
  service, with visor 22, 69, 70, 81, 82, 97; *see also* Caps, "50-mission crush"
Caribou 110
Casualty bag 74
Casualty blankets 30, 79
Cavallo, Stefan A. 95

Chanute field, IL 34
Chennault, Maj. Gen. Claire L. 18, 20, 72
China 20, 64, 70, 72, 79, 82
China-Burma-India Theater of Operations (CBI) 20, 70, 71, 72, 79, 82
Chinese Nuchwang dog fur lining *see* Suits, flying, winter, Type B-1
"Chino" clothing 82
Clometer 30, 108; *see also* Appendix E
Clothing:
  alpaca pile 9, 12, 46, 53, 55
  Army Ground Forces 55, 81–8
  civilian 3, 8
  commercial 9
  flying:
    down insulated 26
    electrically heated 8, 9, 12, 15, 43–50; *see also* Glove inserts; Shoes; Suits; Wires, electrical
    defects 5–11, 12, 31, 45–50
    foreign 9, 24, 38, 72, 74, 81, 126, 132
    fur-lined 32–33, 88, 108, 110
    intermediate 55–57
    RAF 9, 12, 38, 72, 74, 81, 126, 132
    sheep shearling 6, 8, 12, 28, 34, 35, 36, 40, 41, 42, 46, 53, 54, 79, 94, 96, 97, 111, 119, 120, 121, 126; *see also* Appendix G
    finishing process (Korsseal water-proofing treatment) 35, 119–120; *see also* Appendix D
    permeability 125
    requirements for 38–40
    standard issue 11; *see also* Appendices B and C
  summer 9, 14–17
  U.S. Navy 11, 24
  winter 9, 11, 32–42, 108
  women's 83–86
  mechanics sheep shearling 35
  multilayer fabric 29, 38
  nonstandard 1, 81
  obsolete 81
  preservation of 100; *see also* Appendix D
  quilted 26
  ski and mountain troops 6
  summer 29, 61–67
  U.S. Army tank crew 12
Clothing Board, Aviation (World War I) 5, 32, 119
Clothing Branch, Wright Field, OH 6, 8, 9, 13, 29, 38, 46, 50, 60, 78
Clothing colors 20–21
Clothing comfort 8, 9

Clothing contracts 6–11
Clothing design and designers 5, 11, 32
Clothing industry, American 3, 11–14, 32, 35
Clothing inspectors and inspection 9
Clothing labels 17, 18
Clothing materials 5–11
Clothing pooling 13–14
Clothing preservation *see* Appendix G
Clothing procurement 11–23
Clothing production 3, 5–11
Clothing shortages 9–10, 11, 108
Clothing specifications 12
Clothing standardization 2, 4, 28, 81; *see also* Appendix F
Clothing supply 3, 12–14
Clothing testing 12, 24–31, 53, 54, 81; *see also* Appendix E
  desert 30
  flight 25
  opinion survey 26
  tropical 30
  winter and cold 25, 27, 32–42, 39–49
Clothing testing facilities 24; *see also* Wright Field, OH
  all-weather chamber 27, 29, 46
  cold chambers 27, 29, 46
  General Electric cold chamber 27
  Harvard Fatigue Laboratory 27
  McCook Field 13
  Mayo Clinic high-altitude chamber 27
  Monmouth Field cold chamber 27
  tropical 27
  Yale University cold chamber 27
Clothing variations 1, 80–81
"Clo" Unit 30, 108–109
Coats:
  flying, leather 3, 63, 68
  Spalding "ATC Non-sink" 74
Cockpits:
  enclosed 35, 87, 97–99
  open 3, 33, 34, 87, 88, 98
Cold Weather Test Detachment, AK 8, 55; *see also* Alaskan Test Expedition; Ladd Field
Colvinex Corp. 45, 117
Combat casualties 10
Communions equipment 89, 90–92; *see also* Gosport Communition System; Headsets; Microphones; Radio equipment; Receivers
Coney fur "pocket" mittens *see* Mittens, flying, coney fur "pocket type"
Consolidated Vultee B-24 Liberator 45, 99, 108
Continental Textile Mills, Philadelphia, PA 54–55

Copper man *see* Thermal man
Corduroy *see* Suits, flying, winter, corduroy cloth
Cork 75
Cotton 10, 61, 91–82, 130
Cotton twill cloth (Byrd Cloth) 65, 66
Coveralls *see* Suits, flying, summer and winter
Crewmen 21–22
Curtiss C-46 Commando 37
Curtiss NC flying boats 74
Curtiss P-40 fighter 71, 79

Deerskin 110, 114
de Havilland 4 aircraft 7
Department of Agriculture, U.S. 42
Depression years 5, 35
Dibble, M/Sgt. E. H. 82
Doeskin 92, 93
Douglas C-54 Skymaster transport 57, 112
Down lining and insulation *see* Clothing, flying, down insulated
Dreadnaught Safety Suit *see* Suits, dreadnaught safety
Dubbing (for shoes) 119

Early aviators 3, 77, 87
Earphones (receivers) Spec. ANB-1 *see* Receivers, radio, Spec. ANB-H-1; Headsets
Eglin Field, FL 25, 30, 76
Eiderdown 61
Eisenhower or "Ike" jacket *see* Jackets, field, wool, M-44
Electrically heated clothing 43–50; *see also* Casualty blankets; Clothing, flying, electrically heated; Gloves, flying, electrically heated; Shoes, flying, electrically heated; Suits, flying, electrically heated
Electrified lambskin *see* Clothing, flying, sheep shearling
Engineering Division, Wright Field 29, 30
Engineering Section, Experimental 5, 15, 54, 60
England *see* United Kingdom
Equipment Board, AAF, Orlando, FL 13, 41
Equipment Laboratory: (formerly Equipment Section, later Branch) 24, 34, 54, 60, 92
Escape flags: *see* "Blood chits"
European Theater of Operations (ETO) 11, 72, 73
exposure 74, 77; *see also* Frostbite

Fabric testing 24–31
Fasteners, electrical connection, for clothing 43–51, 118

Feather lining *see* Clothing, flying, down insulated
Federal Aviation Administration (FAA) 92
Felt 46–47
"50-mission crush" cap *see* Caps, "50-mission crush"
Fireproofing 10, 31, 65
Flags, American 20
Flak vest *see* Vests, flyers, armored
Flame proofing *see* Fireproofing
Flight testing *see* Clothing testing, flight
flotation garments 74–77; *see also* Coats, Spalding "ATC Non-Sink"; Suits, exposure; Suits, flotation; Vests, life preserver
"Flying Tigers" (American Volunteer Group) 71, 72
Focke-Wulf Fw 190 fighter 63
Football helmets *see* Helmets, football
Footwear 10, 12, 119–132; *see also* Shoes, flying; Boots; Socks
France 30, 43
Frey, Royal D. 7, 13
Frostbite 10, 108–109
Funds, Air Corps 95
Fur 32, 33, 92, 93

"G" forces 29; *see also* Anti-G garments
Gabardine 60, 82
Gagge, Col. (Dr.) A. P. 2, 5, 10, 11, 13, 38, 98
Gauntlets, flying:
  British 13
  U.S. 110–111; *see also* Gloves, flying; Mittens, flying, coney fur
General Athletic Co. 7, 76
General Electric Co. (G.E.) 27, 45, 46, 70, 116, 128
Geneva Convention 20, 81, 82
German Luftwaffe 42
Germany 11, 67, 87
Glasses:
  arctic sun, Type F-1 105
  flying, sun (comfort cable) 104, 105
  flying, sun rose smoke, Type 2 104, 105
Glove inserts 108, 112; *see also* Gloves, flying, electrically heated, insert and shell, for Type F-2 and F-3 suits electrically heated, Colvinex 45, 108
Glove testing 29, 109
Glove training 109
Gloves 23, 32, 108–117
  anti-exposure, Type F-1 (for R-1 suit) 77, 113
  emergency rescue, Type N-1 113–114

flying
  electrically heated, insert and shell, for Type F-2 and F-3 suits 108–110, 112, 115–116
  silk, inner 108
  Type C-1 116; Type C-2 116; Type C-3 116; Type C-4 116, 117; Type C-5 117; C-6 45, 117; Type E-1 45, 117; USAAS 43
  Royal Air Force (RAF) 38
  silk, RAF 23
  summer 114; Type B-2 114; Type B-3 114; Type B-3A 86, 114, 115
  winter 110–112; Type A-1 110; Type A-2 110; Type A-3 110; Type A-4 110, 116; Type A-5 110; Type A-6 40, 110, 111; Type A-7 111; Type A-8 110, 111; Type A-9 34, 39, 41, 108, 111, 112, 116, 117; Type A-9A 108, 111; Type A-10 39, 112; Type A-11 57, 58, 6186, 92, 112; Type A-11A 112; Type A-12 (Arctic) 60, 112
  mechanics, Type D-3 114
Goatskin 110, 116
Goggles 100, 104
  all-purpose (Polaroid No. 1021) (DA) 95, 103, 104
  assembly
    flying, Navy mask type 101
    flying, Type D-1 104; Type D-2 104; Type D-3 104
  contrast, Type G-1 105
  dark adaptation, Type E-1 102, 103–104
  emergency protection, Type H-1 104
  flying 104
    "Aviglas" 100
    electrically heated 88, 100–101; Type C-1 101
    Meyrowitz "Lixor" 88, 101
    "Resistal" 88, 100, 101
    "Skyway" 102
    "Triplex" 100
    Type A-1 100, 101; Type B-1 101: B-1A 101; Type B-2 101; Type B-3 101; Type B-4 101; Type B-5 101; Type B-6 32, 100; Type B-7 39, 65, 79, 101; Type B-8 23, 46, 57, 61, 63, 64, 96, 97, 100, 102–103, 104
    USAAS Type 1 100; Type 2 100; Type 3 100
  "Wilson" 102
gunners (Polaroid No. 1021) (DA) *see* Goggles, all-purpose
M-1944 103

Polaroid fog-free No. 1040 with face pad 104
Gosport Aerodrome 106
Gosport communication system 106–107
Gowen Field, ID 25
Graham M/Sgt. J. A. 82
Great Britain *see* United Kingdom (UK)
Ground crews 81
Grow, Maj. Gen. (Dr.) Malcolm C. 34
Gunners 3, 8, 108–109

Handwear 108–118; *see also* Gloves, flying
Headgear 87–97; *see also* Caps, flying; Helmets, flying
Headsets:
  earphone pads 92
  earphone receptacles 92
  Radio, Type HS-33 106; Type HS-38 105; *see also* Receivers, radio
Heater, oxygen mask 46
Heating, aircraft 12, 32, 33
Helmet and speaking tube earpiece assembly, summer and winter training 107; *see also* Gosport communication system
Helmets 88, 87–107
  armored, Type M3 23; Type M5 21, 23
  combat vehicle crewman (CVC) 97
  crash 87, 96, 97
  flak *see* Helmets, armored
  flying
    chamois 88
    electrically heated, World War I 43, 88
    fawn reindeer-lined 88
    gunners auxiliary, Type G-1 96
    heavy, Type N-1 96
    high-altitude 88
    intermediate, Type A-11 18, 58, 91, 92, 96, 97, 99, 112, 113
    protective 95, 96
    experimental 95, 96
    improvised 95
    Roold 87
    Style B 94
    Type P-1 97
    RAF Type "C" 13, 22, 79, 92
    RCAF 90
    summer 88–92
    Spec. AN-H-15 12, 17, 18, 57, 62, 64, 65, 66, 68, 69, 91, 95, 97, 103
    Type A-1 88; Type A-2 88; Type A-3 88; Type A-4 88, 89; Type A-5 89;

Type A-6 89; Type A-7 88; Type A-8 90, 91; Type A-10 91, 97; Type A-10A 91, 97; Type 1-A 88
  with visor, Spec. 3016 97
  winter 92–96
    fur chin pad 98
    Spec. AN-H-14 93; AN-H-16 9, 12, 23, 41, 47, 57, 61, 91, 94, 96, 97
    Type B-1 90, 92; Type B-2 92; Type B-3 92, 93; Type B-4 93; Type B-5 34, 88, 93; Type B-6 93, 94, 107; Type B-7 93; Type B-9 94, 95, 96
football 3, 87
protective, tank crew 97
Hoffman, Lt. Col. E. L. 34, 50
Hood, flying, winter, fur-lined 96
Hooton, Prof. Earnest A. 28
Horsehide 54, 69, 98, 110, 114
Human centrifuge 29
Huxley, Donald 9, 78

"Ike" jacket *see* Jackets, field, wool, M-1944
India 132
Inserts:
  glove *see* Glove inserts
  helmet, electrically heated 88
  shoe, flying *see* Shoe inserts, flying
Insignia, AAF 17, 18, 20, 69, 70, 72, 73, 81, 82
  aircraft 69
  aircrew (wings) 13, 20, 69
  flag, U.S. 20, 70
  grade (rank), enlisted personnel 19, 20; officers 19, 20, 69, 70, 71
  leather 19, 71
  unit (organizational) 20, 70, 71, 74
Insoles 119
Irvine, Capt. C. S. 36

Jackets:
  aircraft, pilot's (vest) Type C-1 *see* Vests, flying, winter, Type C-1
  field, M-1943 73; Type M-1944 "Ike jacket" 72, 73, 74, 82
  flight, Type B-13 71, 72, 73, 74, 81; Type B-14 72, 73, 74
  flying 72–74, 83
    electrically heated Type F-2, F-2A, F-3, F-3A *see* Suits, flying, electrically heated Type F-2, F-2A, F-3, F-3A
    intermediate
      Spec. AN-J-3 11, 73
      Type B-5 37, 89; Type B-6 36, 37; Type B-10 22, 55, 56, 57; Type B-15 21, 22, 26, 55, 56, 58, 85; Type B-15A 57, 58; Type B-15B 71
    light utility, Type L-2 74
    nurses,' light, Type L-1 74; very light, Type K-1 86
    Spec. AN-J-3 69, 71, 73
    summer 68–72
      Type A-1 68; Type A-2 17, 18, 19, 20, 38, 68, 70, 71, 3, 99; Type A-3 70; Type A-4 89; Type A-5 70; Type A-6 70; Type A-7 84, 70
    winter
      Spec. AN-J-4 (Spec. 6553-AN-J-44) 41, 42
      Type B-1 33, 36, 53, 54, 116; Type B-2 17, 36, 53; Type B-3 34, 35, 36, 37, 40, 54, 70; Type B-4 35, 70, 89; Type B-7 "Alaskan suit" 40, 126; Type B-8 55, 126; Type B-9 60, 61; Type B-11 9, 55, 56; Type B-12 71
    winter, inner, Type B-8 55, 126
  life *see* Vests, life preserver
  nurses, Flying, Type F-1 83
  nurses, flying, intermediate, Type B-17 83
Japan 11
Jet aircraft 95, 96, 97
Joint Research and Test Board 30

Kapok 60, 74, 71
Kellogg Co. 106
Kelsey, Brig. Gen. Benjamin S. 32, 54
Kelsey, Maj. M. P. 76
Keviczky, I. V. 74
Kits:
  para-raft, Type C-2A 14
  survival (emergency) 70, 99, 114; Type B-2 22; Type B-4 104; Type C-1 104
Korean War 14, 62, 92, 102
Korsseal waterproofing treatment 35; *see also* Appendix D; Clothing, flying, sheep shearling

Labels *see* Clothing labels
Ladd Field, AK 25, 44, 45, 55, 112; *see also* Alaskan Test Expedition; Cold Weather Test Detachment
Lamb shearling *see* Clothing, flying, sheep shearling
Leather 35, 38, 51, 52, 54, 68, 69, 88, 92, 93, 97, 98, 109, 110, 114, 119; *see also* Capeskin; Gloves, flying; Helmets, flying; Horsehide; Jackets, flying; Pigskin

Life raft, Type C-2 14
Llama-pile lining 54
Lockeed P-38 Lightning fighter 9, 13
Lopez, Lt. Col. Donald S. 79
Lundquist, Maj. Gust. 63

Macready, Lt. J. A. 52, 59, 60, 98
"Mae West" *see* Vests, life preserver, Type B-4
Manson, Paul 38
Marshall-Field Co., Chicago, IL 74
Martin B-26 Marauder bomber 45
Masks 97–99
  flying, face 97
    chamois-lined 98
    cloth-lined 98
    extra heavy, Type P-1 99
    soft leather, USAAS 98
    summer, Type A-1 98; Type A-2 98, 119; Type A-3 98: Type A-4 98, 99
    winter, Type B-1 99; Type B-2 98, 99; Type B-3 99; Type B-4 98, 99
    with goggles 99
  flying, oxygen, face:
    summer, Type A-5 98–99; Type A-6 98, 99
    winter (1921) 59; Type B-5 98–99
  mechanics, Type D-1 99
  oxygen:
    Type A-9 90, 94; Type A-10 39, 90, 91; Type A-10A 66, 90; Type A-10R 90; Type A-13 91; Type A-13A 95, 96, 97, 113; Type A-14 13, 21, 22, 57, 58, 61, 79, 91, 95, 113; USAAS 88
Material Center, AAF, Wright Field, OH 8
Material Command, Wright Field, OH 5–6, 54
Materials:
  raw 11–12
  substitute 12, 92
  synthetic 11, 26
Materials Laboratory, Wright Field, OH 24, 25, 27, 29
"May West" (Type B-4 vest) 75
McCook Field, Dayton, OH 8, 13, 24, 52, 60, 98, 119
Messerschmitt Bf 109E fighter 42
Meyrowitz Co. 88
Microphones:
  hand, Type T-17
  oxygen mask, Type ANB-M-C1 106
  throat, Type T-30 37, 76, 89, 97, 106
Milkweed "batt" 76
Miller, Maj. F. E. 13
Mittens, flying, coney fur "pocket" type 47, 108

Moccasins, aviators 32, 119, 120; Type A-1 120; Type A-2 121–122
Moleskin 104; *see also* Suits, flying, summer, moleskin
"Monkey Suit" *see* Suits, flying winter, Type B-1
Monmouth Field, NJ 27
Moore, William L. 96
Morris, Lt. Richard 70, 104
Mothproofing 10
Mount McKinley, AK 25
Mouton material 9
Muff, electrically heated 108
Mufflers 80; *see also* Scarves
Mukluks 125–127; *see also* Shoes, flying, winter, Type A-13 and A-14
"Murder Incorporated" 69
Muroc Flight Test Base, CA 97

Name tags 20, 70
National Advisory Committee for Aeronautics (NACA) 95
North American A-36 Apache 103
North American AT-6 Texan trainer 84
North American B-25 Mitchell bomber 45
North American P-51 Mustang fighter 9, 79
Nuchwang dog fur 33; *see also* Suits, flying, winter, Type B-1
Nurses, flight clothing 83–86
Nutria fur 33, 34
Nylon 10, 69, 112

Office of Production Management, U.S., Washington, D.C. 38
Olson, Col. A. D. 82
Ort, Karl, Aviation Co. 88
Overseas cap *see* Caps, garrison
Overshoes, flying, intermediate, Type M-1 127
Oxygen equipment *see* Masks, oxygen
Oxygen unit, portable (walk-around bottle) 39

Parachutes 62
Parkas:
 alpaca and wool pile, Type B-11 55, 57
 down-filled, Type B-9 60–61
 shearling, Type B-4 34; Type B-7 36
Patterson Field, OH 36
Pensacola U.S. Naval Station, FL 74
permeability 34, 35, 108, 109, 130; *see also* Clothing, flying, sheep shearling
Personal Equipment Laboratory, Wright Field, OH 9, 14, 25, 50, 76, 96; *see also* Appendix A
Personal equipment officers 15, 16

Pigskin 110
"Pinks and greens" (uniform) 81, 82
Plug, electric, Type PL-354 106
Polyacrylate leather dye *see* Clothing, flying, sheep shearling, finishing process
Ponyhide 110
Poplin cloth 65
Porter, Capt. Carter C. 103
Post Exchange 78
Pratt, Brig. Gen. H. C. 5
Prisoners of War (POW) 20
Procurement *see* Clothing procurement

Quality control 11, 12
Quartermaster Corps *see* U.S. Army Quartermaster Corps

Radio equipment 6, 37, 105–108; *see also* Communications equipment; Headsets; Microphones; Receivers
Rayon 10, 46, 49, 113
Receivers, radio, Spec. ANB-H-1 37, 105, 106
Red Cross 78
Red linings in clothing 57, 70
Reindeer skin 34
Reproductions and replicas 1, 70, 160
Republic P-47 Thunderbolt fighter 65
Research and development 5–6, 24–31, 108–109
Rheostat, electrical, temperature control, Type Q-1A 45
 temperature regulator 22, 43–44, 45
Robey, Capt. Pearl 36
Rochester Optical Co. 103
Roold Co., France 3, 87
Royal Air Force (RAF) *see* Clothing, flying, RAF
Rubber 11, 101, 103, 106, 127; *see also* Appendix G

Satin lining 60
Scarves, flying 49, 80
 flying, heavy, Type N-1 81
Selfridge Field, MI 45
Shearling clothing *see* Clothing, flying, sheep shearling
Sheepskin and sheepskin lining 33, 34; *see also* Clothing flying, sheep shearling
Shilling, Col. D. C. 92
Shirts, flying, heavy, Type A-1 80
Shirts, service 81
Shoe inserts, flying:
 electric, Type Q-1 18, 130–131
 electrically heated, for F-2 and F-3 suits 43–50
 winter, Type A-7 125–126

Shoes, flying 119, 121–132
 arctic, Type A-14 (mukluk) 57, 126–127
 black felt *see* Boots, felt, outer shell, for Type F-2 electrically heated suit
 electrically heated
  Type C-1 45, 123, 124, 127, 128; Type D-1 45, 123, 124, 128; Type F-2 128: USAAS 127
 intermediate, Type A-15 "Mosquito Boot" 127; women's Type A-16 86, 127
 light, Type L-1 131
 light combat Type E-1 131; Type E-2 65, 131
 winter
  Type A-1 12; Type A-2 119; Type A-3 121; Type A-4 121; Type A-5 34, 121, 122; Type A-6 21, 23, 58, 122–123, 124, 130; Type A-6A 23, 41, 52, 60, 123; Type A-7 121, 124, 130; Type A-8 124; Type A-9 83, 123, 124; Type A-10 40, 125–126; Type A-12 126; Type A-13 (mukluk) 126; type M-1 127; USAAS 119
Shoe, Type F-2 131
Shoes, service, GI (high top) 9, 13, 66, 119, 127, 130; (low quarter) 119
Shure Brothers Co., Chicago, IL 106
Signal Corps *see* U.S. Army Signal Corps
Silk pile lining 54, 69
Silver *see* Wires, electrical
Skilled labor 11
Skirt, nurses' aviation, light, Type A-1 83
Slacks, flying, nurses' light, Type L-1 85, 86
 nurses' aviation, Type A-1 83
 very light, Type K-1 86
Slide fasteners *see* Zippers
Socks 44, 119, 126, 130
Spalding, A. G. and Bros. Co., NY 74, 106
Standardization of clothing and equipment *see* A-N Standardization System; Clothing standardization
Straus ans Buegeleisen Co. 101
Suits:
 dreadnaught safety 74
 ever-warm safety 74
 flying:
  anti-exposure, Type R-1 76, 77, 113
  electrically heated 12, 18, 20, 22, 25, 32, 35, 43–50, 112, 117, 118, 129, 130

experimental, U.S. Rubber Co. 44, 45
Type B-3 44; Type E-1 45–46, 117, 128; Type F-1 ("Blue Bunny") or "Bunny Rabbit" suit 12, 18, 22, 25, 44, 45, 46, 47, 48; Type F-2A 45; Type F-3 12, 22, 46, 48, 103, 117, 118; Type F-3A 118, 129, 130; USAAS (World War I) 43
floatation, Type C-1 74; Type C-2 74, 75
leather 38, 51, 54
light
Type L-1 17, 66, 67; Type L-1A 67; Type L-1B 67; Type L-2 67
nurses,' winter, Type A-1 83
summer 61–67
moleskin 64
Spec. AN-S-31 22, 62, 64, 65, 66; AN-S-31A 64, 66; M44 66; Spec. AN-6550 66; Spec. AN-6550-AN-S-31 66; Spec. AN-6550-M34 66
Type A-1 63; Type A-2 63; Type A-3 33, 61, 63; Type A-4 62, 63, 64, 65, 66; Type A-5 63, 64; Type A-6 64, 66
two-piece 33
very light, Type K-1 18, 20, 64, 66; Type K-1A 67: Type K-2 67; Type K-2B 67
winter 32–40, 56
bedford cloth 34, 52
corduroy cloth 33
fur-lined 32
RCAF, Type "E" 38
rescue, electrically heated 77
Taylor buoyant (RAF) 77
Type B-1 ("Monkey Suit") 32, 33, 53; Type B-2 33, 54; Type B-3 33; see also Suits, flying, electrically heated, Type B-3; Type B-4 33; Type B-5 33; Type B-6 33; Type B-7 33, 34, 51, 53, 54; Type B-8 33, 34, 51, 53, 54; Type B-9 34, 51, 64; Type B-10 54, 55; Type B-11 54
Sunglasses 79, 101–102, 104; see also Glasses
Supply see Clothing supply
Supply Division, Wright Field, OH 12
Suspenders 57
Sweaters 61, 77–78
mechanics, Type A-1 77–78
Swofford, Lt. R. P. 36

Tactical Center and Equipment Board, Orlando, FL 25
Tags, identification (dog tags) 81
Temperature zones 14–17
Testing see Clothing testing
Thermal man (copper man) 28
Thermocouples 27
Thermostats 45
Training, in use of clothing 10, 108–109
Trousers:
flying:
electrically heated, Type F-2, F-2SA, F-3, F-3A see Suits, flying, electrically heated, Type F-2, Type F-2A, Type F-3, Type F-3A
inner, Type E-1 80
intermediate
Type A-4 37; Type A-5 35, 36, 40; Type A-9 55, 56, 57; Type A-11 21, 22, 55, 56, 57, 58, 85; Type A-11A 57; Type A-11B 58; WASP Type A-12 84, 86
winter
inner, Type A-7 55, 126
Spec. AN-T-35 41, 42
Type A-1 23, 36, 53, 54, 116; Type A-2 36, 53, 54; Type A-3 34, 36, 37, 54; Type A-6 "Alaskan Suit" 29, 40, 126; Type A-8 60, 61; Type A-10 9, 56, 57
nurses,' flying, intermediate, Type A-13 83, 85
service 21, 46, 48
Type L-1 85
Turrets, gun 37, 43–44
Type designation numbers 17; type designation sheets 71; see also Appendix F
Typical airman (AAF, World War II) 21–23

Underwear 12, 22, 45, 80
Uniforms, service 17, 19, 20, 46, 63, 64, 70, 72, 80, 81, 82, 83, 103
United Kingdom (UK) 72, 74, 77, 92, 132
U.S. Air Force (USAF) 6, 9, 10, 59
U.S. Army Air Corps USAAC) 7, 53, 54, 54, 55, 74, 100, 114
U.S. Army Air Service (USAAS) 5, 53, 63, 74, 87, 88, 115
U.S. Army Quartermaster Corps (QMC) 6, 8, 12, 55, 61, 72, 74, 78, 80, 81, 119, 131
AAF cooperation with QMC 5–8
jurisdictional relationship with AAF 5, 12
U.S. Army Signal Corps (SC) 20, 100, 106

U.S. Coast Guard (USCG) 74
U.S. Marine Corps (USMC) 74, 131
U.S. Navy (USN) 11, 24, 38, 42, 53, 54, 69, 71, 73, 74, 75, 76, 81, 91, 94, 101, 102, 104
U.S. Navy Aeronautics Board 38
U.S. Rubber Co. 45
Universal Microphone Co. 106
Urbanoski, T/Sgt. Joe 56

Vests 78–80
flyer's armored, M1 15, 21
flying, electrically heated, Colvinex 45, 79–80
winter 79
fur-lined 79–80
pile-lined 79
Type C-1 79; Type C-2 78, 79; Type C-3 79
life preserver
Type A-1 74; Type A-2 74; Type B-1 75; Type B-2 75; Type B-3 75; Type B-4 (AN-V-18, AN 6519-1) "Mae West" 14, 22, 23, 58, 75; Type B-5 23, 75–76
survival, Type C-1 114
Vietnam War 91
Visor, flying, attachable, Type A-1 97

Waltz, Brig. Gen. Robert W. 68, 69
War art 69, 72
War Production Board, U.S. 38, 109
Washburn, Bradford 8
Waterproofing (weatherproofing) 35, 36, 7, 121; see also Appendix D
Western Electric Co. 88, 89, 106
Wilkins, Sir Hubert 55
Williams, Lt. Kenneth 69
Willis, E. J. Co., NY 3
Willis and Geiger Co., NY 55
Wires, electrical 8, 12, 43–50, 116, 117, 118
Wolf fur 40
Women's Airforce Service Pilots (WASP) 83, 84, 86
Wool 10, 17, 33, 45, 46, 83, 112
Wool, "elastique" 47
Wool pile see Clothing, alpaca pile
World War I 5, 24, 25, 43, 45, 52, 63, 68, 87, 88, 92, 98, 100, 110, 114, 119, 127
Wright Field, Dayton, OH 5, 8, 14, 24, 27, 29, 31, 34, 40, 41, 50, 53, 54, 55, 60, 98, 109

Zippers (slide fasteners) 7, 12, 35, 36, 46, 60, 61, 63, 64, 66, 67, 70, 77, 120

www.ingramcontent.com/pod-product-compliance
Lightning Source LLC
Chambersburg PA
CBHW081600300426
44116CB00015B/2942